Contributions to Management Science

The series *Contributions to Management Science* contains research publications in all fields of business and management science. These publications are primarily monographs and multiple author works containing new research results, and also feature selected conference-based publications are also considered. The focus of the series lies in presenting the development of latest theoretical and empirical research across different viewpoints.

This book series is indexed in Scopus.

More information about this series at http://www.springer.com/series/1505

Tiziana Russo Spena • Francesco Bifulco
Editors

Digital Transformation in the Cultural Heritage Sector

Challenges to Marketing in the New Digital Era

Springer

Editors
Tiziana Russo Spena
Department of Economics Management Institutions
University of Naples Federico II
Naples, Italy

Francesco Bifulco
Department of Humanities
University of Naples Federico II
Naples, Italy

ISSN 1431-1941 ISSN 2197-716X (electronic)
Contributions to Management Science
ISBN 978-3-030-63375-2 ISBN 978-3-030-63376-9 (eBook)
https://doi.org/10.1007/978-3-030-63376-9

This Springer imprint is published by the registered company Springer Nature Switzerland AG.
The registered company address is: Gewerbestrasse 11, 6330 Cham, Switzerland

Foreword

Changes in society, people, and technology all affect the world of museums. This consideration is further confirmed by what the ICOM Committee affirmed in the 2016 meeting to describe the three-year plan (2017–2019); i.e. museums operate in different and constantly evolving conditions because they are inserted in rapidly changing societies. As a result, museums are not only the essence of the ongoing changes in the art and culture business but are one of several ways in which changes in societies can be observed and have direct and indirect effects.

Museums are not just spaces that house works of art; they have long since changed their role in society. By the way, this role is not only based on culture, arts conservation, and heritage, but is a blend of multiple goals in a social context. Indeed, museums have been defined by ICOM as "democratizing, inclusive and polyphonic spaces for critical dialogue on the past and the future. [...] Museums are not for profit. They are participatory and transparent and work in active collaboration with and for different communities to collect, preserve, research, interpret, exhibit, and improve understanding of the world, with the aim of contributing to human dignity and social justice, global equality, and to planetary well-being".

I agree with the above definition, because a museum would not exist without people, the ones working behind the scenes, the ones providing the service to visitors, and visitors themselves. The pandemic we experienced in 2020 challenged museums as other firms, because we were unable to meet our visitors and offer what we set in the spaces we manage. These moments made me, my staff, and other colleagues further reflect on how to describe what we offer every day and I am even more convinced than in the past that its purpose is not just a visit, but is an experience, starting before the visit itself and continuing after it, due to the emotions, the knowledge, and the beauty we make available for our visitor.

The experience is the result of our efforts, as well as visitors' actions before, during, and after the visit, and this combination allows us to understand the changes I mentioned above: society is changing, technologies are being brought into play, and social interactions have been turned upside down in several ways. When I am asked about the target of the museum I am managing, I always answer "whoever". I am sure arts and museums are not something for small groups of people, since museums embed and transfer along time our history and represent a journey from the past to the future to be experienced in present time. Therefore, a museum may be seen as an instrument in the hands of a society to further knowledge, stimulate interests, to open mind, and set the ground for future generations willing experience arts and history.

Nowadays, all the tasks a museum can perform are activated through new technologies; this is due to how society has changed. Social media, real-time interactions, mobile technologies, robots, and artificial intelligence are permeating the life and the activities of people and businesses; consequently, museums cannot disregard the effects on society, since visitors are different than in the past, they can live their experience through technology, they want to share what they feel, and they are more and more attracted by the opportunities depending on new advanced tools.

Online exhibits are part of a museum offering and the integration between the physical realm and the digital world is a not-to-be-missed goal, while I have often heard comments about technologies as a dangerous enemy for physical offerings. On-site and online are two ingredients of the same recipe for success, since they both shape an experience, leading to services to be provided before, during, and after the visit. The fruitful combination of these two components of the experience may lead to empowered emotions, with positive effects on memorability, and word-of-mouth.

This book offers a fresh view on the changes I referred to above; thus, I am sure it can stimulate further debate among museum managers and curators, as well as clarify what is occurring around the world and offer interesting insights for the upcoming months.

I feel changes are just around the corner; thus, everyone should be as more aware as possible about what these changes can bring and how to get the best from them and improve the experience visitors would have in a museum. Anyway, this consideration should not limit how the changes may affect visitors also before and after the visit; this is particularly true with reference to online contexts and social media: these are the two key changes impacting museum lastly and they would most likely lead the way towards the museums of future.

Future is a word frequently used in this book; it is considered in almost every chapter, because of two reasons I am even more convinced about after reading it: the future is now for museums, and the future should be foreseen today to be ready to offer what visitors want. I made several efforts in predicting what the future will offer to museums and visitors; thus, I always considered communication and innovation as two pillars of a forward-looking strategy. I am glad to find wide evidence about these two elements in this book, with two lessons everyone should learn as soon as possible, namely that communication is the way to be in touch with visitors and to feed relationships, and innovation has reshaped museum as well as society.

Finally, I really feel the contributions proposed in this book can further advance the understanding of changing consumers in a changing society, leading us to pinpoint what museum managers and curators should do. Moreover, the combination of theoretical advances and practical observations in this book suggests that academics and practitioners should continue working together and, whenever possible, try to merge their knowledge. This would be the most suitable way to anticipate change and be appealing for visitors, also in the future.

Museo Archeologico Nazionale di Napoli, Naples, Italy
September 2020

Paolo Giulierini

Progetto REMIAM EX OPS - POR FESR 2014-2020 Asse I O.S. 1.2 – Azione 1.2.2. DGR n. 798 del 28/12/2016.

Contents

Contributors

Cristina Caterina Amitrano PoliS-Lombardia, Milan, Italy

Francesco Bifulco Department of Humanities, University of Naples Federico II, Naples, Italy

Mariarosaria Coppola Italian National Commission for Listed Companies and the Stock Exchange - Corporate Governance Division, Rome, Italy

Anna D'Auria Department of Economics Management Institutions, University of Naples Federico II, Naples, Italy

Roberta Gargiulo Department of Economics Management Institutions, University of Naples Federico II, Naples, Italy

Angelo Ranieri Department of Economics Management Institutions, University of Naples Federico II, Naples, Italy

Tiziana Russo Spena Department of Economics Management Institutions, University of Naples Federico II, Naples, Italy

Marco Tregua Department of Economics Management Institutions, University of Naples Federico II, Naples, Italy

Introduction

Tiziana Russo Spena and Francesco Bifulco

1 Digital Transformation and Cultural Heritage Challenges

Transformation in the science and technology field brings many changes; one of the biggest challenges is the interaction between multiple skills, tools, and competences. When we talk about the digital transformation, we know that it seeks to produce a better, faster, and more innovative way of pursuing business, social, and economic development (Brennen and Kreiss 2016; Mele et al. 2018; Matt et al. 2015; Russo Spena et al. 2017; Russo Spena et al. 2018).

Digital transformation impacts a considerable number of industries and covers various processes, evolutions, factors, and transactions within and outside the organizations.

In this book, we discuss how digital transformation is involved in—and changing—the cultural heritage sector.

The first Digital Agenda for Europe launched in March 2010, the new 2020 version (The European Union 2020) and the Challenge 8 "Digital Culture" of the EU's seventh Framework Research Programme (FP7), have been conceived to encourage research efforts and applications to make digitized cultural content an economic asset. In particular, as some scholars (Dulong de Rosnay and De Mati 2012) have remarked, the digitization of European cultural heritage is a key aspect of the recently implemented Digital Agenda for Europe. Since 2006, the Lisbon

T. Russo Spena (✉)
Department of Economics Management Institutions, University of Naples Federico II, Naples, Italy
e-mail: russospe@unina.it

F. Bifulco
Department of Humanities, University of Naples Federico II, Naples, Italy
e-mail: fbifulco@unina.it

T. Russo Spena, F. Bifulco (eds.), *Digital Transformation in the Cultural Heritage Sector*, Contributions to Management Science,
https://doi.org/10.1007/978-3-030-63376-9_1

Agenda has presented culture as a strategic asset in terms of its potential to promote European growth and competitiveness. The "four-circle view" of the cultural sectors described by KEA (2006) and O'Connor (2007) broaden cultural industries to include, besides activities connected to heritage, literature, music, entertainment, the arts, and media, any related beneficiary sectors of cultural goods made available via ICTs, such as education and tourism. Culture is a tool for social integration and territorial cohesion in Europe, and technologies are seen as agents spurring the economic and social potential at the foundation of cultural industry development (Li 2020).

However, the effective use of technologies helps create a renewed, integrated, and sustainable approach to the cultural heritage sector. Its economic value, stemming from a variety of sectors and sub-sectors, ranging from the conservation and preservation of historic buildings to activities in the natural environment, is expected to increase due to the spillover contributions of technology in this sector (Katsoni et al. 2017).

On the one hand, technologies are seen as essential engines for combining cultural, aesthetic, symbolic, social, historical, and economic values. By providing different types of interaction with heritage material, technology applications promote an understanding of cultural heritage and encourage users to value and appreciate that heritage. This is ultimately the best long-term investment for the preservation and valorization of cultural heritage. On the other hand, the importance of culture in the recent uncertain times of crisis (i.e., the COVID pandemic era) is seeing unprecedented creative digital use and technology development with and through cultural heritage businesses throughout the world. In the actual pandemic era, digital cultural heritage is contributing to people's enjoyment and creativity more than ever. The customer and the audience are moving towards a new form of digital fruition, and many cultural organizations have quickly started responding to these unique needs (Baiyere et al. 2020; Devine and Tarr 2019).

Digital and new intelligent technologies are being used to document, conserve, and communicate with regard to cultural heritage. New technologies have also been demonstrated to augment cultural service quality, create new customer experiences, and improve the performance of cultural heritage sectors (Devine and Tarr 2019). Digital platforms enable interconnections involving more different actors; new smart devices and virtual reality within the new paradigm of the Future Internet are changing how heritage goods and services are being modelled and delivered. In much the same way that technologies have changed how actors communicate, several fruitful opportunities for cultural industries have emerged, including issues related to adoption and patterns of use, the effects of such tools on outcomes, and how these tools may change business and market relationships.

Some scholars have recently proposed a perspective on cultural heritage studies that considers, together, the new social and technology landscape (Devine and Tarr 2019; Bifulco and Russo Spena 2016). However, to address the challenges that new technologies pose, there is a need to go more in-depth to analyze these changes and depict the complex context in which the cultural heritage services are being innovated and differently proposed to the market (Baiyere et al. 2020; Bifulco and Russo Spena 2016).

The focus on new technologies implies not merely a matter of data digitization, storage, and use for the elaboration of a new digital strategy, but also how technologies are related to the transformation of cultural heritage sectors and market processes as a whole. There is a need to move to the forefront of cultural heritage efforts to understand and help firms and policymakers respond to the challenges of managing cultural heritage businesses in the new technology era.

Web 2.0 technologies that have a collaborative vocation enable the proliferation of new cultural goods and services, evolving towards an enriched range of actors involved in the cultural economy. New technologies can assist in the broader-based distributed generation of cultural content by a broad community of participants so that the generated products, services, and content, are no longer products in a traditional sense; they are always unfinished and continually under development (Filip et al. 2015). High-quality content can be re-used to create experience services, and digital resources facilitate the creation of new thematic content that takes account of the varied interests of users and encourages the development of innovative services delivered via mobile devices.

As a result, cultural industries, especially the heritage sector, are forced to work for stronger digital awareness and responses in their digital strategy in the future, including a new approach to renewing their business models and service processes (Parmentier and Gandia 2017).

In this book, the business approach and market methods in the cultural heritage sector have been questioned in light of the new challenges imposed by the recent digital transformation and how they should be renewed to consider the new future of the cultural heritage sector.

2 Novelty of the Book

The purpose of this book is to devise an alternative conceptual framework for understanding the digital transformation in the cultural heritage sector by taking seriously the role of technology in the strategic process of the modelling and development of cultural heritage services in the digital era.

The focus here is on how marketing activities and customer processes are being transformed by digital technologies to provide better interactions, improve communication, and create value with customers by involving multiple actors through an engaged and personalized approach.

Much of the digital debate in cultural heritage is still in its infancy. Some existing studies are anecdotal and often developed within the domain of established research streams, including the cultural and technological domains that address the topic partially and from the episodic and punctual perspective (Pok and Weihsin 2014). A great part of the debate focuses on digitization in heritage conservation or reproduction (i.e. digitalized) deals with how it has radically changed the promotion, communication, and distribution of cultural content. This also makes it necessary to modify methods of organizing and delivering cultural products to meet the needs of new categories of users (Devine and Tarr 2019). Studies are intended to demonstrate how technologies can preserve cultural heritage and provide access to a wide range of historical and cultural resources in electronic format (Katsoni et al. 2017).

In the management domain, the recent service framework (Lusch and Vargo 2014) is useful for gathering the above-discussed reflections and summarizing the evolutionary dynamics of the concept of cultural goods, highlighting how it is well-tuned to the systems view of the new digital era. The service framework advances the consideration of the dynamic and holistic dimension of cultural heritage services rather than the static and reductionist view of cultural goods. It addresses the conception of the enjoinment of cultural value as a service interaction that overcomes the traditional division between pure goods and pure service (Barile et al. 2012), therefore, centring the interpretative key role of cultural goods seen as a service for the benefit of others. Thus, cultural service is imbued with social value, from which the user recovers an active role in cultural value creation. Conservation and protection assume an integral role within the enjoyment of cultural service, as they are related not only to the consideration of the physical and material structure and artefact but also, and above all, to the effective expressive capacity of cultural value in various contexts of enjoyment (Golinelli 2015). In such a view, technology is seen as resources providing a new venue to extend both the user's involvement in terms of participation in the cultural value creation process and the potential for systemic integration in terms of the possibilities of interactiveness among multiple service providers (arts, ICT media industries, etc.) and market actors (public and individual actors). The cultural value proposition is stated to emerge from an ecosystem perspective (Barile and Saviano 2012; Bifulco and Russo Spena 2014; Bifulco and Russo Spena 2016), whereas the use of digital technology provides new value-creating and revenue-generating opportunities involving a multitude of business and social actors. This logic typically goes hand in hand with the adoption of a servitization strategy promoting a complete shift from a product-centric to a service-centric business model and logic.

The number and diversity of more recent books (Giannini and Bowen 2020; Katsoni et al. 2017; Bifulco and Russo Spena 2016) underscore the importance and significance of technology and digital transformation in cultural heritage. Still, they show a limited recognition or incorporation of the key changes that have emerged in the cultural management landscape. Digital technologies and the internet create unprecedented opportunities to access cultural material for leisure, study and to reuse it to develop learning and educational content, or work, to reach out to broader audiences, to engage in new user experiences, documentaries, tourism applications, games, and other innovative applications (Li 2020). However, the focus is still on how to better approach the use of digital tools, pointing out the difficulties inherent in the type of digital objects, e.g. their complexity, their software-dependence, or the technological obsolescence of equipment for their reproduction.

A substantial body of models, methods, and data relevant to defining and conducting an in-depth investigation of cultural heritage sectors in the digital era and their potentialities for business is still missing (Minoska-Pavlovska 2019). Cultural heritage concerning value creation processes, users, and market actors' interactions and new market issues remains partially recognized and not adequately defined or incorporated into an integrated framework to take together technology transformation and customer focus.

We must be thinking about the digitalization of value creation and marketing processes in cultural heritage because the digital contexts and the increased possibilities of interactions play an increasingly central role in the marketing debate that goes far beyond a simple communication or social marketing programme.

In this book, we convey a more inclusive perspective that addresses the marketing strategy in the digital era as a proactive, technology-enabled process by which firms collaborate with customers and other actors and jointly create, communicate, deliver, and sustain experience and value co-creation in an ecosystems view.

3 Table of Contents

This book presents the results of interdisciplinary projects developed at the Department of Economics, Management, Institutions of University of Naples Federico II. The projects—namely, REMIAM—are part of a bigger interdisciplinary research project on smart technologies for culture, called DATABENC (High-Technology District for Cultural Heritage). It is a project promoted by the national government to advance the development of the cultural services industry of the Campania region as a creative engine for the development and viability of local and regional innovation systems (EX PON03PE_00161). Specifically, the REMIAM project is designed to use the new technologies to design a new model of cultural heritage service provision, where art, technology, new interaction models, and innovative communication techniques are the direction of MUSEI 4.0. The goal is to provide a unique value proposition that can reach a higher differentiated segment of the cultural market by providing a more integrated approach with the local context. Interactive visits, gamification methodologies, new interaction models involving the technological tools that the REMIAM project develops also support quality production activities—both those already in existence and those being developed. Museums become a new space to co-create by involving local crafts and favouring new mechanisms of artistic production through the use of innovative technological tools such as modern 3D printers.

Based on this renewed idea of what the cultural heritage sector should be, this book provides the first outcome of the Project by offering a fresh view of how digital transformation is involved in the cultural heritage sector and changing its strategies and marketing approach.

The book includes nine contributions and one introductory chapter. The chapters offer original theoretical, empirical, and applied content. The new paradigm of digital transformation is also at the forefront of this book's efforts to understand and help firms and policymakers respond to the challenges posed by the new role and complexity of cultural heritage management.

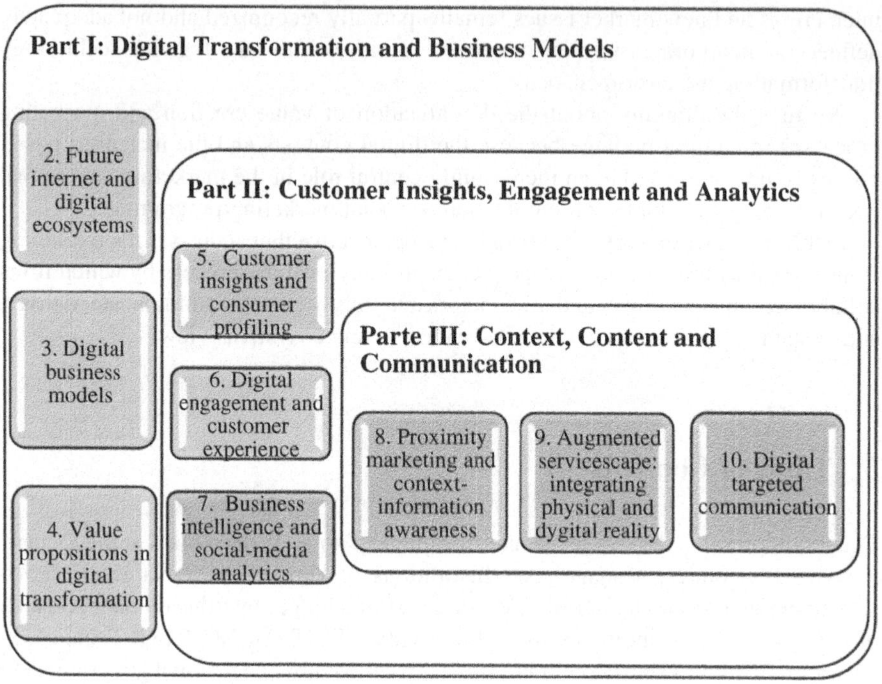

Fig. 1 The structure of the book

The nine chapters in the book are organized into three sections including concepts, practices, and illustrations (Fig. 1). Specifically, case studies referring to the national and international experience from leading cultural organizations underpin the discussion, demonstrating the clear and vital link between theory and practice (Table 1).

The first part—"Digital Transformation and Business Models"—provides theoretical and conceptual content about digital transformation in the cultural heritage sector with a focus on the renewed business models and new value propositions. More specifically, Chap. 2 goes in-depth into the analysis of the new phenomena labelled under the umbrella of "future Internet" and "digital ecosystem." The debate over the digital ecosystem as a new emerging concept represents a step towards the achievement of a better understanding of how cultural heritage services are being transformed. The chapter proposes a more detailed approach to digital ecosystems in business literature and how they are being shaped into practice, with particular reference to the cultural heritage context. Chap. 3 aims to explore conceptual and theoretical frameworks considered relevant to the subject of digital business transformation. Analysis and comparison of different concepts and tools of business models were conducted as a pathway for achieving and maintaining competitiveness for businesses as digital technologies continue to shape and transform the cultural business landscape. By adding a comprehensive analysis and examples to the body

Table 1 Case studies and descriptive elements

Chapter	Cases/main issues		
2	*Linked heritage* (content generation, collaboration, digital tools)	*Christa project* (innovation, cooperation, digital tools)	*Databenc* (community building; knowledge combination; digital tools) *Athena Europe* (B2B relationships; resources integration; digital tools)
3	*Foxfire museum* (partners collaboration, actors' integration, working team) *Tate Museum* (digital contents, digitalised archives, social online collections, digital platforms)	*British music experience* (value propositions, experience propositions, visual experience, learning programme) *The Van Abbemuseum* (personas and crowd actors, game masters) *MoMA (New York)* (social CRM, salesforces dashboard, data integration)	*MANN* (omnichannel strategy, mobile apps, game tools) *Museum of Contemporary art Querétaro* (economic social and cultural outcomes, cultural infrastructure, social themes, local artists, local community)
4	*Cooper Hewitt Smithsonian design museum* (immersive visitor experience, digital pen, gesture match experience, immersion room)	*The American Museum of Natural History* (innovative apps; digital totem, digital project)	*The British museum* (virtual tours, ask A curator project; Soundcloud initiatives)
5	*The Metropolitan Museum of art* (profiling, users' needs and expectations, user experience, google analytics)	*HI. Stories* (profiling, personalization, narratives, data analytics, google play)	*American Museum of Natural History* (profiling, personalization, comments, online rereview) *The National Gallery of London* (profiling, personalization, comments, online rereview)
6	*Louvre museum* (information, exhibitions, events, learning art, video and tales for children, audio guide)	*Museum del Prado* (interactive itinerary, online tickets mobile apps, interactive guide)	*Rijksmuseum* (digitalized collection, online tickets, digital game, mobile app, interactive guide)
7	*Norman Rockwell Museum* (big data, analytics, data-based decision-making process) *The Museum of Fine Arts* (data-based decision-making process, scenarios simulation)	*La Sagrada Familia* (data-based decision-making process, data-based service design process)	*Museum of Modern art* (social media analytics, data-based content development) *Museum of London* (social media analytics, data-based content development) *San Francisco Museum of Modern art* (social media analytics, data-based content development)

(continued)

Table 1 (continued)

Chapter	Cases/main issues		
8	*Palazzo Farnese* (visitor experience, personalization, proximity marketing)	*MUSE* (visitor experience, beacons, 3D images, proximity marketing)	*ARTLENS gallery* (interactive visitor experience, digital wall, proximity marketing, museum app)
9	*British museum* (digital discovery Centre, social media, interactive touchpad, VR headset, VR Google cultural	*Casa Battlò* (digital exhibition, employees' engagement, social media, virtual tour online, mobile app)	*La Cité du vin* (social media, digital apps, interactive and digital games)

of the existing business models, the chapter provides a framework to address a new base for future researchers on this important topic. Chap. 4 explores the role of digital technology in shaping the value propositions of cultural heritage organizations. In a technologies-based context, value propositions are formed through the mutual exchange of knowledge between multiple actors who integrate resources to the value creation process in a digital realm. On the one hand, the technologies help service providers better integrate their understanding of the offered service and what the customers can do; on the other hand, the customers are supported and perform activities that increase the market value of service offerings. Technologies have amplified the way value proposition contributes to both providers' and customers' co-creation.

The second part—"Customer Insights, Engagement and Analytics"—is based on three chapters and deals with the big questions of how to catch and integrate data from multiple touchpoints to profile customers and connect to the customer to provide an engaging and personalized experience. It also includes the analysis of business intelligence and social analytics tools to support marketing processes. More in detail, Chap. 5 addresses the analysis of the new approach to segmentation and consumer profiling. The growing use of analytics means that companies are getting better at knowing what consumers want (and do not want) and are adapting their operations and offerings to respond accordingly. Depending on the degree of personalization offered, dynamic data and analytics tools are critical in matching the right consumer to the right outcomes. True personalization requires cultural businesses to rethink their consumer insights process as well as their analysis and segmentation approaches. Chap. 6 aims to analyze the impact of digital technologies on the customer engagement strategy, namely visitor engagement, proposed by cultural heritage organizations. The analysis of customer engagement and digital technologies highlights the contribution of new forms of touchpoints and engagement strategies reached through interactive websites, new guide devices, mobile apps, and social media. In particular, the analysis of different case studies helps identify the different impacts of digital technologies along the customer journey, namely, digital engagement before, during, and after the visit. Thus, in chap. 7, business intelligence and social media analytics (SMA) are brought into focus to address the strategies, methods, and technologies for managing the data analysis processes. The overall goal is to identify differences in categories, tools, and techniques concerning the development of various analytics processes as well as their application and obtained results in cultural heritage businesses.

The third part—"Context, Content and Communication"—includes three chapters and analyses in depth: (1) proximity marketing and the role of context-information awareness as a new operative marketing approach to actualize personalized experience (2) how the effective design of the cultural heritage servicescape can enable more immersive and interactive service experiences; (3) the role of digital and targeting communication content. Chap. 8 investigates the role of new digital devices in marketing initiatives to provide personalized offerings thanks to context-aware information. Despite scholars' suggestion to create a two-way relationship between provider and user to achieve mutual benefits, the technological tools are used mainly to spread information (i.e. points of interest, opening hours, and other practical information) from an existing database. Some solid evidence related to proximity marketing initiatives in the cultural heritage sector has been further explored. An integrative framework is advanced, by identifying the key elements of museums' proximity initiatives, i.e. people, process, and context. Chap. 9 goes in-depth in the analysis of the museum servicescape in a new combination of physical and virtual contexts including multiple dimensions of visitors' interactions. The chapter proposes a conceptual model to analyze how companies face the increasing complexity in managing the customer experience in the heritage sector by integrating multi-sided aspects of the virtual and physical context. Finally, the increasing amount of content created on social media platforms is calling for sophisticated analysis that separates relevant from non-relevant content and data. Indeed, chap. 10 deals with digital communication by addressing how, through its infrastructure, it multiplies opportunities for customer participation, exchange, or accessibility. The new cultural heritage audiences grow up through new communication strategies aimed at producing different kinds of digital content (e.g. blog posts, videos, photos, etc.). These create the ability to share and reproduce collections and atmosphere across digital and physical spaces with high and active customer participation. New forms of personalized and targeted communication have moved from businesses "pushing" content towards consumers to consumers "pulling" content.

A summary of practical challenges and a snapshot of the lessons learned are presented at the beginning and end of each chapter. The aim is to arouse the audience's interest and improve the readability of the chapters.

The book explores novel topics and is aimed at both graduate and master student audiences. It also provides a knowledge resource for managers, decision-makers, and other practitioners interested in exploring digital marketing in the main cultural heritage business.

4 Where Are we Now?

At the end of each research project, much exciting work remains to be done to link the experience of the researchers who took part in the project to the experience of the reader interested in deepening this book. We must continue questioning the more significant implications of our story, the next steps to be taken, and the lessons we have learned from what we have already researched.

To appreciate in-depth the opportunities and threats of digital transformation, some key aspects of digital marketing in the cultural heritage sector must be clearly assumed.

As the first point, there is a common agreement that technology alone cannot produce "magical results" (Hammer et al. 2016) and that the reality depends on how people use it—mainly, if they can use it to amplify longstanding skills and expertise. Also, the faith in the power of technology does not mean that spending money and time on projects could be enough; the focus will be on how to combine the technology, organizational, and human sides of the new digital era. Driving digital transformation does not imply replacing old business assets and capabilities. However, like any significant building addition, doing it well requires modifying the business process and organization. Technology is taken less as a mere tool or technique and more as a new "mindset" necessary for viewing the market and society differently. The lack of strategic vision or priorities, the lack of knowledge about digital challenges, the reliance on under-empowered human capabilities, and the lack of collaborative and organizational culture can be seen as the soft mechanisms that hinder digital transformation in all industries. The cultural heritage sector is no exception.

Second, there is an awareness that a new form of competition arises thanks to the new technologies. The higher competition is expected, especially by newcomers, and will not be confined to the cultural heritage sector. The rise of new media companies, i.e. Amazon Video, Netflix, and YouTube, prompts the evolution towards a new form of cultural offering. Here, the focus on products and services starts to disappear in favour of the new "content," including stories, videos, books, and more. This new content is intended to connect with and engage new and different customers rather than to pitch a product or service. However, the main scope of the cultural heritage sector is to preserve treasures and deliver "wonder." Many museums embrace these challenges by breaking down their physical spaces and actively expanding exhibitions, activities, and resources through different digital touchpoints. We are witnessing the development of value propositions by companies that, alongside the support and enhancement of products and services, are substantiated in systematic structures for creating, editing, and distributing new content (narrations, storytelling, experiences) conveyed through different channels made available by digital technologies. Cultural heritage organizations directly offer not products and services but, rather, meanings and experiential content. But this content does not fall into a specific form defined and pre-packaged by the organizations in response to the characteristics of each customer; instead, they acquire sense and fulfilment above all through the relationships that are established with the surrounding space and time of the customer, where his/her experiential context takes form and in which the consumer is dropped. As a result, we can state that digital is in the cultural heritage service mission to enhance customers' personalized experiences.

Moreover, the adoption of digital technologies helps cultural heritage businesses to reach their customers in a relatively efficient and straightforward manner, but these technologies are also implemented to streamline all the business and organizational processes. The experience of the cultural heritage business is being transformed and enriched by the new opportunities of technologies thanks to the possibilities that they deliver, i.e. connection, cooperation, sharing, and innovating. We are beginning to see broader adoption of technologies not merely in the sense of digitizing collections but also regarding the use of data to learn more about the customer experience and personalize and contextualize the experience. For example during the still-in-progress pandemic era, many cultural heritage businesses have received a big push to improve their integration of technology to create a more innovative development environment. In this sense, the smart museum sought to employ data to facilitate everything from scheduling to the realization of exhibitions, from the conservation of information management to micro and macro market monitoring, to smart services, as well as to develop multimedia digital interactive touchpoints. Museums have expanded their physical and virtual space to break down the boundaries between experience proposition and their visitors.

Fourth, focusing attention on experience means referring to the personal experience of the consumer, recognizing the active role that he has in shaping it. Consequently, we note that the consumer is no longer considered a "target" and that the effort of companies in the face of behaviour in detail to direct the offer no longer suffices. The fundamental approach changes. That is, it is not the company that manages the experience; instead, it is the consumer who decides how to live his own consumer experience. The new digital technologies, some of which do not require large investments (above all, beacons, intelligent devices, smartphones, and app systems), become generators of new forms of content, starting from the activation of the dimensions of time and space of the consumer. The common trait among these technologies is that they allow for a strong interconnection between people, data processes, and objects by eliminating the limits existing in the physical sphere, enabling consumers to reach levels of involvement that, until recently, could only be imagined. An example is the new mobile revolution. Here the term "mobile, "is detached from the product from which it derives (for example the mobile phone) and ends up increasingly acquiring a meaning close to "mobility, "i.e. the possibility of having information and searching for, creating, and sharing content in any place and in real-time. In addition to the moments when users check emails or social networks or exchange messages with their network of contacts, there are highly intentional situations in which a user shows a specific interest, such as the need to deepen, look, document, or experience something. These are the situations in which the relevant decisions are made, and consumer expectations are very high. It is precisely in the same as situations that companies need to be able to offer customers exactly what they are looking for at the right time. However, the principle of contextuality, on the one hand, expands the possibilities offered to the company but, on the other hand, imposes new challenges. First of all, companies must eliminate unnecessary steps in the customer engagement process, whether it is documentation, a registration, or a museum visit. To be satisfactory, the experience must not only influence the emotional sphere of the individual but also be useful and easy to manage to avoid stressful situations.

Finally, new metrics and rules are needed to manage the new complexity of the cultural heritage sector. Cultural institutions should take into account the new role of crowdsourcing and the rules to engage others in creating new digital resources (images, videos). Collaboration requires permissive regimes of engagement based on competencies more than ownership and it employs new copyright systems that strengthen ongoing collaboration for further content enhancement. In a digitalized society, with an ever-increasing variety of systems and applications, interoperability makes it possible to re-use digital content and develop global markets and systems, including those related to tourism, while preventing the undesired effects of fragmentation. Releasing digital cultural information as open data can have economic benefits for the various stakeholders along the production chain (from the cultural institution that owns the cultural object to creative industries, digital artisans, and tour operators), and more generally in terms of improved knowledge of cultural heritage. Cultural institutions should assess the opportunities provided by new technologies to put together stimulating digital exhibitions and itineraries, exploiting the potential provided by digital storytelling and transmedia storytelling and accounting for the contributions of the various types of users, including specialized ones (related to school visits, sports, social memories, conferences, religions, food and wine, and movies). Compatible with the organizational structure and the availability of professional skills, cultural institutions should evaluate the suitability of establishing ad hoc departments collaborating with or dedicated to the digitization and development of multimedia resources.

Acknowledgements This book is the result of a collaborative effort undertaken over time and from multiple points of view.

First, our initial thoughts were developed in close collaboration with the authors of this book. Researchers whose management and marketing studies fully engaged in the Remiam project discussed with us the seminal ideas of this book and what structure it should take to address the management of cultural heritage in the new era of social and technological evolution. As co-creators of this book, thanks to their expertise and work in the field, they contributed to the development and refining of our initial concepts and their relationships, to see how well they reflected our observations of reality, ultimately creating a clear picture of the investigated phenomenon. Throughout one to 2 years of meetings, workshops, and conference debates and presentations, we shared common knowledge and interest in providing a comprehensive collection of new contributions, developing research areas of digital cultural heritage, and conceiving and developing a joint book project. Thus, we express our deepest gratitude and appreciation to all authors for their outstanding contributions; without them, this book's format could not have been developed.

Also, during our participation in workshops and conferences on the topic, we discussed many ideas as the basis of this book, with colleagues and researchers from different research domains and contexts. We owe an enormous debt of gratitude to those who took part in constructive comments to discuss nuances of the text and pushed us to clarify concepts, explore particular facets of new terms and concepts, and explain the rationale for specific arguments.

Our special thanks also go to all actors of the REMIAM ecosystem, especially the members of the district board, the scientific committee, and all partners, including research centres, universities, and SMEs, representing leading actors in technological, research, and business contexts at both the national and international levels.

We also extend our sincere thanks to all reviewers for their support and the donation of their precious time spent providing constructive and critical reviews. Their positive feedback and encouraging comments helped us work on the manuscript in a targeted and detailed way. We hope that by following them, we were able to create a book that shows logical consistency and greater clarity and impact.

Our special thanks also go to the publisher, Springer, and especially Prashanth Mahagaonkar, who guided us through the publishing process. He was kind enough to invite us to consider including this book in the "Contributions to Management Science" series. We have greatly appreciated his counsel during the final stages of the manuscript completion. Finally, we are deeply indebted to Ramya Prakas and the other members of the publisher's staff for their wonderful editorial support and guidance.

References

Baiyere A, Salmela H, Tapanainen T (2020) Digital transformation and the new logics of business process management. Eur J Inf Syst:1–22

Barile S, Montella M, Saviano M (2012) A service-based systems view of cultural heritage. J Bus Mark Manag 5(2):106–136

Barile S, Saviano M (2012) Dalla gestione del patrimonio di beni culturali al governo del sistema dei beni culturali. In: Golinelli GM (ed) Patrimonio culturale e creazione di valore, verso nuovi percorsi. Padova, Cedam, pp 97–148

Bifulco F, Russo Spena T (2014) Dal Distretto tecnologico all'eco-sistema dell'innovazione: sfide e opportunità imprenditoriali. Sinergie - Rivista di studi e Ricerche 17:67–86

Bifulco F, Russo Spena T (2016) Managing cultural heritage: innovation perspectives, customer experience, resources enhancement, performance management. Milan, Mc Graw Hill

Brennen JS, Kreiss D (2016) Digitalization The international encyclopedia of communication theory and philosophy, 1–11

Devine C, Tarr M (2019) The digital layer in the museum experience. In: Giannini T, Bowen JP (eds) Museums and digital culture. Springer, Cham: Switzerland, pp 295–307

Dulong de Rosnay M, De Mati JC (2012) The digital public domain. In: *Foundations of an open culture*. Open Book Publishers, Cambridge

Filip FG, Ciurea C, Dragomirescu H, Ivan I (2015) Cultural heritage and modern information and communication technologies. Technol Econ Dev Econ 21(3):441–459

Giannini T, Bowen JP (2020) Museums and digital culture: new perspectives and research. Springer, Cham, Switzerland

Golinelli GM (2015) Cultural heritage and value creation. In: Towards new pathways. Switzerland, Springer

Hammer M, Hippe M, Schmitz C, Sellschop R, Somers K (2016) The dirty little secret about digitally transforming operations. Harv Bus Rev 31

Katsoni V, Upadhya A, Strategies A (2017) Tourism, culture and heritage in a smart economy. Springer, Switzerland

KEA (2006) *The Economy of Culture in Europe*. Report prepared for the European Commission. Directorate-General for Education and Culture, Brussels

Li F (2020) The digital transformation of business models in the creative industries: a holistic framework and emerging trends. Technovation 92:102012

Lusch RF, Vargo SL (2014) Service-dominant logic: premises, perspectives, possibilities. Cambridge University Press, Cambridge
Matt C, Hess T, Benlian A (2015) Digital transformation strategies. Bus Inf Syst Eng 57 (5):339–343
Mele C, Russo Spena T, Peschiera S (2018) Value creation and cognitive technologies: opportunities and challenges. J Creating Value 4(2):182–195
Minoska-Pavlovska M (2019) Digital strategies for museums. J Sustain Develop 9(22):145–161
O'Connor J (2007) The cultural and creative industries: a review of the literature. Art Council England, Creative Partnership Series. London, p 69
Parmentier G, Gandia R (2017) Redesigning the business model: from one-sided to multi-sided. J Bus Strateg 38(2):52–61
Pok WSW, Weihsin DH (2014) Digital heritage and culture: strategy and implementation. World Scientific
Russo Spena T, Mele C, Nuutinen M (2017) Innovating in practice: perspectives and experience. Springer Publisher, Switzerland
Russo Spena T, Mele C, Marzullo M (2018) Practising value innovation through artificial intelligence: the IBM Watson case. J Creating Value 4(1):1–14
The European Union (2020) Digital agenda for Europe. Available from https://europa.eu/european-union/file/1497/download_es?token=l4yW0Ijx

Part I
Digital Transformation and Business Models

Future Internet and Digital Ecosystems

Tiziana Russo Spena, Marco Tregua, and Francesco Bifulco

Abstract This chapter goes in-depth into the analysis of the new phenomena labelled under the umbrella of "future Internet" and "digital ecosystem". The Future Internet (FI) is defined as a collection of data communication network technologies in the future. In this chapter the FI is discussed in relation to the Digital Ecosystems i.e. the peer to peer structures of support for a networked architecture and collaborative environment. The debate over the digital ecosystem as a new emerging concept represents a step towards the achievement of a better understanding of how cultural heritage services are being transformed. Here, the attention is not only on the definition of a possible best structure for a networked environment but to the ways in which networked environments evolve along time and with reference to the dimensions, dynamics, and variables that affect their emergence. The chapter proposes a more detailed approach to digital ecosystems in business literature and how they are being shaped into practice, with particular reference to the cultural heritage context.

1 Introduction

Digital transformation is a term that is fuelling an increasing debate in business, public, and academic discourse (Kreiss and Brennen 2016; Matt et al. 2015). Over several decades, computing capabilities have grown exponentially in power, while their costs are relatively decreasing (Moore 1974). Today's broad spectrum of IT-based solution has transformed the activities and processes of organizations as well as their human users.

T. Russo Spena (✉) · M. Tregua
Department of Economics Management Institutions, University of Naples Federico II, Naples, Italy
e-mail: tiziana.russospena@unina.it; marco.tregua@unina.it

F. Bifulco
Department of Humanities, University of Naples Federico II, Naples, Italy
e-mail: fbifulco@unina.it

T. Russo Spena, F. Bifulco (eds.), *Digital Transformation in the Cultural Heritage Sector*, Contributions to Management Science,
https://doi.org/10.1007/978-3-030-63376-9_2

New technologies and their applications, such as smart devices, apps, sensors, and so on, provide companies with data on the products' uses, allowing for the development of new data-driven services. Also, smart technologies develop into connected platforms enabling the delivery of new and augmented services and offerings from a distance (Beverungen et al. 2017; Amitrano et al. 2018).

The Internet of Things uses a digital IT infrastructure to virtually network physical items such as "smart" objects to human users and other objects (Oriwoh et al. 2013). Evans (2012) called the resulting infrastructure an "Internet of Everything" (IoE) that links smart objects, humans, and data via connected digital processes to deliver value. In these systems, smart objects enable the monitoring, optimizing, or remote controlling of smart devices, or smart devices can autonomously adapt to their environment (Beverungen et al. 2017). In several cases, companies have successfully built new forms of business models, based on an ecosystem that connects customers to a range of services, other customers, and/or other providers and actors (Larivière et al. 2017; Vargo and Lusch 2017). Due to digital connectivity and network effects, formerly separate industries increasingly collaborate to offer new and better service provision. In some cases, they also conflate contributing to the emergence of systems with few players dominating a new digital hub economy (Iansiti and Lakhani 2017). The emergence of these new forms of relationships and business models has consequences for the entire market structure, the competitive forces within these "new markets" (including providers on different levels of the service network), and consumers and society (Ng and Wakenshaw 2017). More recently, Langley et al. (2020) showed, in more detail, the impacts of IoE on business models and highlighted the changes occurring at micro-, meso-, and macro-levels; moreover, they set a research agenda in the business domain to further understand how digital technologies change business models and societies.

Some industries have already experienced a far-reaching shift in their business models due to digitalization (i.e. the music business, the computer and software market, entertainment, and e-commerce (Li 2020; Matzner et al. 2018; Ng and Wakenshaw 2017). Yet, many other companies still must face notable challenges regarding digital transformation to grasp the profitable opportunities of smart and more effective service provision (Spohrer 2017).

This chapter aims to analyze, in-depth, the new phenomena labelled under the umbrella of the "Future Internet" and "digital ecosystem". More in detail, it is self-evident how technologies are shaping both contexts, but a more comprehensive framework is needed to better depict the role of the Future Internet and its tools in digital ecosystems. Additionally, the role of the digital ecosystem in business literature and service research should still be depicted, as the literature review highlighted. Some contributions are available, but scholars are simply proposing an understanding of the digital ecosystem through the lens of some business conceptualizations (Russo Spena et al. 2017). They emphasize the support offered to new opportunities for value creation (Kopalle et al. 2020) while stressing the need to investigate the outcomes for firms in terms of the offering, value dynamics, competitiveness, and resource allocation.

The debate over the digital ecosystem as a new emerging concept represents a step towards the achievement of a better understanding of how cultural heritage services are being transformed (Li 2020; Russo Spena et al. 2017). The emerging technological trends in creative industries have been addressed by Li (2020), who describes them as the new conditions for their sustainability. However, the effect of increasing adoption of technology-driven businesses and new management challenges in creating new cultural service contexts require far more insights from both scholars and practitioners.

In this chapter, we propose a more detailed approach to what digital ecosystems are in the business literature and how they are being shaped into practice, with particular reference to the cultural heritage context, in line with the call by Li (2020). To achieve such an aim, we identify some empirical contexts to illustrate how the elements proposed in the literature can contribute to understanding a new way of carrying out cultural business activities in the new digital and ecosystem perspectives.

2 The Paradigm of the Future Internet

The Future Internet (FI) is defined as "a collection of data communication network technologies in the future" (Chang et al. 2011, p. 1). The Future Internet as global and common communication and distributed information system may be considered from various interrelated perspectives: the networks and shared infrastructure perspective, the services and application perspective as well as the media and content perspective.

FI has previously been proposed as the shift from a communication highway to a hybrid network controlling or operating virtually any device (Ulieru and Grobbelaar 2007) and even as "an enabling technology for a number of contemporary applications" (Naqvi et al. 2010, p. 90). Furthermore, FI is even considered an empowerment of the previously available tools to share data, as it should provide more resiliency to the hardware network and improve the quality of services (Tomkos et al. 2009). Resilience should also be applied to the FI architecture to avoid the negative consequences of failures affecting service continuity (Csikor et al. 2013, Papazoglou et al. 2010). Therefore, FI is aimed at favouring the creation of powerful infrastructures, supporting applications, and allowing for the achievement of new business models (Demestichas et al. 2013). These advances in service quality are performed thanks to the adaptability of the Future Internet to users' needs and to the contexts in which FI applications can be used (Karnouskos et al. 2012); the applications are, quite paradoxically, linked to both ease of use and complexity, as they appear to be easy to use by final users, while the complexity is related to two elements, namely (a) the technological infrastructure providing workability and services and (b) the interactions taking place in a wide and intertwined context made of services and systems.

Ben Hamida et al. (2012) proposed a focus on services and their provision when depicting the context of FI as consisting of a plethora of services, interacting one with another, and determining the scale of the FI itself. The linkages among services shaping FI are based on data, as users create data and content, and the open data approach chosen in lots of conditions is leading both public and private actors to share available data and contribute to the creation of new data (Davey et al. 2012). Additionally, data are sourced both consciously (as with crowdsourcing and social computing) and unconsciously (as in the case of tracing systems) (Antoniou et al. 2012). In sum, users are not thought of just as data consumers or service end-users, but as participants in the new Internet, namely, the FI (Oostveen et al. 2013). Thus, efforts are required to identify and understand the approaches favouring users' involvement in FI communities.

A focus on the linked systems is mirrored in the statement offered by Karnouskos et al. (2012), who expect that "FI will be a very complex system of systems" (p. xvi). These ties among systems are represented in different ways and with different conceptualizations, as in Wainwright and Papanikolaou (2012) when proposing data networks as both one of the main features of FI-based interactions (namely, a horizontal capability) and the output of these technologies. The concept of network is used by Matsubara et al. (2013) in considering the infrastructure connecting and orchestrating the FI of "people, devices, content, clouds, and things" (p. 28). One more approach proposed by FI scholars is related to ecosystem, as service ecosystems are thought of as scenarios in which FI can be suitable for use (Wajid et al. 2013); this last contribution is particularly useful for service scholars, as the previous linkages between FI and services were general, while Wajid et al. proposed a theoretical framework hosting the proposed tie. In the same vein, and leaning on Matsubara et al. (2013), Kumar and Krishna (2017) investigated FI as a lever for service universalization, as this would reduce the gap between areas in service provision; indeed, they observed the availability of new means of service provision with limited development of the communication infrastructure.

The Future Internet has been thought of as a relevant and effective set of instruments in relation to collective adaptive systems (Kos et al. 2012) and within service studies too, thanks to the cue previously proposed by Galis et al. (2009), framing FI as "a service- and self-aware network" (p. 112). The notion of awareness is carefully described by Świątek et al. (2012) when dealing with content awareness, context awareness, and user awareness. Content awareness is the choice of the right process to deliver data to the final users. Context awareness is the choice of the right channel to deliver data, while user awareness is a way to make explicit the two choices above in relation to a specific user; namely, it is the expression of customization. The feasibility of customization was stressed by Lu et al. (2018) as a result of the implementation of business platforms in supply chains, as innovation is designed, tested, implemented, and experienced through the efforts of multiple actors, including customers.

An increasing number of scholars in different fields of science is paying attention to changes and opportunities emerging because of the Future Internet, as several areas are being affected by it, such as digital media, enterprises, smart cities, healthcare, energy management, and transportation (Wainwright and Papanikolaou

2012). Thus, FI is affecting the ways firms conduct business and the chance to improve relationships among different actors in complex service-providing contexts (Bagur-Femenias et al. 2016).

3 The Technologies of the Future Internet

The Future Internet consists of several technologies and aspects, such as the Internet of Services (IoS), the Internet of Things (IoT), artificial intelligence (AI), cloud computing (CC), Network of the Future, and so on (Baker et al. 2009; Tselentis et al. 2009; Tregua et al. 2016). The above-cited elements can be considered together because they have some commonalities; indeed, cloud computing is a network of computers running the same application(s) at the same time, and three paradigms emerge to better describe it, viz. infrastructure-as-a-service, platform-as-a-service, and software-as-a-service (Alias et al. 2014). All of them are clearly focused on how solutions can be provided through the usage of new technologies. The distribution of data and instruments in a wide network is key even when one is defining the Internet of Services, as the same services can be accessed from different locations due to Internet connections (Vaz et al. 2012). The same logic is applied to data depending on objects and to the software favouring such a process; this is how the notion of IoT emerged (Tan and Wang 2010). Similarly, the Network of the Future is embedding all of the previous novel elements in defining how connectivity can lead to a wider network, with ubiquitous accessibility and a wide number of actors linked to one another (Alias et al. 2014). The usage of technologies is deeply changing the way firms behave, and the recent paradigm of the Future Internet is representing these changes. In any event, the definitions of such a paradigm are still emerging and sometimes conflict with one another (Hernández-Muñoz et al. 2011). One of the most commonly accepted definitions of the Future Internet is proposed by Boniface and Surridge (2013), who consider it as "a sociotechnical system comprising Internet-accessible information and services, coupled to the physical environment and human behaviour, and supporting smart applications of societal importance." Nowadays, many industries are implementing new instruments to improve the efficiency of their processes, as is happening in cultural heritage (Amato et al. 2013; Li 2020), tourism (Corigliano and Baggio 2013), the agri-food business (El Yasmine et al. 2014), and city management and safety systems (Vargas-Hernández and Pallagst 2020).

3.1 Internet of Things and Internet of Everything

The Internet of Things (IoT) is one of the technologies embedded in the paradigm of the Future Internet; some authors consider IoT to be the most relevant concept deriving from the notion of the Future Internet (Haller et al. 2009; Chang et al.

2011; Tregua et al. 2016). IoT is shaped by sensors and other tools connecting objects and making them communicate (Petrov et al. 2012, Wang et al. 2019); this communication is performed thanks to the software embedded in the objects and the software also facilitates the processing of an increasing number of data exchanged and collected (Haller et al. 2009).

One of the most commonly considered definitions considers IoT as a variety of things or objects—such as Radio-Frequency Identification (RFID) tags, sensors, actuators, mobile phones, etc.—which, through unique addressing schemes, are able to interact with each other and cooperate with their neighbours to reach common goals (Atzori et al. 2010). Additionally, the Internet of Everything (IoE) emerged as an evolution; this concept proposed a wider set of connections than IoT, as people are connecting among themselves and with objects (Barakat 2016). These definitions recall the comprehensive approach contained in the European Research Projects on the Internet of Things (2009), as IoT is thought of as addressing convergence, content, collections, computing, communication, and connectivity between people and things. Additionally, one of the areas of research for the Future Internet is the Internet of Services, a vision of the Internet in which everything (e.g. information, software, platforms, and infrastructure) is available as a "service," i.e. as the application of "digital competencies [. . .] for the benefit of another entity or the entity itself" (Matzner et al. 2018; p. 6).

Even service scholars have recently started paying attention to the linkages between IoT/IoE and the main service features; one of the most recent contributions is proposed by Andersson and Mattsson (2015), with a focus on service innovation, due to the great novelties brought by IoT. The authors proposed four elements of service innovation as potentially depending on IoT; objectification of actors, overlapping, intermediating, and business modelling were affected by IoT and led to service innovation, thanks to the interplay among them. Moreover, IoT acts as a set of mechanisms favouring the needed linkage between cloud services and end-user Internet service (Wang et al. 2013). Due to this focus on users, it is becoming more common to observe the shift from IoT to IoE, as people are integrated with things, services, and the context (Rahman and Rahmani 2018). This approach mirrors and empowers the statement by Winter and Ono (2015), who described the Internet of Everything (IoE) as the alignment and ties between the physical and virtual worlds. Moreover, Leminen et al. (2012) referred to IoT ecosystems and business models; in these new business models, firms use service applications to favour resource integration. However, they did not refer to IoE, while Langley et al. (2020) did and described the level of smartness for *things* with implications for business models and effects on the economy, due to the leverage on the capabilities and connectivity of smart things.

Furthermore, IoT is seen as the element favouring interactions (Gretzel et al. 2015) and the development of relationships oriented to value co-creation by providing the tools necessary to allow the integration of firms' and customers' instruments. IoT—as well as IoE—is providing the chance to better connect objects, services, and actors, so that actors' involvement in creating experiences is greater than before (Wang et al. 2013; Russo Spena et al. 2016; Tregua et al. 2016). The interactions depicted above can be observed even in the assemblage of things and objects as described by Ng and Wakenshaw (2017); this assemblage should not be thought of as something static such as a mere accumulation of resources, but as a continuous adjustment towards the optimized combination to increase value potentialities.

Some practical consequences have been highlighted by Ehret and Wirtz (2017) when proposing the industrial IoT, namely, the implementation of IoT in an industrial context aimed at the achievement of a more responsive design of solutions to users and, thus, to a higher value to be created. Another recent advance has been proposed by Antonova (2018) when depicting IoT as a way to favour partners' integration in a complex and dynamic network; due to this new chance to interact, actors can share their competitive advantages and shape new business models to achieve more complete value creation for both the partners and the end-users.

3.2 *Cloud Computing and Artificial Intelligence*

Cloud computing (CC) is sometimes considered to be a set of various services provided as computing services, leading to a sharing infrastructure or a platform to deliver applications and services. Dempsey and Kelliher (2018) tried to clarify the jungle of definitions and the differences depending on a series of different perspectives: They depicted CC as the democratization and utilization of computing power favouring the overcoming of technical and financial shortages. They leverage the previous theoretical proposal by Benlian and Hess (2011) when stressing the opportunity to provide on-demand services and software to access resources, data, and applications for several users. As a consequence, CC is offering a new way to provide and distribute software applications, thus leading to changes in the way firms can achieve revenue due to new forms of service provision and subscription. In summary, CC has been defined (Dempsey and Kelliher 2018) as the fifth utility and its effects on human activities are hugely relevant; they can have even more of an impact when considering the connections to be created with artificial intelligence and machine learning.

Artificial intelligence (AI) is one of the changes taking place in the widest scenario of the human-machine interactions; the development of AI is still progressing, even if its deployment is still a bit far (Corea 2017). In any event, AI is just behind the corner in several industries, and the way business is thought about is changing due to the great and still unexplored potentialities that can emerge by using AI in companies and business models. Before one looks at the changes that can take place in some industries, it is necessary to clarify what AI is, due to the novelty of this topic. AI is considered a system leading computer to learn autonomously, namely, to improve the already available algorithms, without explicitly programming the computer for such a task (Corea 2017). The adjective "artificial" stands for the strict relationship with data instead of focusing on physical law as human beings are. Data are crucial in depicting the main features of AI, as data—and especially big data—are the basic input to start the processes of AI; among these processes, the most common one is analyzing data to improve both the way an output can be achieved and the content of the output itself. Corea (2017) described two different types of AI depending on the application of data; if AI leads to knowledge to be applied to several environments because of the possible integration among different skills, it is called Artificial General Intelligence (AGI); if the knowledge created is led by creativity and is featured by social and emotional skills and impacts, it is Superintelligent AI or ASI. One of the environments benefiting from AI is health care, with special reference to start-ups, as it is possible to prevent, diagnose, and cure diseases thanks to the opportunities that AI offers (Garbuio and Lin 2019).

AI provides opportunities to increase the effectiveness and efficiency of service provision and customer interaction (Larivière et al. 2017; Marinova et al. 2017; Rust and Huang 2012), such as in the case of medical diagnoses or intelligent chatbots to support customer interactions. AI threatens human service jobs in a wide range of industries, from bus drivers and call centre agents to financial analysts and even lawyers and doctors (Huang and Rust 2018).

All the expected contributions emerging from AI and its different evolutions can be observed in a business context when paying attention to business models; AI is based on a continuous evolution, with the advantage of a reduced experimentation phase, due to the extremely reduced time of data processing and process improvements. Moreover, the business models of firms focused on AI favour a great spreading of these new tools, as they are provided for free to stimulate all the advantages of open source and open innovation. Due to this approach, it will be easier to decrease the time-to-market of AI, the problems in testing, and the validation of mechanisms.

4 Business Ecosystems at the Digital Forefront

Business scholars are paying attention to the way actors are being interrelated by technology in contexts known as digital ecosystems. Boundaries among industries are being blurred due to the widespread incorporation of technologies. The digital ecosystem represents an industry phenomenon based on the adoption of Internet-based technologies for business accelerating the progress of industry convergence and favouring engagement and its management (Morgan-Thomas et al. 2020); the authors claimed that the management of engagement depends on innovation in devices, new devices, and shifts in connectivity.

More definitions—including well-established ones—of "digital ecosystem" rely on Moore's conceptualizations of business ecosystems, i.e. "an economic community supported by a foundation of interacting organizations and individuals—the organisms of the business world." This economic community produces goods and services of value to customers, who are themselves members of the ecosystem. An ecosystem includes customers, producers, competitors, and other stakeholders, whereas it is not possible to divide economic activities under specific industries. The features of a business ecosystem include fragmentation, interconnectedness, cooperation, and competition (Iansiti and Levien 2002). A wealthy ecosystem sees a balance between cooperation and competition in a dynamic free market. All actors complement one another, leading to a more dynamic division of labour, organized along one-dimensional value chains and two-dimensional value networks.

However, a unique and commonly accepted definition of "digital ecosystem" does not exist. As highlighted by Marinos et al. (2011), the extant contributions by scholars are leading to different meanings in a general way and even because of different interpretations by different actors. Similarly, Jardim-Goncalves et al. (2013) stressed how "current economic theories have difficulty in explaining digital ecosystems" (p. 24). The term "digital ecosystem" is still used to describe a variety of concepts, ranging from the existing networking infrastructure of the Internet to digital ecosystem services which enable customers to use existing e-business solutions. The term is also increasingly linked to the future development of Information and Communications Technology (ICT) adoption for e-business, to support business ecosystems (Chatzoglou and Chatzoudes 2016). However, Iansiti and Lakhani (2020) observed the phenomenon from a different angle, stating the unstoppable growth of some global firms (e.g. Google, Facebook, and Alibaba), as the services they provide are offered through algorithms and the services are mostly automated.

A seminal definition of "digital ecosystem" has been proposed by Chang and West (2006) as an analogy to previous definitions of ecosystems; more in detail, the authors stated that a digital ecosystem is "an open, loosely coupled, domain clustered, demand-driven, self-organising agents' environment, where each *specie* is proactive and responsive for its own benefit or profit" (p. 6). Openness is the feature best representing digital ecosystems as similar to natural ecosystems, while the reference to the loosely coupled agents mirrors the chance to continuously involve new actors from the digital community. Self-organization makes the digital ecosystem different from other perspectives, where there are key actors leading relationships and activities; as a consequence, roles are not fixed, control is decentralized, and collaborations represent the key to a successful collaboration of all the agents (or actors). Scholars from information technology offer some more insights into how to depict a digital ecosystem, by contributing to the debate in business literature, as their definitions take into account economic aspects such as businesses, SMEs, markets, and so on. Ghormley (2012) proposed a digital ecosystem as a community cloud with amalgamations of distributed control.

By focusing on the role of technology, Matopoulos et al. (2012) proposed a different perspective on the digital ecosystem with a more detailed focus on businesses. As a consequence, they proposed a new theorization switching the focus from a digital ecosystem to a "digital business ecosystem" (DBE) when applying its main features to business contexts; consequently, a DBE offers opportunities to firms to operate and collaborate through digital technologies when performing actions depending on their products and services (Maracine and Scarlat 2009). Additionally, a DBE is considered the milieu supporting the creation of contexts in which firms can extend their markets. More in detail, *e-attributes* are individuated to depict SMEs and clusters favouring the emerging of a DBE. The main advantages of operating in digital ecosystems can be categorized as mainly internal and mainly external. The internal advantages are related to the achievement of higher levels of efficiency, the ease in accessing information, and the chance to always be up to date. The external advantages are the ease in finding partners to match resources, knowledge, and experiences, the extension of the potential market, and the combination of services with those of partners.

Some authors (Selander et al. 2013) split a digital ecosystem into a central part and a periphery; they highlighted how the survival of both the ecosystem and the peripheral actors is not mutually influenced. Recently, a similar distinction between the key actor and the other actors was proposed by Nambisan (2017) when highlighting the relevance of the firm leading the platform in a digital ecosystem; the key role of this firm depends on its chance to address both value creation and appropriation. With their digital business models and vast market coverage, companies function as game changers, both in established markets and beyond traditional market boundaries. In several cases, they have successfully built new forms of competitive power, creating a hub economy with one or a few dominant players. Iansiti and Lakhani (2020) refer to this development as the "digital domino effect" to describe a process in which more and more markets and actors that traditionally competed in separate industries are reduced to just a few hub firms that capture growing shares of the overall economic value created (Iansiti and Lakhani 2020). Some more elements depicting a digital ecosystem are learning and interactions. These two topics are influencing actions towards the achievement of specific goals and are taking place in complex contexts, as ecosystems are; this complexity is expressed by ecosystems' main features, namely decentralization, autonomy, diversity, and reception of conflicts. When the role of knowledge is particularly stressed in an ecosystem or in a digital ecosystem, it is common to propose a new conceptualization known as "knowledge ecosystem," where creation, sharing, deploying, and the risk of forgetting can take place (Maracine and Scarlat 2009). Among the four knowledge-based activities, creation is more crucial than the others, and it is thought to start when tacit knowledge becomes explicit.

A digital ecosystem is a context where digital elements—viz., software, components, applications, and services—are acting together to favour the achievement of a specific aim, like the creation of content, a business process, and so on (Kannan et al. 2010). More recently, Conti et al. (2019) defined a digital ecosystem as "a digital environment populated by interacting and competing digital species" (p. 2); digital features permeate services and data too, and these two elements are strictly connected in some specific contexts, as highlighted with reference to smart cities by Zuccalà and Verga (2017), stating that a digital ecosystem favours data sharing useful to synergic applications to different public services, enabling innovative solutions.

The interactions depicted above are also at the forefront of service scholars' studies in which digitalization can be observed mainly in the assemblage of things and objects and services as described by Ng and Wakenshaw (2017). This assemblage should not be thought of as something static, such as a mere accumulation of resources, but as a continuous adjustment towards the optimized combination to increase value potentialities. Digital ecosystems rely on interactions and the development of relationships oriented to value co-creation; in such a view, technologies provide the context to allow for the integration of companies' and customers' propositions (Lusch and Nambisan 2015; Gretzel et al. 2015). Smith et al. (2017) framed the digital ecosystem as interactions offering entrepreneurs access to resources for the achievement of desirable outcomes. The characterization of the effectiveness of digital ecosystems can be made through the concept of bridging and bonding. Bridging refers to connections of actors within the network, ideally reaching as many diverse connections as possible to access new knowledge. Bonding is referred to as the behaviour of actors within the network. Providing others with emotional support, sharing solidarity, and enriching relationships with commitment characterize high levels of bonding.

In sum, digital ecosystems rely on a community or network of actors with common or interdependent purposes which lead to their value-creating activities rather than mere technologies. Therefore, new digital technologies must be thought of from the perspective of the networked collaborations and integration they provide; they do not define what a network is or what communities are but, rather, what they can do together and how they can transform their way of doing to increase the value.

5 The Digital Ecosystem in Cultural-Based Services

Several studies consider the role of technologies in cultural-based services and, more in general, in relation to cultural heritage (Donghui et al. 2017; Kalay et al. 2007; Li 2020; Tengberg et al. 2012). Some of the reasons why scholars are paying a significant amount of attention to how technology is reshaping cultural heritage are the new means of service provision (Strielkowski et al. 2012), the challenges for marketers (Hausmann 2007), the cooperation taking places among actors (McKercher and Du Cros 2002), and the approach to an ecosystem perspective (Lazzeretti and Sartori 2016). In this part, attention will be devoted to the digital ecosystem emerging in—and for—cultural heritage. Eklund et al. (2009) are some of the first scholars to depict a digital ecosystem through cultural heritage and, namely, through a museum. More in detail, they described a digital museum in Australia as a representation of the real-world museum; the digital transformation deployed for this museum inspired the digital exploration of an already existing museum, proposing a digital ecosystem as the transforming of a business ecosystem. Additionally, this ecosystem is thought of as linked to other ecosystems consisting of stakeholders, other museums, and other actors; the ties among ecosystems frame new ecosystems.

Some key features have been discussed as common in the context of cultural heritage. The first aspect involves the need for cultural digital ecosystems to embrace digital solutions for cultural heritage promotion and preservation (Lawson et al. 2010). Companies must take up the opportunities brought in by digitalization and digitization as a means to valorize and preserve their cultural heritage. New technologies bring cultural heritage sites back to life. Virtual museums offer visitors the ability to see artwork residing in different places in context and to experience objects or sites inaccessible to the public. The example of Linked Heritage regarding intangible cultural heritage is a positive step in this direction that could be replicated elsewhere.

Exhibit 1 Linked Heritage

Linked Heritage is an already-completed project contributing to Europeana, as is Athena Europe.

This project was aimed at looking for new content related to cultural heritage across Europe, improving the quality of cultural content, and enlarging the amount of data available to Europeana. In a more general vein, Linked Heritage had, as its main goal, the coordination of standards and technologies to be provided to Europeana, and thus to all EU countries and external partners.

The Internet of Things is deployed in Linked Heritage, as geospatial standards, geographic information, and *e*-infrastructures are the main elements supporting cultural institutions in Europe towards the creation of further knowledge and the achievement of higher efficiency in cultural services.

In Linked Heritage, cooperation was key to building the digital ecosystem itself, as an explicit call for participation was launched at the beginning of the project. Through this call, the partners operating at the launch of the project were joined by participants who stated that they could contribute as content providers and as members of working groups, roundtables, and other seminars to enhance cultural-heritage-based initiatives, or as disseminators of the information collected in the project and already available in Europeana. Public regional and local authorities engaged with relevant stakeholders. These actors included both public and cultural institutions (galleries, libraries, museums, archives, and film heritage institutions) as content providers; cultural industry as re-users of cultural heritage content in applications and added-value services, e.g. in the education, edutainment, design, gaming, and tourism sectors; technology firms as providers of digitization/preservation technologies; and Internet actors such as social networks, online reference works, and philanthropic organizations.

Knowledge sharing is both a result favored by participation and a reward for actors joining Linked Heritage; the joining of new actors favored the creation of a wider community, as nine new partners and four sister projects partnered with the already acting team composed of 37 partners, eight main contributors, and a coordinator taking care of the relationships, both internal to the project and with the external institutions. Finally, complexity is mirrored in the activities and their relationships, as in the Athena Europe project, but in the content of data to be collected and shared; indeed, digital objects are considered aggregators of digital data, so the content providers joining the project had to gather material from the contexts spread all over Europe, standardize

(continued)

them, apply the Europeana guidelines and procedures, and support the administrative tasks. Digital technology is featuring the project because it provides a new way to use data and an unambiguous reference to the content and its provider.

Additional aspects include the need to foster collaboration and create partnerships between regional authorities, museums, and academia to increase the attractiveness of the museums and visitors' experience (Pierroux 2018). There is a need to build the knowledge base and enhance the capacity of public and private actors and institutions to develop and implement digitization strategies for cultural heritage artefacts based on common standards and approaches. Overcoming differences and integrating knowledge and competences from different domains must be addressed as well. Cooperation can contribute to this process by providing a platform for mutual learning and knowledge exchange between actors. The examples of DATABENC and ATHENA demonstrate how to respond to the demand for innovation. The applications of digital technologies for cultural heritage can be inspirational in another context in terms of strengthening knowledge and competences for the rise of innovation and improvement of the cultural heritage context.

Exhibit 2 DATABENC

Databenc is a project established by two universities in Southern Italy that gathers together another university, several SMEs, four research centres, and more than 50 other partners.

This ecosystem is aimed at stressing open innovation as an approach to favouring the activities of a high-technology scientific district dealing with cultural heritage. Integrating knowledge, favouring the conservation of cultural heritage assets, proposing new services through ICT, and making usage sustainable are the main aims of this project. The aims are to gather and communicate the content of the scientific knowledge of an artistic, archaeological, literary, historical, and philosophical nature in the territory of Region Campania. The emphasis is on historic centres, activating, and experiencing new strategies for their representation, organization, dissemination, and promotion based on paradigms of technological intelligence.

The set of actors launched technologies supporting physical visiting paths, virtual re-enactment, and learning-oriented contexts to favour the spread of knowledge about the local area's cultural heritage. The partners of Databenc aim to propose the safeguarding, conservation, and fruition of cultural heritage through cloud computing; more in detail, the development of a web platform allows for an integrated approach towards data management and the standardization of service processes. The technological equipment provides intelligence tools that support transparency and economic growth as well as they

(continued)

allow to coordinate the different business and economic models and the real and participatory actions of local governance and of other actors.

The community consists not just of the wide set of project partners but also of local actors such as schools, museums, and other private associations. These actors constantly took part in the activities, shared content online, and contributed to the dissemination of the results achieved through the project. The complexity of the project not only depends on the wide range of actors but is mirrored by the ties among different fields of science needed to improve the solutions to be proposed in relation to the cultural heritage assets. The uniqueness of the cultural and natural heritage is particularly stressed to identify the interventions to be carried out and the need to preserve local areas. The partners of the project particularly stressed the relevance of cloud-based, web-based, and Internet of Things-oriented services as the three main pillars of the platform identified as crucial in furthering the cultural services. Innovation, sustainability, and service provision are the three outputs to be achieved through the technology-based platform, built through the support of all actors cooperating with each other, plus the interventions of the local community.

Exhibit 3 Athena Europe

Athena Europe is a project carried out by several partners all over Europe under the coordination of the European Commission.

This project aims to favour the participation of museums and other institutions in Europeana, the digital library collecting all digital products from institutions in the countries of the European Union. Moreover, Athena Europe aims to coordinate the activities of museums all over Europe, looking for digital content in these museums, favouring the integration of the several sectors of cultural heritage, and developing tools to support access to digital content. All of these aims can be achieved by mapping and coordinating stakeholders and content all over Europe and by enforcing the relationship with Europeana.

In Athena Europe, cooperation is a key process, as there are partners with specific roles—namely, 23 content providers, six technology providers, six actors dealing with dissemination, one evaluation body, and one coordinator taking care of the relationships with the European agencies. The cooperation among these actors takes place to favour knowledge collection, transformation into a digital version if needed, and dissemination through digital tools all over Europe and even outside the European area, thanks to the involvement of other partners. The focus on data collection and dissemination is useful to show the setting up of a community that enables the workability of this ecosystem based on digital tools; more in detail, additional partners were appointed to favour

(continued)

collection and dissemination in each of the countries joining the project. Following the choice of these partners, local communities emerged, and a coordinator of communities was appointed at Europeana. Finally, complexity is not only self-evident in the context described in the previous lines but can also be observed when looking at the activities to be performed, as they are greatly intertwined with one another. The main activities described in Athena Europe are monitoring and evaluation, awareness and dissemination, identifying of standards and recommendations, integration of data, coordination of content, analysis of issues, and development of plug-ins to be integrated into Europeana. These activities are all linked to one another and are not just a sequence of tasks to be done. The redundancies, interconnections, and mutual influence among them take place through technologies, as the set of tools favouring the performing of these activities and the integration and dissemination of data.

In many cases, cultural heritage is thought of differently when one is dealing with a digital ecosystem; namely, it is considered part of a wider digital ecosystem including city or tourism business. Amato et al. (2013) considered cultural heritage to be an element of a city undergoing a digital transformation enabling the integration of a heterogeneous range of cultural, architectural, technological, social, and natural artefacts to provide new experiences for leisure and business. Additionally, Li (2020) paid attention to the multiple business models adopted by firms in different markets and also in the so-called multi-sided markets. Therefore, an ecosystem represents the upstream, downstream, and horizontal complexity of multiple stakeholder contexts. In such contexts, digital platforms enable the management of multi-sided relations.

The example of the CHRISTA PROJECT is a positive step in citizens' engagement and attracting the interest of different actors (tourists, youth, citizens, etc.) in the city's history and the culture of the county.

Exhibit 4 Christa Project

The *Christa project* is an interregional project of cooperation acting at both the national and European levels to favour the sustainable development of culture-based initiatives through innovation and aimed at developing tourism.

In Christa, heritage is thought of as natural and cultural, so cultural tourism, heritage tourism, and ecotourism are the main contexts to which the results are aimed and expected. Ten partners from 10 countries are collaborating in this project, but each of the partners has its main responsibilities in an area close to where it operates. Sharing initiatives, disseminating knowledge, and cross-supporting are the key approaches of this project.

In the Christa project, the partners carry out their main efforts in relation to the local area where they operate, but they cooperate to identify and define

(continued)

policies for sustainable and responsible actions in relation to cultural and natural tourism development. The partners of this project act together to deploy all-embedding actions—namely, interventions aimed at preserving, conserving, offering, and restoring cultural heritage assets. The goals of the project are defined in line with the framework proposed by the European Union and the Horizon 2020 targets. The community is built around these goals, as the partners identified public authorities and stakeholders as both contributors and beneficiaries of the project, since the summarizing aim is to provide environmental and resource-oriented efficiency. Additionally, the community is further developing, as during the dissemination of events, new ideas were launched, and new partnerships were created to favour similar interventions. Finally, the complexity of this project is based on the need to operate on two different layers, as each member must act on a local base and a national base, due to the nature of the project. Hence, the definition of local interventions, standards, and policies requires a process of negotiation and adaptation to achieve a result that can be applied all over Europe in the areas featuring the project. Moreover, the complexity is represented by the intricacy of the aims related to protecting cultural heritage assets and making them available to users. Digital tools are supporting this project, as they are favouring the analysis of good practices, mutual learning among partners, capacity building through the involvement of local communities, and scenario evaluation to test the adaptability of policies in different areas.

6 Discussion

The rise of the concept of the digital ecosystem has been proposed in the literature as related to cultural heritage.

As mentioned above, digital technology provided cultural businesses with a necessary infrastructure to build a new digital business integrating different technologies (IoT and IoE, cloud computing AI technologies) that made it possible for users and different businesses and actors to come together and build a digital ecosystem of interactions (Antonova 2018). Interactions within the digital surroundings and the material context of digital technology change the means of doing in the cultural heritage context and become a key focus in the cultural ecosystem (Li 2020). Indeed, the cooperation among firms to set a digital ecosystem (Maracine and Scarlat 2009), the community shaped by this ecosystem (Ghormley 2012) and the complexity depending on knowledge are the key factors shaping new digital cultural activities. In the same vein, Li (2020) addressed a call for research on the effects of technology in digital ecosystems based on cultural heritage by describing the contribution of platforms for mutual learning and knowledge exchange between multiple actors ecosystems.

Mutual adjustments within the digital ecosystem regarding products, services, and locations include consideration of all the social and technological components fostering interactions within digital ecosystems. Instead of exchanging property as in the traditional market-based economy, made up of sellers and buyers, the parties in this new network-based economy share access to services and experiences. For example new technology-enabled services are increasing the complexity of the cultural experience and connecting previously distinct digital, physical, and social realms (Bolton et al. 2014); they are increasingly nested within complex self-adjusting service ecosystems (Subramony et al. 2018), and the ongoing changes in the service ecosystem context trigger innovation which, in turn, may lead to further complexity (Edvardsson et al. 2018).

Thus, the digital cultural ecosystem (Matopoulos et al. 2012) is more consistent with a view of the networking of different actors and businesses and the adjustment of the players to the new realities of the digital economy. Multiple actors can be seen as providers and clients in a cultural ecosystem; therefore, it is not just a matter of how complex an ecosystem's structure is, as companies have a series of portfolios and the ties among ecosystems shape new ones. Formally, a digital cultural ecosystem can be huge, covering joint content management systems of one country or region, but it can also be small, such as a virtual museum or private collection of artefacts. In the digital ecosystem, local and global actors concurrently operate to determine solutions to satisfy different problems. Digital ecosystems are platforms for the network-based economy of business ecosystems, providing mechanisms for the creation of new business and value; these results emerge as a consequence of how digital ecosystems are shaped; indeed, they consist of both internal and external advantages, such as increasing efficiency, the availability of more information, and the chance to benefit from the activities of multiple partners. These features mirror, and are mirrored in, the notion of the ecosystem itself, namely, a context continuously reshaped by actors. The cooperation of actors is one factor depicting the essence of ecosystems, including when they are framed as digital ecosystems (Maracine and Scarlat 2009). Digital cultural ecosystems have a kind of self-generative nature working on a service-oriented logic in which users can act as providers at the same time; these interchanging roles were described in ecosystems in general, but the characteristics of cultural heritage provide much more evidence on how actors participate in these joint processes with synergic efforts. These efforts are not driven or steered by one single actor, but the trigger point may vary because of the changing roles of actors. Also, the new technologies created an open space to provide and access information, knowledge, data, and new resources. The digitization and online accessibility of cultural resources become input for added-value products and services which can fuel innovation in areas such as tourism, education, advertising, and gaming. In detail, the new view proposed by Iansiti and Lakhani (2020) considering firms as drivers of new technologies is spreading, as some of these firms have grown too much and IT-based solutions may help in dealing with such relevant numbers.

References

Alias C, Qzgiir C, Jawale M, Noche B (2014) Evaluating the potential of Future-Internet-based transportation control tower solutions using the example of a logistics service provider. In: Proceedings of the 2014 Biennial CSME International Congress. Toronto (ON), CAN

Amato F, Chianese A, Mazzeo A, Moscato V, Picariello A, Piccialli F (2013) The talking museum projects. Procedia Computer Science 21:114–121

Amitrano C, Tregua M, Russo Spena T, Bifulco F (2018) On Technology in Innovation Systems and Innovation-Ecosystem Perspectives: A Cross-Linking Analysis. Sustainability 10 (10):37–44

Andersson P, Mattsson LG (2015) Service innovations enabled by the "internet of things". IMP J 9 (1):85–106

Antoniou A, Theodoridis E, Chatzigiannakis I, Mylonas G (2012) Using future internet infrastructure and smartphones for mobility trace acquisition and social interactions monitoring. In: Álvarez F et al (eds) The Future Internet Assembly. Berlin, Springer, pp 117–129

Antonova A (2018) Smart services as scenarios for digital transformation. Industry 40 3 (6):301–304

Atzori L, Iera A, Morabito G (2010) The internet of things: A survey. Comput Netw 54 (15):2787–2805

Bagur-Femenias L, Perramon J, Barquero JD (2016) Does intensive social network management lead to positive effects in quality practices? Total Qual Manag Bus Excell 27 (11–12):1246–1260

Baker N, Zafar M, Moltchanov B, Knappmeyer M (2009) Context-Aware Systems and Implications for Future Internet. In: Tselentis G et al (eds) Towards the Future Internet. IOS Press, Berlin, pp 335–345

Barakat SM (2016) Internet of things: Ecosystem and applications. J Curr Res Sci 4(1):32

Ben Hamida A, Kon F, Oliva GA, Dos Santos CEM, Lorré JP, Autili M et al (2012) An integrated development and runtime environment for the future internet. In: Álvarez F et al (eds) The Future Internet Assembly. Berlin, Heidelberg, Springer, pp 81–92

Benlian A, Hess T (2011) Opportunities and risks of software-as-a-service: Findings from a survey of IT executives. Decis Support Syst 52(1):232–246

Beverungen, D., Matzner, M., & Janiesch, C. (2017). Information systems for smart services, 15, 781–787

Bolton RN, Gustafsson A, McColl-Kennedy J, Sirianni NJ, Tse DK (2014) Small details that make big differences: A radical approach to consumption experience as a firm's differentiating strategy. J Serv Manag 25(2):253–274

Boniface M, Surridge CU (2013) Research Challenges for the Core Platform for the Future Internet.. Retrieved from http://ec.europa.eu/information_society/activities/foi/library/docs/fippp-research-challenges-for-coreplatform-issue-1-1.pdf

Chang RS, Kim TH, Peng SL (2011) Security-Enriched Urban Computing and Smart Grid: Second International Conference, SUComS 2011, Hualien, Taiwan, September 21–23, 2011. Proceedings (Vol. 223). Springer Science & Business Media

Chang E, West M (2006) Digital ecosystems and comparison to existing collaboration environment. WSEAS Trans Environ Dev 2(11):1396–1404

Chatzoglou P, Chatzoudes D (2016) Factors affecting e-business adoption in SMEs: an empirical research. J Enterp Inf Manag 29(3):327–358

Conti V, Ruffo SS, Vitabile S, Barolli L (2019) BIAM: a new bio-inspired analysis methodology for digital ecosystems based on a scale-free architecture. Soft Comput 23(4):1133–1150

Corea F (2017) Artificial intelligence and exponential technologies: business models evolution and new investment opportunities. Springer, London

Corigliano MA, Baggio R (2013) Creatività, innovazione, tecnologie e competitività nel turismo. Rivista di Scienze del Turismo-Ambiente Cultura Diritto Economia 4(1–2):53–82

Csikor L, Rétvári G, Tapolcai J (2013) High availability in the future internet. In: Galis A, Gavras A (eds) The Future Internet Assembly. Springer, Berlin, Heidelberg, pp 64–76

Davey J, Mansmann F, Kohlhammer J, Keim D (2012) Visual analytics: Towards intelligent interactive internet and security solutions. In: Álvarez F et al (eds) The Future Internet Assembly. Berlin, Heidelberg, Springer, pp 93–104

Ehret M, Wirtz J (2017) Unlocking value from machines: business models and the industrial internet of things. J Mark Manag 33(1-2):111–130

Demestichas P, Georgakopoulos A, Karvounas D, Tsagkaris K, Stavroulaki V, Lu J et al (2013) 5G on the horizon: Key challenges for the radio-access network. IEEE Veh Technol Mag 8 (3):47–53

Dempsey D, Kelliher F (2018) Industry Trends in Cloud Computing. Pallgrave McMillian, New York

Donghui C, Guanfa L, Wensheng Z, Qiyuan L, Shuping B, Xiaokang L (2017) Virtual reality technology applied in digitalization of cultural heritage. Cluster Computing, 1–12

Edvardsson B, Frow P, Jaakkola E, Keiningham TL, Koskela-Huotari K, Mele C, Tombs A (2018) Examining how context change foster service innovation. J Serv Manag 29(5):932–955

Eklund P, Goodall P, Wray T, Bunt B, Lawson A, Christidis L, Van Olffen M (2009) Designing the digital ecosystem of the virtual museum of the pacific. In 2009 3rd IEEE International Conference on Digital Ecosystems and Technologies (pp. 377–383). IEEE

El Yasmine ASL, Ghani BA, Trentesaux D, Bouziane B (2014) Supply chain management using multi-agent systems in the agri-food industry. In: Chaib-draa B, Müller J (eds) Service Orientation in Holonic and Multi-Agent Manufacturing and Robotics. Switzerland, Springer, Cham, pp 145–155

European Research Projects on the Internet of Things (CERP-IoT) (2009) Strategic Research Agenda (SRA). Internet of Things—Strategic Research Roadmap

Evans D (2012) The internet of everything: How more relevant and valuable connections will change the world. Cisco IBSG:1–9

Galis A, Denazis SG, Bassi A, Giacomin P, Berl A, Fischer A et al (2009) Management Architecture and Systems for Future Internet Networks. In: Tselentis G et al (eds) Future Internet Assembly. IOS press, Amsterdam, pp 112–122

Garbuio M, Lin N (2019) Artificial intelligence as a growth engine for health care startups: Emerging business models. Calif Manag Rev 61(2):59–83

Ghormley Y (2012) Twos company, threes a cloud: Challenges to implementing service models. J Serv Sci 5(1):19–28

Gretzel U, Sigala M, Xiang Z, Koo C (2015) Smart tourism: foundations and developments. Electron Mark 25(3):179–188

Haller S, Karnouskos S, Schroth C (2009) The internet of things in an enterprise context. In: Domingue J, Fensel D, Traverso P (eds) Future Internet Symposium. Berlin, Heidelberg, Springer, pp 14–28

Hausmann A (2007) Cultural tourism: Marketing challenges and opportunities for German cultural heritage. Int J Herit Stud 13(2):170–184

Hernández-Muñoz JM, Vercher JB, Muñoz L, Galache JA, Presser M, Gómez LAH, Pettersson J (2011) Smart cities at the forefront of the future internet. In: Domingue J et al (eds) Future internet assembly. Springer, Berlin, Heidelberg, pp 447–462

Huang MH, Rust RT (2018) Artificial intelligence in service. J Serv Res 21(2):155–172

Iansiti M, Lakhani KR (2017) Managing our hub economy. Harv Bus Rev 95(5):84–92

Iansiti M, Lakhani KR (2020) Competing in the Age of AI. Harvard Business Review, Jan-Feb.

Iansiti M, Levien R (2002) The new operational dynamics of business ecosystems: Implications for policy, operations and technology strategy. Division of Research, Harvard Business School, Boston, MA

Jardim-Goncalves R, Grilo A, Agostinho C, Lampathaki F, Charalabidis Y (2013) Systematisation of Interoperability Body of Knowledge: the foundation for Enterprise Interoperability as a science. Enterprise Information Systems 7(1):7–32

Kalay Y, Kvan T, Affleck J (2007) New heritage: New media and cultural heritage. Routledge, London

Kannan R, Balasundaram SR, Andres F (2010, October) The role of mulsemedia in digital content ecosystem design. In Proceedings of the international conference on management of emergent digital ecosystems (pp. 264-266)

Karnouskos S, Colombo AW, Bangemann T, Manninen K, Camp R, Tilly M, Eliasson J (2012, October) A SOA-based architecture for empowering future collaborative cloud-based industrial automation. In IECON 2012-38th Annual Conference on IEEE Industrial Electronics Society (pp. 5766–5772). IEEE

Kopalle PK, Kumar V, Subramaniam M (2020) How legacy firms can embrace the digital ecosystem via digital customer orientation. J Acad Mark Sci 48(1):114–131

Kos A, Pristov D, Sedlar U, Sterle J, Volk M, Vidonja T et al (2012) Open and scalable IoT platform and its applications for real time access line monitoring and alarm correlation. In: Andreev S, Balandin S, Koucheryavy Y (eds) Internet of Things, Smart Spaces, and Next Generation Networking. Springer, Berlin, Heidelberg, pp 27–38

Kreiss D, Brennen JS (2016) Normative theories of digital journalism. *Sage handbook of digital journalism studies*. New York, Sage

Kumar MR, Krishna YS (2017) Future Networks an SOA perspectives Design Goals. Int J Adv Res Comput Sci 8(9):649–654

Langley DJ, van Doorn J, Ng IC, Stieglitz S, Lazovik A, Boonstra A (2020) The Internet of Everything: Smart things and their impact on business models. J Bus Res, online first

Larivière B, Bowen D, Andreassen TW, Kunz W, Sirianni NJ, Voss C et al (2017) "Service Encounter 2.0": An investigation into the roles of technology, employees and customers. J Bus Res 79:238–246

Lawson A, Eklund PW, Goodall P, Wray T, Daniel V, Van Olffen M (2010) Designing a digital ecosystem for the new museum environment: the Virtual Museum of the Pacific. In: Yeatman H (ed) The SInet 2010 eBook. SInet UOW, Wollongong, pp 227–239

Lazzeretti L, Sartori A (2016) Digitisation of Cultural Heritage and Business Model Innovation: The Case of the Uffizi Gallery in Florence. Studies on the Value of Cultural Heritage 14:945–970

Leminen S, Westerlund M, Rajahonka M, Siuruainen R (2012) Towards IOT ecosystems and business models. In: Andreev S, Balandin S, Koucheryavy Y (eds) Internet of things, smart spaces, and next generation networking. Berlin, Heidelberg, Springer, pp 15–26

Li F (2020) The digital transformation of business models in the creative industries: A holistic framework and emerging trends. Technovation 92:102012

Lu Y, Papagiannidis S, Alamanos E (2018) Internet of Things: A systematic review of the business literature from the user and organisational perspectives. Technol Forecast Soc Chang 136:285–297

Lusch RF, Nambisan S (2015) Service innovation: A service-dominant logic perspective. MIS Q 39 (1):155–176

Maracine V, Scarlat E (2009) Dynamic Knowledge and Healthcare Knowledge Ecosystems. Electron J Knowl Manag 7(1):99–110

Marinos A, Moschoyiannis S, Krause P (2011) Towards a restful infrastructure for digital ecosystems. Int J Electron Bus 9(5–6):484–498

Marinova D, de Ruyter K, Huang MH, Meuter ML, Challagalla G (2017) Getting smart: Learning from technology-empowered frontline interactions. J Serv Res 20(1):29–42

Matopoulos A, Herdon M, Várallyai L, Péntek Á (2012) Digital business ecosystem prototyping for SMEs. J Syst Inf Technol 14(4):286–301

Matsubara D, Egawa T, Nishinaga N, Kafle VP, Shin MK, Galis A (2013) Toward future networks: A viewpoint from ITU-T. IEEE Commun Mag 51(3):112–118

Matt C, Hess T, Benlian A (2015) Digital transformation strategies. Bus Inf Syst Eng 57 (5):339–343

Matzner M, Büttgen M, Demirkan H, Spohrer J, Alter S, Fritzsche A, Ng IC et al (2018) Digital Transformation in Service Management. J Ser Manag Res 2(2):3–21
McKercher B, Du Cros H (2002) Cultural tourism: The partnership between tourism and cultural heritage management. Routledge, London
Moore JM (1974) Computer aided facilities design: an international survey. Int J Prod Res 12 (1):21–44
Morgan-Thomas A, Dessart L, Veloutsou C (2020) Digital ecosystem and consumer engagement: A socio-technical perspective. J Bus Res, online first
Nambisan S (2017) Digital entrepreneurship: Toward a digital technology perspective of entrepreneurship. Entrep Theory Pract 41(6):1029–1055
Naqvi S, Dallons G, Ponsard C (2010, May) Applying digital forensics in the future internet enterprise systems-European SME's perspective. In Systematic Approaches to Digital Forensic Engineering (SADFE), 2010 Fifth IEEE International Workshop on (pp. 89–93). IEEE
Ng IC, Wakenshaw SY (2017) The Internet-of-Things: Review and research directions. Int J Res Mark 34(1):3–21
Oostveen AM, Meyer ET, Pickering B (2013) User involvement in future internet projects. In: Domingue J et al (eds) The Future Internet Assembly. Berlin, Heidelberg, Springer, pp 310–322
Oriwoh E, Jazani D, Epiphaniou G, Sant P (2013) Internet of things forensics: challenges and approaches. In 9th IEEE International Conference on Collaborative computing: networking, Applications and Worksharing (pp. 608–615). IEEE
Papazoglou M, Pohl K, Parkin M, Metzger A (2010) Service research challenges and solutions for the future internet: S-cube-towards engineering, managing and adapting service-based systems. Springer, London
Pierroux P (2018) Learning and engagement in museum mediascapes. In: Drotner K, Dziekan V, Parry R (eds) The Routledge Handbook of Museums, Media and Communication. London, Routledge, pp 128–142
Petrov V, Andreev S, Koucheryavy Y (2012) An applicability assessment of IEEE 802.11 technology for machine-type communications. In 2012 The 11th Annual Mediterranean Ad Hoc Networking Workshop (Med-Hoc-Net) (pp. 24–31). IEEE
Rahman H, Rahmani R (2018) Enabling distributed intelligence assisted future internet of things controller. Applied computing and informatics 14(1):73–87
Russo Spena T, Amitrano CC, Tregua M, Bifulco F (2016) Cultural service experiences and smart technologies. In: Bifulco F, Russo Spena T (eds) Managing Cultural Heritage. Mc Graw Hill, Milan, pp 63–80
Russo Spena T, Tregua M, Bifulco F (2017) Searching Through the Jungle of Innovation Conceptualizations: System, Network and Ecosystem domains. J Serv Theory Pract 27(5):977–1005
Rust RT, Huang MH (2012) Optimizing service productivity. J Mark 76(2):47–66
Selander L, Henfridsson O, Svahn F (2013) Capability search and redeem across digital ecosystems. J Inf Technol 28(3):183–197
Smith C, Smith JB, Shaw E (2017) Embracing digital networks: entrepreneurs' social capital online. J Bus Ventur 32(1):18–34
Spohrer J (2017) IBM's service journey: A summary sketch. Ind Mark Manag 60:167–172
Strielkowski W, Riganti P, Jing W (2012) Tourism, cultural heritage and e-services: Using focus groups to assess consumer preferences. Tourismos: an International Multidisciplinary Journal of Tourism 7(1):41–60
Subramony M, Solnet D, Groth M, Yagil D, Hartley N, Kim PB, Golubovskaya M (2018) Service work in 2050: toward a work ecosystems perspective. J Serv Manag 29(5):956–947
Świątek P, Juszczyszyn K, Brzostowski K, Drapała J, Grzech A (2012) Supporting content, context and user awareness in Future Internet applications. In: Álvarez F et al (eds) The Future Internet Assembly. Springer, Berlin, Heidelberg, pp 154–165
Tan L, Wang N (2010) Future internet: The Internet of Things, Proceeding of 3rd International Conference on Advanced Computer Theory and Engineering (ICACTE), 5: 376–380

Tengberg A, Fredholm S, Eliasson I, Knez I, Saltzman K, Wetterberg O (2012) Cultural ecosystem services provided by landscapes: assessment of heritage values and identity. Ecosyst Serv 2:14–26

Tomkos I, Pointurier Y, Azodolmolky S, Eiselt M, Zami T, Piesiewicz R et al (2009) DICONET: future generation transparent networking with dynamic impairment awareness. In: Tselentis G et al (eds) Toward the future Internet. IOS press, Dublin, pp 173–182

Tselentis G, Domingue J, Galis A, Gavras A, Hausheer D, Krco S, Lotz V, Zahariadis T (2009) Towards the future internet. A European research perspective. IOS Press, Washington, DC:: The Netherlands

Tregua M, Russo Spena T, Bifulco F (2016) The Context of Future of Internet and Cultural Heritage. In: Bifulco F, Russo Spena T (eds) Managing Cultural Heritage. McGraw Hill, Milan, pp 23–45

Ulieru M, Grobbelaar S (2007) Engineering industrial ecosystems in a networked world. In Industrial Informatics, 2007 5th IEEE International Conference, 1: 1–7

Vargas-Hernández JG, Pallagst K (2020) Green Innovation and Sustainable Urban Ecosystems. In: Vargas-Hernández JG, Pallagst K (eds) Building an Entrepreneurial and Sustainable Society. New York, IGI Global, pp 54–74

Vargo SL, Lusch RF (2017) Service-dominant logic 2025. Int J Res Mark 34(1):46–67

Vaz AM, Magalhaes Martins B, Carneiro Brandao R, Alberti AM (2012) Internet of Information and Services: A Conceptual Architecture for Integrating Services and Contents on the Future Internet. IEEE Latin America Transactions, I 6:2292–2300

Wainwright N, Papanikolaou N (2012) Introduction: the FIA research roadmap, priorities for future Internet research. In: Álvarez F et al (eds) The Future Internet Assembly. Springer, Berlin, Heidelberg, pp 1–5

Wajid U, Marín CA, Mehandjiev N (2013) Optimizing service ecosystems in the cloud. In: Galis A, Gavras A (eds) The future internet assembly. Springer, Heidelberg, pp 115–126

Wang T, Luo H, Jia W, Liu A, Xie M (2019) MTES: An intelligent trust evaluation scheme in sensor-cloud-enabled industrial Internet of Things. IEEE Transactions on Industrial Informatics 16(3):2054–2062

Wang W, De S, Cassar G, Moessner K (2013) Knowledge representation in the internet of things: semantic modelling and its applications. Automatika 54(4):388–400

Winter J, Ono R (2015) The Future Internet: Alternatives Visions. Switzerland, Springer, Cham

Zuccalà M, Verga ES (2017) Enabling energy smart cities through urban sharing ecosystems. Energy Procedia 111:826–835

Digital Business Models

Tiziana Russo Spena, Francesco Bifulco, Marco Tregua, and Anna D'Auria

Abstract This chapter aims to explore the conceptual and theoretical frameworks considered relevant to the subject of digital business transformation and that helps increase the general understanding of new business models in the emerging cultural digital context. Analysis and comparison of different concepts and elements of business models are conducted with the aim of better understanding the digital business transformation in the cultural heritage sectors. Analysis of business models is gaining prominence as a pathway for achieving and maintaining competitiveness for businesses as digital technologies continue to shape and transform the cultural business landscape. By adding a comprehensive analysis and examples to the body of the existing business models, the chapter provides a framework for addressing a new basis for future research on this significant topic.

1 Introduction

In recent years, considerable research has been conducted into the "business model" in the age of digital transformation (Frank et al. 2019; Li 2020; Spieth et al. 2019). As technology evolves, both researchers and policymakers must deal with rapid changes in the development of business models. The digital business transformation involves new processes of integrating the growing body of digital technologies and the resulting customer, product, and operational data (insights) into an organization, with results that increase value creation capabilities. Businesses are undertaking their own digital

T. Russo Spena (✉) · M. Tregua · A. D'Auria
Department of Economics Management Institutions, University of Naples Federico II, Naples, Italy
e-mail: tiziana.russospena@unina.it; marco.tregua@unina.it; anna.dauria@unina.it

F. Bifulco
Department of Humanities, University of Naples Federico II, Naples, Italy
e-mail: fbifulco@unina.it

T. Russo Spena, F. Bifulco (eds.), *Digital Transformation in the Cultural Heritage Sector*, Contributions to Management Science,
https://doi.org/10.1007/978-3-030-63376-9_3

transformations, rethinking what customers value most, and creating operating models that take advantage of what is newly possible for competitive differentiation.

New sources of a firm's abilities, based on new resources such as data and analytics, come into focus, which produces competitive differentiation (Shan et al. 2019). Enhanced by technology, firms easily incorporate and elaborate on customer and market insights and the idea of consumers greatly participating in the firms' content production and/or creation process. New business models expose the logic of consumers seen as value creators in a way such that reality reshapes the relationship between producer and consumer. This new interplay has an impact on value propositions and transforms companies' operations using digital technologies for greater customer interaction and collaboration. Various models have been developed, each with its own unique understanding and perspective; for example scholars such as Parmentier and Gandia (2017), Rumble and Mangematin (2015), and Zhao et al. (2019) propose multi-sided business models, as models that allow for "defining and organizing the value transactions made on the platform between the firm and the user groups" (Parmentier and Gandia 2017, p. 53).

However, when it comes to business models in cultural heritage, the academic literature and the related empirical research is less developed, if not scarce. A great part of the debate is on business models in commercial sectors, including wide cultural and creative ecosystems such as the publishing sector, music, and others; however, very little is known about new business, despite the attention paid to the novel elements brought about by technology in cultural heritage business (Bec et al. 2019; Navarrete 2013). In any event, business models in cultural organizations are a relevant part of the debate due to the specific features of this business. Therefore, further efforts are needed.

Over the last years, museums, archives, and other cultural heritage institutions have made a good start at digitizing important cultural heritage collections and developing digital services based on new technologies. Also, in the case of cultural heritage, the impetus to invent new business models comes from the same drive towards the digital. It should be noted that actors in the cultural heritage industry are particularly challenged by rapid changes; as technology evolves, both researchers and practitioners must address new and often unexpected challenges. Thus, experimentations with different tools and frameworks in the heritage business are currently taking place at various levels. Some of the new business models are still practical in nature yet continue to gain more strategic significance as they strengthen the role of cultural heritage in society. Analysis of business models is gaining prominence as a pathway for achieving and maintaining competitiveness for businesses as digital technologies continue to shape and transform the cultural business landscape.

This chapter aims to explore the conceptual and theoretical frameworks considered relevant to the subject of digital business transformation, and that helps increase the general understanding of new business models in the emerging cultural digital context. Analysis and comparison of different concepts and elements of business models are conducted with the aim of better understanding the digital business transformation in the cultural heritage sectors. By adding a comprehensive analysis and examples to the body of the existing business models, the chapter provides a framework for addressing a new basis for future research on this significant topic.

We first address the evolution of business models in the literature, with a focus on the recent digital resources to show the evolution of their conceptualization and to identify the main elements constituting it. The elements emerging from literature drive the provision of a novel framework to address the business models in cultural organizations and expand their current understanding from practical and theoretical views.

2 Business Models

In the last decade, considerable research has been conducted into the "business model" to advance the ideas and concepts in business sectors. As has been widely discussed recently (Fiorentino et al. 2020; Parmentier and Gandia 2017; Weerawardena et al. 2019) a business model is much more than the financial transactions that an organization undertakes. While scholars agree on what a business model is not, there is no generally accepted definition of the term "business model" through which to provide a systematic discussion (Müller et al. 2011; Shafer et al. 2005). In fact, multiple definitions of "business model" exist, which poses significant challenges for understanding its essential components.

The business model is defined as a conceptual tool created to clarify who the business actors are and what their roles are and to describe the potential benefits for various business actors and of the sources of revenue (Timmers 2000).

Many scholars have stressed the focus on economic aspects, as it has been defined that the model describes the rationale of how an organization creates, delivers, and captures value (Amit and Zott 2001; Osterwalder and Pigneur 2010; Weerawardena et al. 2019). According to other scholars, a business model is the representation of a given aspect of a firm's strategy; it outlines the essential details of how a firm selects its customers, defines, and differentiates its offerings, creates utility for its customers, defines the tasks it will perform or outsource, configures its resources, and, ultimately, captures profits (Slywotzky 1996). Many of the definitions include a great confusion in terminology as *"business model, strategy, business concept, revenue model and economic model are often used interchangeably"* (Sharma et al. 2010). Additionally, Shafer et al. (2005) stated that a *"business model is a representation of a firm's underlying core logic and strategic choices for creating and capturing value within a value network"* (p. 204). The business model has also been referred to *"as architecture, design, pattern, plan, method, assumption and statement"* (Morris et al. 2005; p. 726) that make the strategic choices explicit. For this, its architecture encompasses all the aspects of companies including the revenues, costs, and profits associated with the business delivering value. Teece (2010) defines business models as depending on a firm's capabilities and articulates its view with reference to the architecture providing and delivering value to customers. In

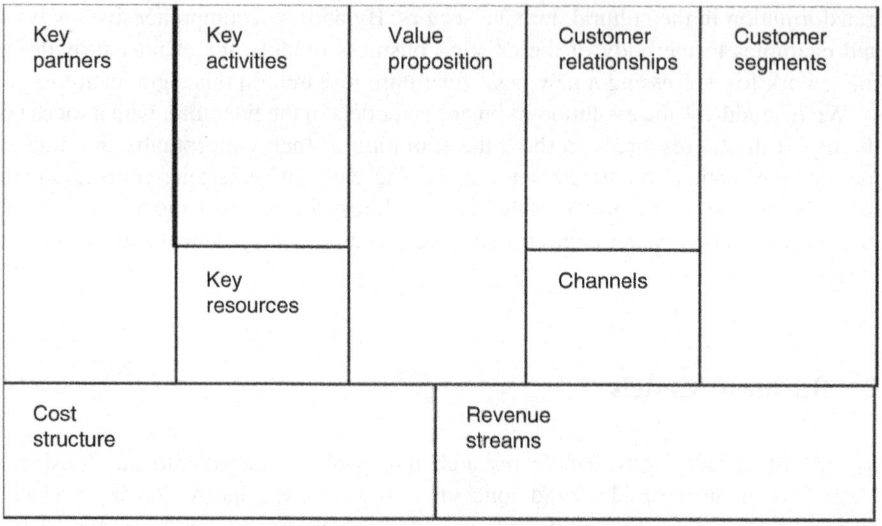

Fig. 1 The business model canvas. Source: adapted from Osterwalder and Pigneur (2010)

another sense, the business model is also seen as a communication or planning tool that allows entrepreneurs, investors, and partners to examine strategic choices for internal consistency, to surface the assumptions of the business plan, and to understand the vision towards which the business is being built. It is often just as useful in sense-making around a going concern, or when new opportunities and threats indicate a need for reinvention (Li 2020).

From a different perspective, other scholars clearly focused on the notion of a business model as a set of interrelated activities that transcends the boundaries of the firm into its wider environment (Zott and Amit 2017). As business models explain how value is created, they outlined that there is a strict linkage to the concept of the value chain and a value-creating entity and suggested that the focus is on stakeholders identification, value creation, visions, values, and networks and alliances. In this sense, a business model is a well-specified system of interdependent components or building blocks (i.e. activities and processes) that serves as a firm's organizing logic for value creation (for its customers) and value appropriation (for itself and its partners) (Sorescu et al. 2011).

More in practice, Osterwalder et al. (2005) provide a framework for analyzing business ideas and visualizing business model elements that have become part of the most adopted practice for business (Shan et al. 2019; Weerawardena et al. 2019). In their earlier business model canvas (Osterwalder and Pigneur 2010) (see Fig. 1) and in the more recent value proposition canvas (Osterwalder and Pigneur 2014), the authors take a feature-based approach, suggesting the importance of infrastructure, offering, customers, finances, and resources. It is a description of the value a company offers to one or several segments of customers and of the architecture of the firm and its network of partners for creating, marketing, and delivering this value relationship capital, to generate profitable and sustainable revenue streams.

2.1 *The Business Models Canvas*

In 2010 Osterwalder and Pigneur defined the Business Model Canvas as a "shared visual language" (p. 155); they added that the sharing of such a view set on nine building blocks would have facilitated the understanding of what a business model is and enabled a debate over its main elements. Indeed, the focus offered through canvas creates a chance to favour idea exchange and to discuss the effects of changes in firms. More in detail, a change in one of the building blocks doubtless has effects on the others; therefore, it may represent a tool to analyze a firm's path towards change through its key elements and the ties among them.

The right side of the BMC describes key partners, key activities, and key resources—i.e. the premises to set a firm's offering. The partners are the entities other than the firm itself that enable the workability of the business model. On the operational side, the activities describe what a firm should do to achieve the workability of its business model. Similarly, and in relation to the two previous blocks, resources are the elements and assets a firm should have to attain the workability of its business model. The aforementioned offering is then presented in the central part of the model as the value proposition; it represents the entire offering of a firm, namely, the combination of products and services as a bundle.

On the right side, the authors focused on customers, as they proposed the relationships to be taken care of, the segments grouping customers, and the channels useful to make concrete the value propositions. The relationships are the actions needed to acquire and keep a customer and how these relationships should be set with reference to each customer segment, namely, the groups of addressees of a value offering. Moreover, channels are the ways a firm communicates and reaches customer segments to accomplish the delivery of the value proposition.

Finally, on the lower side of the canvas, there are the economic elements of the business model, namely, revenue streams and cost structure. They respectively represent what a firm gets and what it sacrifices from an economic perspective to perform the operations of the business model.

3 Business Models and Digital Age

The increasing embeddedness of digital technologies in products and services (Bharadwaj et al. 2013; Ekman et al. 2019; Markovich et al. 2019) points to new ways of creating and delivering value and a need for new insights relating to the role of business models in the development of business (Chesbrough 2012; Yoo et al. 2010;). Digital business ecosystems enable the possibility of combining capabilities

Table 1 Digital business transformation: Key focuses

Focus	Elements	Content
Customer	Customer insights	Professional web controlling enables the analysis of usage behaviour and generation insights: firms have new opportunities to be in touch with customers through social-intelligence tool kit. (Harrysson et al. 2012)
	Customer experience and engagement	Cross-media customer experiences through mobile, social, and online platforms; online channels overwhelm traditional ones, but they are used for both online and offline purchases. (Voorveld et al. 2016)
Product	New products and services	New digital services and products (e.g. apps offer added value for customers); product and service innovation are one of the domains of digital transformation: separate business unit may focus on this digital infusion. (Wiesböck and Hess 2019)
	New technology	New technologies enable advanced services such as apps or digital signage terminals; new technologies expand the range of innovation to be brought in a firm, but they need a supportive culture. (Power and Heavin 2018)
Processes	Cost and time savings	Reduced sales, delivery, and service costs for fast time to market; indeed, firms can now decide between working more or working smarter, thanks to the support of technologies to resource allocation and business processes. (Yeow and Huat Goh 2015)
	Increase in productivity	Increase process and employees' productivity through the use of digital applications, as they support new and more efficient business architectures. (Xu et al. 2018)

across boundaries into innovative new offerings and solutions to create and capture value (Schlagwein and Schoder 2011). Digital business ecosystems feature not only idiosyncratic technological architectures (Yoo et al. 2010) but also important new interorganizational business architectures and new ways of competing in the business (Frank et al. 2019; Zott and Amit 2017). The digital transformation is maybe one of the most important drivers of business model innovation, as it is continuously challenging firms to innovate their business model. Businesses that restrain themselves from engaging in digital innovation are more exposed to the competition of other firms that are able to capture the latent value of technology (Tesch and Brillinger 2019).

One of the first contributions stressing the way new technologies can favour the emergence of new business models was proposed by Demestichas et al. (2013). They framed new business models as one of the goals achievable through technologies, as new technologies can favour the better management of all stakeholders, more fruitful business collaborations, and the creation of added value. Winter and Ono (2015) edited a book that grouped several contributions depicting the different pillars of the Future Internet and their role in shaping new ways of doing business (Table 1). Specifically, they describe the Future Internet as a "social engineer" with positive effects on businesses, as both public policies and research activities may now be driven by ubiquitous computing, ambient intelligence, and IoT towards economic growth, higher levels of efficiency, and sustainability. Furthermore, the expected effects may be wide if one thinks about the variety of business processes affected by data collection and data analysis, and the role of data on decision-making.

One of the most all-embedding approaches is the service-based business model (Kindström 2010), as customers and firms are expected to cooperate towards the achievement of value creation and IoT is something to elaborate on to lever all the assets available. Data are among these assets and can favour better service provision. In addition, a business model based on Cloud Computing (CC) relies on the already established and well-known definition of software as a service (Dempsey and Kelliher 2018). CC changed the ways software is distributed among firms and the revenue to be achieved through subscriptions, leading to more complicated conditions to achieve a profit. CC providers are willing to participate in the growth of this new market, but they are not encouraged by the perceived risk in enforcing the revenue.

Also, business models based on artificial intelligence (Corea 2017) take the focus of the mutual influence between these two elements: business models are changed because of AI, but AI is affected by business models. This mutual impact depends on the differences emerging over time, as actors' behaviour can be hugely affected by the free availability of AI. As observed in the short term, it would be easy to spread AI and to achieve better versions, but in the long term, the risk of free riding is relevant, simply because of the free availability (Müller 2016).

Critical aspects of new business models include reconfiguring the customer value proposition (i.e. what is being offered) and reshaping the operating model (i.e. how it is delivered) (Weerawardena et al. 2019). For example due to the digital transformation, images of artwork have become more mobile and travel easily between different platforms. As a result, products and services, information and customer engagement can be completely reshaped using the new capabilities for mobility, interactivity, and information access. The challenge then becomes how to monetize these new customer value propositions. The operating model can be realigned, so that customer preferences and requirements inform every activity in the value chain (Ellis et al. 2019; Madhani 2017). Doing this requires integrating all business activities and optimizing how data related to those activities are managed and tracked. For example by taking advantage of the digital affordance of modularity, platforms enable firms to focus their attention (and innovation) on one part of a system at a time, and to assemble those parts—whether they are products or activities—into a variety of configurations. The challenge is to determine the new business requirements and tools needed to achieve the full benefit for companies, customers, and all partners.

Consequently, the key features of the digital business model are the offering and interactions favouring the value proposition, the new revenue model, the new roles, the rewards reshaping the value chain, and the new customer segmentation and differentiation strategy leading to the setting up of a value network (Prem 2015).

4 Business Models and Cultural Context

As shown in the previous sections, in recent years technological innovation has reshaped the whole global market, also affecting the cultural sector. Additionally, new technologies have favoured and enabled the configuration of new kinds of services; in particular, there have been several investigations into how digitalization is affecting visiting experiences considered technologies as both challenges and opportunities for this sector, as in the case of collections and services available only online (Lazzeretti and Sartori 2016).

Literature contributions show that the digitization of cultural heritage is growing up together with the improvement of the quality of technical equipment and digital tools, as well as to create and propose to customers accurate reproductions of cultural artefacts and sites (Lazzeretti and Sartori 2016).

In this regard, it must be noted that cultural heritage businesses are particularly challenged by a rapid pace of change in their activities and competitive context and that many examples show that the companies in this kind of industry are far from reaching a standard in business models (Zhao et al. 2019).

The cultural heritage industry requires a logic that embeds multiple aspects (Klamer et al. 2013; Towse and Hernández 2020); indeed, in many companies that belong to the cultural and creative sectors, a firm delivers value to the customer, gets payment and converts those payments into an economic benefit. However, many organizations that are part of the cultural industry are more "welfare-dependent" or "publicly funded" and, in many countries, (still) less entrepreneurial (Landoni et al. 2020; Weerawardena et al. 2019). Nevertheless, most cultural organizations deliver cultural, social, and economic value; these firms are also changing both their language and behaviour and finally they find their way through and towards new business models.

Therefore, the internet and the digitization process led to a great and radical transformation of the whole global market, with special reference to distribution and communication channels, and in relationships with clients and partners, whose role as resources is even more pivotal. However, despite the increasing number of contributions on the business model, the literature on business models in the cultural sector is still scarce, although some scholars have identified two types of literature: "*consultancy literature (especially of the prescriptive variety) and scientific articles, which are themselves subdivided between basic research articles (descriptive and analytic) and applied research (prescriptive) aimed at professionals*" (Sutermeister 2018; p. 184).

With special reference to the consultancy-oriented literature, several contributions stress that the cultural sector is still having problems incorporating a commercial logic and defining innovative business models appropriate to the context

Key partners	Key activities	Value proposition	Customer relationships	Customer segments
State/Regional State and local governments Education Development bodies Creative arts sector Aboriginal communities National/International Governments Research institutions State/National/International Museums and collecting organisations Not for profit and community groups Funding bodies Cultural and scientific agencies Museum industry Tourism industry Other Industries	Public engagement and co-creation Planning and programme development Education and learning Exhibition and events Regional outreach Community advocacy Collections activity Research Promoting tourism Asset management Retail, hospitality and commercial services Staff development Industry development Regulatory work	«To be the heart of the state and the spirit of the people» «Creating opportunities to connect peoples, cultures, histories, knowledge and collections so that people can explore, understand, express and share their identity, culture and sense of place. «Pushing the boundaries to explore new ways to view the world and uncover the power in shared ideas and experiences»	Adding value Facilitating partners Building social capital Inclusive and accessible Social Learning Community engagement Content co-creation Research-based Face to face at events and show	All Western Australians Aboriginal people Intrastate, interstate and overseas tourists Families Children and young people Local, state and national government Research institutions Industry
	Key resources		**Channels**	
	Brand New Museum 7 museums/sites Collections Staff Intellectual property		Print, radio, tv adverts Collection online Social media Specialist networks Regional outreach Outreach via community networks	

Cost structure	Revenue streams
Staff Buildings Accommodation Depreciation Programme supplies/services	State government Admissions Fees for services Venue hire Retail Grants WAM Foundation

Fig. 2 Western Australian museum business model canvas. Source: adapted from https://www.culturehive.co.uk/

(Asfoura et al. 2010). On the other hand, applied or prescriptive research highlights the lack of professionalism in cultural heritage management, as well as the scant attention that the institutions pay to the sector (Sutermeister 2018; p. 184).

Indeed, apart from scholars' contributions, some cultural organizations have already adopted a structured business model inspired by Osterwalder and Pigneur's proposal. A very representative example is the Western Australian Museum (WAM), which shaped a "cultural" version of the business model canvas (Fig. 2) focusing on two building boxes, namely, *"value proposition" and "key partners,"* highlighting the social and cultural role of the museum, with special reference to its ability to create opportunities to connect peoples, cultures, histories, knowledge, and collections, to allow people to live and share enriching experiences. In detail, WAM brings together a unique set of assets and Key Resources that encompass heritage, culture, science, and the environment. It connects these with the interests of a broad range of Customer Segments. Assets, resources, and customers are united through a new people-focused Value Proposition that positions WAM as "of the people, by the people and for the people." The responsible and prepositive approach towards the community can also be detected in the description of the key activities as well as in the customer relationships building box; furthermore, in the canvas emerges the variety of key customers that are divided into international, national, and regional actors. Finally, the adoption of an omnichannel strategy is evident when one considers the channels list and the interplay among them.

5 Digital Business Models in Cultural Business: A Proposed Framework

This section offers the proposal of a framework to describe the new emerging business models based on digital transformation and affecting the cultural heritage business. To do that, we lean on the previous literature review on business models and digital business models. We analyzed the most recent contributions dealing with these two topics. Indeed, we launched a query on "business model*" on Web of Science–Web of Knowledge and built a dataset consisting of 1559 contributions in international journals published in the time frame from 2015 on. This dataset led us to identify the most recent and frequent advances based on the building blocks; to deal with this huge dataset, we looked for the nine building blocks in the keywords and abstract, then analyzed, in more detail, the content of the articles dealing with building blocks and offering a fresh view on them. Also, we discussed and analyzed these topics in the context of cultural heritage literature and deepened how the recent contributions addressed the themes. Finally, illustrations provided us with additional details and arguments on the building blocks of business models in the cultural heritage sector.

For purposes of the present chapter, a digital business model in cultural heritage is understood as a set of assumptions about how an organization, by relying on new technologies, creates new value and delivers it to a customer and other stakeholders, and how the value is turned into economic, social, and cultural outcomes.

Based on these aspects, the new theoretical and practical evidence led us to identify a new version of each building block as represented and described below (Fig. 3. In detail, seven pillars have been identified, namely, "actors integration," "content and users resources generation," "experience proposition," "personas and crowd actor," "social customer relationship management" "omnichannel strategy,"

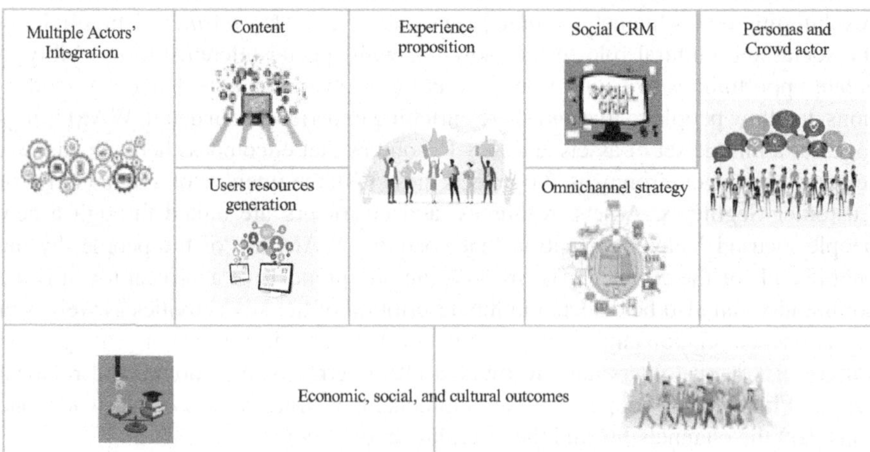

Fig. 3 The new proposed framework. Source: Author's elaboration

and "economic, social, and cultural outcomes." Therefore, in the following sections, a comprehensive analysis and examples will be provided to shape a more solid base for future research on this important topic.

5.1 From Partners' Collaboration to Actors' Integration

Market dynamics are today substantially changed, as all the actors have now acquired an active role. Nowadays, new forms of interaction have been developed, moving from collaboration, or cooperation, to the integration of sources of knowledge and resources in line with Osterwalder's definition of key partners (Osterwalder and Pigneur 2010).

One of the main elements leading to this new approach is the diffusion of new technologies in all the economic sectors, and, in particular, in the service market.

As technologies are changing our everyday lives, making them smarter and always connected through digital tools and devices, companies must concentrate on acquiring more heterogeneous resources involving a wider range of partners to create the applications, software platforms, tools, and services needed to create integrated solutions (Storbacka 2011; Wieland et al. 2017).

More complex ecosystem perspectives are now emerging throughout the business landscape and across industries, with new ways to create, deliver, and capture value (Fuchs et al. 2000). In line with the new approach and goals, the need for integration and collaboration is further amplified and made possible thanks to the even-faster-changing technologies and consumers' behaviour, leading to a demand for a highly customized user experience (McKinsey 2017). More in detail, the resources are brought by the actors contributing to the various processes, from production to consumption, and all of them favour access to these resources (Amit and Han 2017). These make it evident that a proper integration process is a needed aspect to shape more valuable services and capture values. However, in an ecosystem view, it became apparent that capability/resource integration can be considered effective only if the consequences are beneficial for all participants and the focus is on continuous value creation (Fuchs et al. 2000; Mandrella et al. 2020). Within the cultural heritage context, integration among local agencies, local communities, and businesses need to be considered due to their ecosystem effects (Li et al. 2020).

Exhibit 1 Foxfire Museum

The Foxfire Museum was formed in 1974 and is located in Georgia. Its main aim is to preserve and enhance local heritage—both natural and cultural—through a learner-centred approach, involving students and local communities to build connections across generations.

(continued)

In detail, Foxfire's mission is "to preserve the diverse traditions of Southern Appalachia and advance the understanding and appreciation of cultural heritage through public programs, publications, and learner-centered education."

Since its inception, Foxfire has become a national phenomenon, and students purchased land establishing a physical and solid presence in the community.

At the moment, the museum comprises over 106 acres where students can build structures from period materials after learning traditional construction methods, thereby transforming the open-air area of the museum into a space filled with artefacts, tools, and folk art pieces that provide a glimpse into the lives of the people who inhabited that area over 180 years ago.

The museum has been able to accomplish its mission thanks to members and donors who have supported the museum for over 50 years.

Therefore, Foxfire can be considered as being built from the community. In exchange, members receive access to everything the museum offers—exhibitions, historic structures, gardens and trails, special activities, as well as craft classes and workshops throughout the year. In its experience, collaboration is based not only on sharing projects; instead, it involves a new way of doing based on identifying all the stakeholders, providing a new way to form a working team to achieve a specific purpose, creating collaborative working planning and designing and facilitating collaborative tasks. Integration is not simply an extension of collaborative work; it includes an entire process that involves new ways of identifying partners and establishing parity among them, the building of mutual goals, shared responsibility, and decision-making. Through collaborative processes, the museum plays an important role in helping partners keep sight of the goal and stay motivated and in tune with the shared objectives.

5.2 *From a Focus on Activities and Resources to the Generation of Content and User Resources*

Information is gaining more relevance in the relations between a company and its customers. Sometimes this relevance is greater than that of the products themselves; therefore, companies pay more attention to content creation, which paves the way to content delivery. Content is significant, such as information that is personal and timely when accessed by the customer. "Content" refers to photos, images, texts, scans, metadata, blog posts, videos, tags, audio files, and all other online representations of companies' resources or assets.

Studies on business models focused on content at the core of what business models provide to perform activities, thereby supporting the shaping of value propositions. Cristofaro (2020) observed the new emerging business models as a consequence of digital transformation and the shift towards digital service. He investigated the evolution of business models in line with the pervasive development of apps and claimed the content to be pillars of the value offerings that companies address through mobile apps. Similarly, Casais et al. (2020) investigated the business models of companies dealing with the sharing economy in the tourism industry and the process of describing how these companies and their customers integrate efforts into online platforms. Content is crucial in the cultural heritage domain too, as witnessed by the relevance of online reviews and communication strategies (Bigné et al. 2020) or as a process affecting both service provision and the achievement of innovation outcomes (Narangajavana Kaosiri et al. 2019). Therefore, content plays a key role in the design of the value proposition and its related aspects regarding how to engage the customer (Prebensen 2017).

Moreover, user-generated content provides an example of the additional resources that the interactions of the platforms favour by multiplying the opportunities for marketing activities as well as innovation. The tie between innovation and content as a resource had been proposed by Musteen et al. (2018) with reference to virtual worlds as *loci* hosting the user-generated innovation. This innovation has multiple positive impacts, such as revenue generation for firms, an increasing interest in online platforms and virtual contexts, and a stimulus towards entrepreneurship; therefore, the authors consider, as a not-to-be-missed feature, the interdependency of multiple areas of business models, such as resources (to be combined), partnerships (to be expanded), and activities (to be framed in a wider and also virtual context). Additionally, content generation by users led to the reconsidering of activities in traditional business models, as the participation of multiple actors in creating content may offer a new view of activities. The support brought by users is framed in the wider perspective of innovation; companies can leverage the insights offered by users and set strategies based on these new sources of information. This unleashes creativity and enlarges business opportunities in cultural heritage (Cerisola 2019). Digital content (blog posts, videos, polls, infographics) is the translation of a resource—or an asset—into something that the audience and other actors can use or work within the digital realm (Tom Dieck and Jung 2017).

Exhibit 2 Tate Museum Digital Strategy

In 2013, Tate launched a digital strategy for the 3 years to come with the headline: Digital as a Dimension of Everything; which outlined a guide for the digital transformation of the Tate organization.

In this strategy, the previous Head of Digital at Tate, John Stack, developed a holistic digital proposition to achieve Tate's goal to endorse public pleasure and understanding of art. The digital mission proceeds from Tate Director Sir Nicholas Serota's idea is that the future museum will be rooted in the very buildings it occupies but will address audiences around the globe.

(continued)

According to Serota, the authority of the future museum will depend on how well this is done (Stack 2013). When the digital strategy was written for the four Tate galleries, Tate's art collection was already digitized and a new goal to digitize the archive, special library collections, and artist books was set. Another goal highlighted in the digital strategy is greater curatorial engagement with the online art and archive collection and in the digital spaces overall. The experience of the galleries is also mentioned in the digital strategy, aiming at transforming visitor experiences with Wi-Fi connections to enable the use of the extended websites for on-site use. Another dimension of the visitor experiences mentioned in the digital strategy is interactive comment walls linked to social media, which Tate Modern wishes to deploy more widely (Ibid.).

Other important digital aspects that affect the way Tate addresses the collection are mentioned in the strategy, i.e. the aim at creating short films and blog posts using the website, social media, and emails. Tate's curators are encouraged to write blog posts relating to Tate's exhibitions. The use of social media is a way to engage the current audience and reach out to new audiences. Another way to engage the audience is through social collections online. The audience is encouraged to use social learning features connected to online art and archive collection. This is mentioned as a way to enter into a "wider digital ecosystem," increase audience engagement, and "augment the digitized collection with audience voices and ideas." Another way to increase the engagement mentioned in the strategy is through smartphone apps offering digital content connected to the galleries (Ibid.).

Tate aims to use digital platforms and channels to provide rich content for existing and new audiences for art, create, and nurture an engaged arts community, and maximize the associated revenue opportunities. It achieves this by embracing digital activity and developing digital skills across the organization.

(*source:Aadapted from Tate Gallery official website—www.tate.org.uk)*

5.3 *From the Value Proposition to the Experience Proposition*

The value proposition plays a central role in the business model, as well as in its representation through the canvas. The pivotal role of the value proposition stems from its impact on addressing an offering to consumers, including ways to manage the relationship with these consumers (Amitrano et al. 2017).

The complexity of offerings is mirrored in value propositions, leading to expand what consumers can access and includes every interaction between the customer and the business (Lanzolla and Markides 2020). Indeed, it has been stated that the value proposition itself begins to offer something to consumers, even before service is offered (Leroi-Weldens et al. 2017; Pencarelli et al. 2017), due to the effect on the cognitive side. Similarly, the long-term effects and the memory of an offering may bring potential value to consumers; therefore, its consequences can be better represented with reference to the notion of experience. The experience represents a pivotal part of the new business models (Fissi et al. 2020). The notion of experience is proposed with reference to the integration of emotional, cognitive, and relational elements instead of just functional ones (Ladhari et al. 2017). Moreover, the shift towards experience is also depicted as a consequence of digitalization; therefore, customers are at the centre of companies' activities and their business models, especially in light of a change brought about by technologies (Georgopoulos et al. 2017). A value-oriented business model has been proposed that recalled the experience as the final essence of the interactive process between a firm and a customer (To et al. 2019). The experience is both pivotal and complex due to the multiple elements affecting the interactions with customers. The business model overcomes the traditional competitive view towards a more integrated and experience-based perspective. The core offering of business models is no longer properly represented by value proposition; the experience is more suitable in describing what is offered to consumers and how firms make offers to focus on multiple benefits—not just functional ones—and in a wider time frame.

Exhibit 3 British Music Experience

The British Music Experience is a museum of popular music in the UK. It offers content describing the lives and careers of the best-known singers in the history of pop music in Britain and the rest of the world.

The core offering of the museum is brand-new and imbues new technologies to make the visit more immersive. Visitors are driven into a hall filled with musical instruments, dresses, pictures, and screens showing the best of pop music. Additionally, music and lights will complete a multi-sensorial experience of music. Therefore, technologies would give dynamicity to the visit, as visitors would not just see pictures, instruments, and dresses, but also take a trip into the past and into the world of the music of various decades. All in all, the visit would lead to a cognitive, emotional, and multi-sensorial experience driven by technologies.

The British Music Experience tells the story of British Music through costumes, instruments, performance, and memorabilia from the Beatles and Bowie to Adele, Oasis, and X-Factor. Book in advance and get a free audio-guide.

Discover the ultimate history of British Rock and Pop, through over 600 artefacts on display in Liverpool's iconic Cunard Building.

From the Beatles, The Rolling Stones, and Bowie to The Spice Girls, Oasis, Adele, and X-Factor, the BME boasts an unrivalled collection of memorabilia, stage outfits, instruments, images, and footage. It charts the beginnings, rise,

(continued)

and influence of British pop from 1945 to the present day. We have got outfits worn by artists from Freddie Mercury and Dusty Springfield, to the Spice Girls, Adam Ant and Little Mix, and musical instruments played by some of the world's most renowned artists from Noel Gallagher to the Sex Pistols. The museum even has handwritten song lyrics from Adele, the original statues from the Brits and the Apple Corp front door from Saville Row.

The museum includes galleries, interactive zones, audiovisual experiences, and hologram performances. Visitors can get hands-on in the Gibson Brands Interactive Studio by learning to play guitar, drums, or keyboards. Try your hand at being a rock star by testing the vocal booth and dance your way through the eras in our Dance the Decades studio. Star Café and Merch Store are located in the foyer and are open to the general public (no ticket required) during museum opening hours.

Learning and Public Programmes, together with our events programme and temporary exhibitions further add to the experience. Museum offers educational workshops and bespoke tours for school children, and a range of public events including masterclasses hosted by industry experts, film screenings, Q&As, book launches, and live gigs. We are even available for private hire if you are looking to host an event with a wow factor.

Source: Adapted from the British Music Experience official website—www.britishmuseumexperience.com

5.4 From Customer Segment to Personas and Crowd Actors

Customer segmentation has always been a fundamental step in planning and implementing marketing strategies. In his proposal of a business model, Osterwalder recalled the traditional conception of the market structure mentioning the mass market, the niche market, the segmented market, and the diversified market.

Nowadays, more customer data is available to offer complete profiling of the customer, thus supporting the segmentation and offering more insights into data as a way to improve the segmentation (Sivarajah et al. 2017). A so-called persona represents a new approach to the segmentation process in which the focus is on *"the process of creating representative groups of similar users"* (Laporte et al. 2012; p. 265). Personas offer more than segments, as the description is more complete and also embeds additional elements, such as personality and values (Lee et al. 2020). Thanks to new technology and digital tools, companies are now able to occupy their own "persona segment," adopting the most suitable technology (An et al. 2018).

In addition to expressing the reality of the new social context, scholars talk about crowd acting as a single actor—or "crowd actor" (Bigham et al. 2015; Raj and Kar 2015)—as a new vision of community concept through the lens of new technologies, and tracing a path from customer to the community to the crowd. Bigham et al. (2015) describe the crowd as *"a dynamic group of individuals* (that) *collectively form a single actor that responds to real-time performance tasks,* e.g., *controlling an on-screen character, driving a robot, or operating an existing desktop interface"* (p. 101). In museum research, Cappa et al. (2020), described the role of the crowd by focusing on the concept of actors as resources. Crowd involvement is the inclusion of visitors as a resource to act in a process that improves the cultural experience and connects the visitor's individual experience to those of others (Vermeeren et al. 2018).

Crowd-based initiatives are strongly focused on ICTs as tools able to facilitate the involvement of dispersed individuals from different geographical, social, and cultural belongings. This allowed companies to benefit from the various types of expertise and resources with which people are endowed (Cappa et al. 2020) and conceive of the museum experiences as interconnected through the contribution of the crowd. An example of the persona method applied to museums is represented by the Van Abbemuseum in Eindhoven, Netherland, in particular, with reference to the exhibition programme named Play Van Abbe.

Exhibit 4 The Van Abbemuseum, Eindhoven, the Netherlands

The Van Abbemuseum exhibition presents a selection of important art pieces and guests several special guest artists.

Visitors are invited to a role whilst visiting the museum, choosing among four categories, namely the pilgrim, the tourist, the flaneur, and the worker, and become themselves a part of the exhibition.

In shaping the categories, the museum focuses on the criteria that visitors usually use to evaluate or criticize art. Each of these roles lets the visitor live the museum in a different way, according to their own attitude; in line with this, roles are not fixed, and the visitors can choose to change them during their visit, adopting a new character. They can also play different roles to visit the same rooms or areas more than once.

More in detail, the Pilgrim is identified as someone that seeks enlightenment through contemplative observation. Texts and objects are continuous reinforcements of the pilgrim's belief. Consequently, the journey itself becomes as significant as the destination."

The visitor is someone looking for a way to break from the daily routine thanks to unusual experiences; he/she enjoys things that are declared "authentic" and aims at understanding "the essence of things back home by exploring new environments."

The Flaneur represents a very open-minded visitor, interested in everything, although not committing to nothing; he/she seems to have to aim—or, at least, does not declare it—appearing "always distant from reality and using encounters to illustrate own internal narratives."

(continued)

Differently, the Worker has a specific interest in the exhibition, he/she is involved and engaged in visiting the museum, while figuring out "reality via action and production."

In their visiting experience, guests are assisted by "game masters" that guide them, help with orientation, and giving feedback.

Source: Adapted from the Van Abbemuseum official website—www.vanabbemuseum.nl/

5.5 From Customer Relationship Management (CRM) to Social Customer Relationship Management

Customer relationships must be managed to create fruitful ties between a firm and consumers and to favour the emerging of long-term relationships, as this would be beneficial for firms' profitability, word-of-mouth, and a company image (Karjaluoto et al. 2016).

New media are also channels favouring the development and managing of relationships with customers, both current and potential. Some scholars address the role of social media platforms and their technical features as new elements for managing customer engagement; completeness, flexibility, and integration are the key novelties that social media bring to customer relationship management (Di Gangi and Wasko 2016). A switch from traditional CRM to new social forms is suggested. Indeed, since 2011, scholars (Baird and Parasnis 2011) started dealing with social CRM as a consequence of the unstoppable growth of social media. Social CRM has started being considered a new phenomenon offering the chance to manage relationships with customers, and relevant for recognizing customers' voices and taking into account their opinions and the willingness to get engaged. With the further development of social CRM, models started to appear, as it was with the Social CRM House (Malthouse et al. 2013)—namely, the combination of the CRM dimension and social media dimension. This combination leads to a consideration of the influence among components of social media, the typologies of social media, and the space and applications in which they act. The consideration of both elements leads to a consideration of social CRM consisting of dynamic capabilities, due to the orientation towards customers and the implementation of technology (Harrigan et al. 2015). Therefore, the relation itself is the outcome of a social CRM process, shifting the attention of firms towards relationship-building before focusing on other performances. More recently, social CRM has been considered the cornerstone of engagement actions addressed towards actors (Hakimi and Mehdi 2020); in any event, social CRM is not shown as directly affecting firm performance, but it may lead to the improvement of social media-based relationships, thus creating fertile ground for further and fruitful activities.

According to the same perspective, social media may partner with traditional media in customer relationship media, but it cannot be the only option that a firm chooses; however, the SCRM is seen especially as a new and beneficial way to support the activity of salespeople (Piccarozzi et al. 2018). Additionally, and with special reference to cultural heritage, a recent perspective also considered the effects of social CRM on the hospitality industry (Jung et al. 2018); indeed, the authors described the opportunities offered by technologies to improve the offering and increase the effectiveness of managing customer relationships through social media and based on new applications.

Other scholars stressed that social media is not just a communication instrument but that it provides the opportunity to perform different business activities (Han and Trimi 2017). They described social media as more than a single tool, as social media is a context hosting marketing strategy. SCRM can guide the process of designing online strategies, and the benefits are centred around increasing "customer insights and engagement;" they are not peripheral but fundamental to driving business performance (Li et al. 2017).

Exhibit 5 Museum of Modern Art (MoMA—New York)

The Museum of Modern Art (MoMA) is one of the best-known museums in the world. MoMA has many visitors and events; therefore, managing customer relationships is not an easy task. With that in mind, the board chose to adopt Salesforce to manage all the platforms and the wide array of information arising from the museum's more than 2.5 million visitors per year.

On-site collected data, social media pages, reviews, and internally available information were all combined in a unique set of data to properly deal with visitors' inquiries. Additionally, the advantage of using such an all-embedding solution stands on both the collection and the usage of information, as data are collected in 15 channels and used in seven facilities throughout the museum. The museum migrated all data-driven operations 9 years ago and all employees are using the same instruments; this has promoted dialogue among departments and may lead to further improvements in the activities. Additionally, the use of the software was recently further enlarged; indeed, through Salesforce, MoMA created a system to manage the relationship with customers and engage them in new experiences.

When they decided to implement Salesforce as their CRM platform in 2011, the MoMA was really a pioneer. At that time, there was not a Salesforce-based customized application for Museums, so the MoMA had to do all the hard work on their own. But because the MoMA is ... well, the MoMA, they had the means, the team and—let us be honest—the "guts" to do the whole project on their own. It has been a success for them, and the great news is that all museums can now benefit from their experience.

When the project was initiated, the museum had several criteria around the "must do" of their future CRM platform:

(continued)

- The solution had to offer the capacity to integrate all data from the 15 channels and Points of sales of the institution.
- Reporting was previously done the old way: extracting data from their different platforms and merging them under Excel. The museum's team obviously wanted to get rid of that and looked for a solution with impressive reporting capabilities and automations.
- MoMA was not better than any other museum when they started: they too were previously storing their data in their basement! Because of the logistical constraints, maintenance, and risks related to the—unfortunately still too frequently seen—"basement storage," the new solution had to be in the cloud.
- The team wanted a mobile solution that could follow them in their growth and enable them to work anywhere within the seven facilities of the museum . . . and so they went with Salesforce.

They observed two types of improvement; those they anticipated, and those they did not.

- They are now able to take a holistic look at their members and donors and can more accurately gauge their interaction with the museum.
- Using Salesforce's real-time dashboard, they can monitor areas such as membership, lead-conversion, fundraising, ticketing sales, and email campaign effectiveness.
- They now understand their retailing channel such as: what is selling; who is buying; how much they are spending; the demographics of buyers such as students, families, couples, patrons, etc.
- Their mobile app has increased cloud-sourced membership and has resulted in reduced physical queues and improved visitor experience.
- The increased transparency among internal MoMA departments has increased the cultivation of donors and prospects.
- They can now run specific targeted marketing campaigns based on customer data. This has increased success rates and increased membership conversion.
- The centralized solution has reduced the cost of ownership through the reduction of internal hardware and minimized service and maintenance costs.
- The improved time to market means that the museum can react quickly to trends and changes.

Sources: moma.org, veevart.com, artsandculture.google.com, cetrixcloudservices.com

5.6 *From Channels to an Omnichannel Strategy*

Digital transformation is affecting the distribution and choice of market channels; indeed, firms are competing on wider and multiple markets, aiming at being in touch with customers who were previously out of reach or making business transactions more comfortable and widely available, with no space and time constraints. This change affects business models, as the business environment changes according to the availability of different channels and points of interactions; this tie has been highlighted by scholars investigating business models and tying them to the so-called omnichannel strategy (Davis-Sramek et al. 2020).

An omnichannel strategy integrates the offline (or on-site) experience and the online one (Rigby 2011); this combination is both a challenge and an opportunity for firms, as customers look for the opportunity to be served as soon as possible and in the most comfortable place. The challenge depends on the intricacies of integrating channels and touchpoints considering the impact of social media and new technologies. The omnichannel strategy provides more chances to personalize a customer journey and results in a strategy more prone to creating successful experiences for customers by overcoming the most atomistic paths of the multichannel approach (Rusanen 2019).

The omnichannel perspective applied to business models affects a firm and its propositions. The issues the authors focus on are tied to the e-business notion by Zott and Amit (2017) and offer a transformation that is structural, cross-segment, and contextual. As some scholars have outlined (Siqueira Jr et al. 2020), it is hard to separate the on-site and online markets, with both of them being equally relevant. The rising popularity of the omnichannel strategy emerges as a response to more complex and demanding consumers (Tan and Gligor 2019). Within the cultural heritage service sector, studies on the integration of the online and offline are mirrored in communication activities first, as museums and other institutional organizations are oriented to spread digital content and information through different channels. The overlapping between the online and the offline environment also leads to a reconfiguration of the museum value proposition (Pavoni 2019) in relation to the increased opportunities to provide new learning experiences and innovate the value creation activities (Frontoni et al. 2019).

Exhibit 6 MANN—National Archaeological Museum of Naples

The National Archaeological Museum of Naples managed both service provision and its communication through multiple channels.

Indeed, through the website, the on-site collection is described carefully to invite people to visit the facilities and experience unique cultural heritage settings consisting of various collections based on marbles, mosaics, bronze statues, Egyptian artefacts, busts, and several remains from Pompeii. Additionally, the MANN app combines history with high-tech, as the app leads

(continued)

visitors through both the traditional on-site visit and an augmented reality environment involving Pompeii and related events, to be experienced through a tablet or mobile phone. Additionally, the extension of the visitor experience is geographical; the section "Mann in the world" describes all the events that have taken place around the world based on pieces of art that MANN lent to other museums, including museums in Grosseto, Rome, New York, Portland, Paris, New York, Guangzhou, Atlanta, Perth, and Athens, to name just a few. This extension took place in some unconventional locations, such as the Airport of Naples and the European Court of Justice in Luxembourg. Furthermore, a game was launched to get people around the world interested in the museum offerings while allowing them to experience something new.

In a similar vein, MANN's communication has grown a lot in recent years. The museum launched a project—named OBVIA—proposing comics, books, events, and partnerships with other museums and businesses from the tourism sector. All these efforts led to a huge increase in both the number of people interacting with the museum through different channels and a very relevant increase in the number of visitors. One of the most recent interventions related to communication consists of 50 short videos to launch a storytelling campaign. These videos are broadcast on underground stations in Naples, through the official website of the museum, and through a blog with a worldwide audience. The videos show some of the most interesting pieces of art and remain exhibited at MANN and are partnered with an audio description of both historic and artistic features.

Source: Adapted from the official website of the museum—www.museoarcheologiconapoli.it

5.7 From Cost and Revenue to Economic, Social, and Cultural Outcomes

The role of companies in society has changed significantly in the last decades; a wider approach is now preferred, as the impact of firms' activities in the community is a hot topic in the scientific debate as well as among practitioners (Zahra and Wright 2016).

In this regard, Spieth et al. (2019) talked about *"hybrid organizational forms that combine commercial and welfare institutional logics and play an increasingly important role in addressing the grand societal challenges we face today"* (p. 427), focusing on the contrast between hybrid social purpose in contrast and commercial business models. Pisano et al. (2016) highlighted the multi-sided outcomes of new business models, with effects to be measured on—and for—the whole context. Therefore, economic measures are not sufficient for assessing the impact of new business models. These measures must also include the political, institutional, and educational outcomes for a given geographical context and the relationships created, seen as useful in generating new value networks for a territory.

New technologies and the multi-actor (or multi-sided) approach amplify the impact of companies' businesses as no longer only economic but also social and cultural; in this regard, some scholars talk about the social engagement paradigm (Hamari et al. 2016). This also affects companies because their main goal is now creating, sharing, and delivering value, for both society and the company itself. The evolution of the role of customers from single actors to crowd actors, described in subsection 3.5.4, turned customers and other actors into co-designers of service, going beyond economic goals and taking into account the social and cultural role of companies and all the other actors (Cappa et al. 2020). Other scholars (Stubbs and Cocklin 2008) introduced the concept of sustainable business models (SBMs), further deepened by Fiorentino and colleagues in 2020, which observed how companies use smart technologies to create and/or improve their sustainable business models. In the cultural heritage sector, Sinapi and Ballereau (2016) proposed the concept of the cultural business model in their study of the sustainable business model in cultural entrepreneurship, aimed at detecting "factors that influence the emergence of sustainable business models in the cultural entrepreneurial process" (p. 336). They stated, in conclusion, that the business model "constitutes a promising analytical grid to investigate sustainability logics within the entrepreneurial process" (p. 340). Differently, Wnuczak (2018) proposed Social Value Added (SVA) as an adaptation of the well-established Economic Value Added (EVA) to incorporate the social costs and benefits, taking into account consequences for public assets, local residents, connected businesses, and the cultural domain as a whole.

Exhibit 7 The Museum of Contemporary Art Querétaro

The Museum of Contemporary Art Querétaro (MACQ) is located in Santiago de Querétaro in Mexico.

Originally, the museum was a monastery and then a military barracks before becoming a public primary school. In 2008 the building was extremely deteriorated. Due to the risk presented by the roofs and mezzanines, the use of the school was removed, leaving the building abandoned for 10 years until the present restoration.

Currently, the MACQ is a 2500-square metre museum with two central galleries, a book shop, and a multimedia library.

The new Museum of Contemporary Art Querétaro is one of the most important projects in the country in terms of cultural infrastructure. In the middle of the twentieth century, it was declared an artistic and historical monument. It is part of the zone of historical monuments of Querétaro and is inscribed on the UNESCO World Heritage list.

The museum aims to promote and disseminate artistic practices through research, dialogue, workshops, and non-formal education processes.

(continued)

Its exhibition is divided into four distinct themes: the history of the building, social themes, poetry, and new technologies.

With special reference to the social theme, art pieces dealing with subjects such as migration, environmental devastation, and the reduction of violence are exhibited. Furthermore, the museum encourages and supports the dialogue between local and international artists. For example ceramic sculptures by Mexican artist Rodrigo Lara are surrounded by photographs by Frenchman Pierre Huyghe. Additionally, modern sculptures by Mexican Antonio O'Connell, made from reclaimed materials to resemble a house construction in an array, are next to pieces by Salvador Dalí.

While portraying such cross-continental exhibitions, the museum also aims to favour local development, including the integration between its community and the various forms of contemporary art production.

In general, the mission of the Museum of Contemporary Art Querétaro is to be a space that shows and establishes relationships between local, regional, and international artists through different forms of contemporary art and to present a high-quality educational program based on workshops, libraries, and other social initiatives. Also, its vision is to be one of the main references at the regional and national levels for the exhibition of, and education about, contemporary art, as well as to be an institution that promotes the integration of the community and contemporary art.

Source: Adapted from the official website of the Museum—www.macq.mx

6 Conclusion

This chapter provides a framework to address the complex layer that digital transformation has added to the way companies conduct business in cultural heritage.

As a unit of analysis, the business model provides a systemic perspective on how companies provide, deliver, and capture value. Digital transformation widely impacts all these processes by reshaping the architecture for the product, service, and information flows, including a consideration of the new role of the customer to be engaged and satisfied as well as of multiple partners to be involved and their integrated benefits.

The most relevant and promising change that emerged with reference to cultural organizations' creation and proposition of value is that digital transformation is transforming these organizations from the point of view of their social role. The audience—both actual and potential—is more than just customers. Consequently, the companies providing cultural services are more than mere providers. The plethora of actors in cultural heritage contexts can contribute to multiple—albeit different—ways to create something valuable, not just for customers. The partners—or, more in general, the actors—represent the new engine of partnerships, based on resource integration rather than simply collaboration. Similarly, customers contribute to firms' activities by highlighting new chances to set up value propositions and as content generators. This latter is a concept useful in describing the new shape of resources in firms' activities, as resources are no longer static; they are constantly refreshed, not only because of firms but also through the participation of multiple actors. Moreover, the way users shape the context in which cultural services are offered changes the value proposition. It is not a process leading to the same effect; rather, the offering in the digital context is perceived differently by any customer due to its interaction with the context itself. As a consequence, it is not just a value proposition; it is an experience that mirrors the uniqueness and personalization of customer interactions with the cultural value propositions.

In addition, information sharing, real-time interactions, and the multiple channels available to communicate and deliver an offering are all changing because of social media. Customer relationship management became social to take care of customers where they are. It is not just a mere switch from a traditional channel to a new one; it is something that represents a wide network of interactions and touchpoints in which the firm and the consumer are not the only entities; rather, a multitude takes part in these processes and may affect them. In a similar vein, the delivery process includes opportunities for market development, as it would be easier to attract new customers because of novelty, interactivity, and participation. The crowd is the innate feature of new technologies, as it represents something brand-new for most industries, i.e. interactivity, because there are additional ways to be in touch with firms. Customers may benefit from these wider chances for interaction and participation, as these instruments lessen the amount of time and space constraints, thereby making available content, experience, and new relations.

Additionally, not only would multiple actors affect the interactions for relationship management and along channels between a firm and a consumer, but also the opposite effect would occur; social actors may be directly interested by the social value created by a firm and a customer in their interaction, as the economic side of a transaction is no longer sufficient for understanding the complexity of the value creation processes in business models addressing technologies as a relevant feature.

Through the proposed framework, it is possible to foresee the cultural heritage domain as described by a new business model, in which the social actors and the multitude of actors and their relations are crucial features. These new characteristics of a business model to be applied to cultural heritage represent a new challenge for cultural organizations. Indeed, technology is both a challenge and an opportunity, as museums and other cultural firms may lever the chances offered by new technologies to stimulate user-generated content to both enhance and refresh the available resources. Similarly, it is necessary to address the new social domain as the cases have shown, as customers increasingly use technologies to select an offer, verify its main characteristics, experience it, and comment on it. Therefore, social tools bring customers a variety of instruments before, during, and after the value experience, leading to new opportunities for value creation.

References

Amit R, Han X (2017) Value creation through novel resource configurations in a digitally enabled world. Strateg Entrep J 11(3):228–242

Amit R, Zott C (2001) Value creation in e-business. Strateg Manag J 22(6–7):493–520

Amitrano C, Tregua M, Russo-Spena T, Bifulco F (2017) Evidenze di service cultural experiences in Castel Nuovo. Implicazioni e prospettive. In: Aveta A (ed) Castel Nuovo in Napoli. Ricerche integrate conoscenza critica per il progetto di restauro e valorizzazione. Art Studio Paparo, Napoli

An J, Kwak H, Jung SG, Salminen J, Jansen BJ (2018) Customer segmentation using online platforms: isolating behavioral and demographic segments for persona creation via aggregated user data. Soc Netw Anal Min 8(1):54–74

Asfoura E, Kassem G, Dumke R (2010) Characterization of business model for federated ERP systems. Int J U- & E-Service, Sci Tech 3(4):19–36

Baird CH, Parasnis G (2011) From social media to social customer relationship management. Strateg Leadersh 39(5):30–37

Bec A, Moyle B, Timms K, Schaffer V, Skavronskaya L, Little C (2019) Management of immersive heritage tourism experiences: A conceptual model. Tour Manag 72:117–120

Bharadwaj A, El Sawy OA, Pavlou PA, Venkatraman N (2013) Digital business strategy: toward a next generation of insights. MIS Q:471–482

Bigham JP, Lasecki WS, Wobbrock J (2015) Target Acquisition and the Crowd Actor. Human Computation 1:101–131

Bigné E, Zanfardino M, Andreu L (2020) How online reviews of destination responsibility influence tourists' evaluations: an exploratory study of mountain tourism. J Sustain Tour 28 (5):686–704

Cappa F, Rosso F, Capaldo A (2020) Visitor-Sensing: Involving the Crowd in Cultural Heritage Organizations. Sustainability 12(4):1445

Casais B, Fernandes J, Sarmento M (2020) Tourism innovation through relationship marketing and value co-creation: A study on peer-to-peer online platforms for sharing accommodation. J Hosp Tour Manag 42:51–57

Cerisola S (2019) A new perspective on the cultural heritage–development nexus: the role of creativity. J Cult Econ 43(1):21–56

Chesbrough H (2012) Open innovation: Where we've been and where we're going. Res Technol Manag 55(4):20–27

Corea F (2017) Artificial intelligence and exponential technologies: Business models evolution and new investment opportunities. Springer, London

Cristofaro M (2020) E-business evolution: an analysis of mobile applications' business models. Tech Anal Strat Manag 32(1):88–103

Davis-Sramek B, Ishfaq R, Gibson BJ, Defee C (2020) Examining retail business model transformation: a longitudinal study of the transition to omnichannel order fulfillment. Int J Phys Distribution Logistics Manag, ahead of print

Demestichas P, Georgakopoulos A, Karvounas D, Tsagkaris K, Stavroulaki V, Lu J et al (2013) 5G on the horizon: Key challenges for the radio-access network. IEEE Veh Technol Mag 8 (3):47–53

Dempsey D, Kelliher F (2018) Industry Trends in Cloud Computing. Pallgrave McMillian, New York

Di Gangi PM, Wasko MM (2016) Social media engagement theory: Exploring the influence of user engagement on social media usage. J Organ End User Com 28(2):53–73

Ekman P, Thilenius P, Thompson S, Whitaker J (2019) Digital transformation of global business processes: the role of dual embeddedness. Bus Process Manag J 26(2):570–592

Ellis E, Kwofie EM, Ngadi M (2019) Value Beyond Price: End User Value Chain Analysis. Int J Food Sys Dynamics 10(4):347–360

Fiorentino R, Grimaldi F, Lamboglia R, Merendino A (2020) How smart technologies can support sustainable business models: insights from an air navigation service provider. Management Decision, ahead of print

Fissi, S., Romolini, A., & Gori, E. (2020). Building a business model for a new form of hospitality: the albergo diffuso. Int J Contemp Hosp Manag, ahead of print

Frank AG, Mendes GH, Ayala NF, Ghezzi A (2019) Servitization and Industry 4.0 convergence in the digital transformation of product firms: A business model innovation perspective. Technol Forecast Soc Chang 141:341–351

Frontoni E, Paolanti M, Puggioni M, Pierdicca R, Sasso M (2019) Measuring and Assessing Augmented Reality Potential for Educational Purposes: Smart Marca Project. In: International Conference on Augmented Reality, Virtual Reality and Computer Graphics. Springer, Cham: Switzerland, pp 319–334

Fuchs PH, Mifflin KE, Miller D, Whitney JO (2000) Strategic integration: Competing in the age of capabilities. Calif Manag Rev 42(3):118–147

Georgopoulos A, Kontogianni G, Koutsaftis C, Skamantzari M (2017) Serious games at the service of cultural heritage and tourism. In: Vicky K, Upadhya A, Stratigea A (eds) Tourism, Culture and Heritage in a Smart Economy. Springer, Cham: Switzerland, pp 3–17

Hakimi WB, Mehdi A (2020) Testing the Impact of Social CRM on Firm Performance: The Role of Customer Engagement, Innovation Performance and Social Media Use. Int J Cust Relationship Market Manag 11(2):71–85

Hamari J, Sjöklint M, Ukkonen A (2016) The sharing economy: Why people participate in collaborative consumption. J Assoc Inf Sci Technol 67(9):2047–2059

Han H, Trimi S (2017) Social commerce design: A framework and application. J Theor Appl Electron Commer Res 12(3):50–68

Harrigan P, Soutar G, Choudhury MM, Lowe M (2015) Modelling CRM in the social media age. Australas Mark J 23(1):27–37

Harrysson M, Metayer E, Sarrazin H (2012) How 'social intelligence' can guide decisions. McKinsey Quarterly 4(1):81–89

Jung TH, Lee H, Chung N, tom Dieck, M. C. (2018) Cross-cultural differences in adopting mobile augmented reality at cultural heritage tourism sites. Int J Contemp Hosp Manag 30 (3):1621–1645

Karjaluoto H, Munnukka J, Kiuru K (2016) Brand love and positive word of mouth: the moderating effects of experience and price. J Prod Brand Manag 25(6):527–537

Kindström D (2010) Towards a service-based business model–Key aspects for future competitive advantage. Eur Manag J 28(6):479–490

Klamer A, Mignosa A, Lyudmila L (2013) Cultural heritage policies: a comparative perspective. In: Rizzo I, Mignosa A (eds) Handbook on the Economics of Cultural Heritage. Edward Elgar Publishing, London

Ladhari R, Souiden N, Dufour B (2017) The role of emotions in utilitarian service settings: The effects of emotional satisfaction on product perception and behavioral intentions. J Retail Consum Serv 34:10–18

Landoni P, Dell'era C, Frattini F, Petruzzelli AM, Verganti R, Manelli L (2020) Business model innovation in cultural and creative industries: Insights from three leading mobile gaming firms. Technovation 92:102084

Lanzolla G, Markides C (2020) A business model view of strategy. J Manag Stud, ahead of print

Laporte L, Slegers K, De Grooff D (2012) Using correspondence analysis to monitor the persona segmentation process. In: Proceedings of the 7th Nordic Conference on Human-Computer Interaction: Making Sense Through Design, pp 265–274

Lazzeretti L, Sartori A (2016) Digitisation of Cultural Heritage and Business Model Innovation: The Case of the Uffizi Gallery in Florence. Il Capitlale Culturale Studies on the Value of Cultural Heritage 14:945–970

Lee M, Kwahk J, Han SH, Jeong D, Park K, Oh S, Chae G (2020) Developing personas & use cases with user survey data: A study on the millennials' media usage. J Retail Consum Serv 54:102051

Leroi-Weldens S, Sandra S, Van Vaerenbergh Y, Grönroos C (2017) Does communicating the customer's resource integrating role improve or diminish value proposition effectiveness? J Serv Manag 28(4):618–639

Li F (2020) The digital transformation of business models in the creative industries: A holistic framework and emerging trends. Technovation 92:102012. ahead of print

Li YM, Lai CY, Lin LF (2017) A diffusion planning mechanism for social marketing. Inf Manag 54 (5):638–650

Madhani PM (2017) Customer-focused supply chain strategy: developing business value-added framework. IUP J Supp Chain Manag 14(4):7–22

Malthouse EC, Haenlein M, Skiera B, Wege E, Zhang M (2013) Managing Customer Relationships in the Social media Era: Introducing the Social CRM House. J Interact Mark 27(4):270–280

Mandrella M, Trang S, Kolbe LM (2020) Synthesizing and Integrating Research on IT-Based Value Co Creation: A Meta-Analysis. J Assoc Inf Syst 21(2):388–427

Markovich A, Efrat K, Raban DR, Souchon AL (2019) Competitive intelligence embeddedness: Drivers and performance consequences. Eur Manag J 37(6):708–718

McKinsey (2017) Putting customer experience at the heart of next-generation operating models. Retrieved from https://www.mckinsey.com/business-functions/mckinsey-digital/our-insights/putting-customer-experience-at-the-heart-of-next-generation-operating-models

Morris M, Schindehutte M, Allen J (2005) The entrepreneur's business model: toward a unified perspective. J Bus Res 58(6):726–735

Müller VC (2016) Fundamental issues of artificial intelligence. Springer, Berlin

Müller RM, Kijl B, Martens JK (2011) A comparison of inter-organizational business models of mobile app stores: There is more than open vs. closed. J Theor Appl Electron Commer Res 6 (2):63–76

Musteen M, Curran R, Arroteia N, Ripollés M, Blesa A (2018) A Community of Practice Approach to Teaching International Entrepreneurship. Admin Sci 8(4):56

Narangajavana Kaosiri Y, Callarisa Fiol LJ, Moliner Tena MA, Rodriguez Artola RM, Sanchez Garcia J (2019) User-generated content sources in social media: A new approach to explore tourist satisfaction. J Travel Res 58(2):253–265

Navarrete T (2013) Digital cultural heritage. In Handbook on the economics of cultural heritage. London, Edward Elgar Publishing

Osterwalder A, Pigneur Y (2010) Business Model Generation: A Handbook For Visionaries, Game Changers, And Challengers. Wiley, New York

Osterwalder A, Pigneur Y (2014) Value Proposition Design. Wiley, New York

Osterwalder A, Pigneur Y, Tucci C (2005) Clarifying Business Models: Origins, Present, and Future of the Concept. Commun Assoc Inf Syst 16(1):1–25

Parmentier G, Gandia R (2017) Redesigning the business model: from one-sided to multi-sided. J Bus Strateg 38(2):52–61

Pavoni R (2019) Virtual appropriations. MoMAR, Audio Tour Hack, Recycle Group. Augmented Reality as a subversion of museum storytelling. Hermes. J Commun 14:13–14

Pencarelli T, Conti E, Splendiani S (2017) The experiential offering system of museums: evidence from Italy. J Cultural Heritage Manag Sustain Develop 7(4):430–448

Piccarozzi M, Aquilani B, Gatti C (2018) Industry 4.0 in management studies: A systematic literature review. Sustainability 10(10):3821

Pisano V, Ferrari ER, Fasone V (2016) The orchestration of business models for territorial development. Meas Bus Excell 20(4):72–83

Power DJ, Heavin C (2018) Data-based decision making and digital transformation. Business Expert Press, London

Prebensen NK (2017) Innovation potentials through value proposals. In: Prebensen NK, Chen J, Uysal M (eds) Co-Creation in Tourist Experiences. London, Routledge, pp 64–75

Prem E (2015, December) A digital transformation business model for innovation. In ISPIM Innovation Symposium (p. 1–11). The International Society for Professional Innovation Management (ISPIM)
Raj PG, Kar S (2015) Design and development of a distributed mobile sensing-based crowd evacuation system: A big actor approach. In 2015 IEEE 39th Annual Computer Software and Applications Conference, 3: 355–360
Rigby D (2011) The future of shopping. Harv Bus Rev, December
Rumble R, Mangematin V (2015) Business model implementation: The antecedents of multi-sidedness. Business Models Modelling 33:97–131
Rusanen O (2019) Crafting an omnichannel strategy: Identifying sources of competitive advantage and implementation barriers. In: Piotrowicz W, Cuthbertson R (eds) Exploring Omnichannel Retailing. Switzerland, Springer, Cham, pp 11–46
Schlagwein D, Schoder D (2011) The management of open value creation. In 2011 44th Hawaii International Conference on System Sciences (pp. 1–11). IEEE
Shafer SM, Smith HJ, Linder JC (2005) The power of business models. Bus Horiz 48(3):199–207
Sharma R, Reynolds P, Scheepers R, Seddon P, Shanks G (2010) Business analytics and competitive advantage: a review and a research agenda. In: Respicio A, Adam F, Phillips-Wren G (eds) Bridging the socio-technical gap in DSS - challenges for the next decade. IOS Press, Amsterdam, NL, pp 187–198
Shan S, Luo Y, Zhou Y, Wei Y (2019) Big data analysis adaptation and enterprises' competitive advantages: the perspective of dynamic capability and resource-based theories. Tech Anal Strat Manag 31(4):406–420
Sinapi C, Ballereau V. (2016) Looking for new sustainable business model in cultural entrepreneurship. Conference Proceedings of 7th Annual Research Session ENCATC October 5–7, 2016 Valencia, Spain, pp. 336–344
Siqueira JR Jr, Peña NG, ter Horst E, Molina G (2020) A 2020 perspective on Spreading the word: How customer experience in a traditional retail setting influences consumer traditional and electronic word-of-mouth intention. Electron Commer Res Appl 40:100930
Sivarajah U, Kamal MM, Irani Z, Weerakkody V (2017) Critical analysis of Big Data challenges and analytical methods. J Bus Res 70:263–286
Slywotzky AJ (1996) Value Migration. Harvard Business School Press, Boston
Sorescu A, Frambach RT, Singh J, Rangaswamy A, Bridges C (2011) Innovations in retail business models. J Retail 87:S3–S16
Spieth P, Schneider S, Clauß T, Eichenberg D (2019) Value drivers of social businesses: A business model perspective. Long Range Plan 52(3):427–444
Stack J (2013) Tate digital strategy: digital as a dimension of everything. In: Proceedings Museums and the web, Portland, OR, USA, 17–20 April
Storbacka K (2011) A solution business model: Capabilities and management practices for integrated solutions. Ind Mark Manag 40(5):699–711
Stubbs W, Cocklin C (2008) Conceptualizing a "sustainability business model". Organ Environ 21 (2):103–127
Sutermeister AC (2018) Innovative business models: an opportunity for the cultural sector? Bringing Together the Logics of Public Service and Business. In Beyond EYCH 2018. What is the cultural horizon? Opening up perspectives to face ongoing transformations, 181–194
Tan AWK, Gligor D (2019) A decision-making framework for inventory positioning in an omnichannel business environment. Int J Inform Sys Supp Chain Manag 12(1):81–94
Teece DJ (2010) Business models, business strategy and innovation. Long Range Plan 43 (2–3):172–194
Tesch JF, Brillinger AS (2019) The evaluation aspect of digital business model innovation. In: Tesch JF (ed) Business Model Innovation in the Era of the Internet of Things. Switzerland, Springer, Cham, pp 67–86
Timmers P (2000) Electronic commerce: marketing strategies and business models. Prentice Hall Publishing, New York

To CK, Au JS, Kan CW (2019) Uncovering business model innovation contexts: a comparative analysis by fsQCA methods. J Bus Res 101:783–796

Tom Dieck MC, Jung TH (2017) Value of augmented reality at cultural heritage sites: a stakeholder approach. J Destin Mark Manag 6(2):110–117

Towse R, Hernández TN (2020) Handbook of cultural economics. Edward Elgar Publishing, London

Vermeeren AP, Calvi L, Sabiescu A, Trocchianesi R, Stuedahl D, Giaccardi E, Radice S (2018) Future museum experience design: crowds, ecosystems and novel technologies. In: Vermeeren A, Calvi L, Sabiescu A (eds) Museum Experience Design. Switzerland, Springer, Cham, pp 1–16

Voorveld HA, Smit EG, Neijens PC, Bronner AF (2016) Consumers' cross-channel use in online and offline purchases: An Analysis of Cross-Media and Cross-Channel Behaviors between Products. J Advert Res 56(4):385–400

Weerawardena J, Salunke S, Haigh N, Mort GS (2019) Business model innovation in social purpose organizations: Conceptualizing dual social-economic value creation. J Bus Res, ahead of print

Wieland H, Hartmann NN, Vargo SL (2017) Business models as service strategy. J Acad Mark Sci 45(6):925–943

Wiesböck F, Hess T (2019) Digital innovations. Electron Mark:1–12

Winter J, Ono R (eds) (2015) The Future Internet: Alternative Visions, vol 17. Springer, London

Wnuczak P (2018) Social value added (SVA) as an adaptation of economic value added (EVA) to the specificity of cultural institutions. J Manag Bus Admin 26(1):100–120

Xu LD, Xu EL, Li L (2018) Industry 4.0: state of the art and future trends. Int J Prod Res 56 (8):2941–2962

Yeow A, Huat Goh K (2015) Work Harder or Work Smarter? Information Technology and Resource Allocation in Healthcare Processes. MIS Q 39(4):763–786

Yoo Y, Henfridsson O, Lyytinen K (2010) Research commentary—the new organizing logic of digital innovation: an agenda for information systems research. Inf Syst Res 21(4):724–735

Zahra SA, Wright M (2016) Understanding the social role of entrepreneurship. J Manag Stud 53 (4):610–629

Zhao Y, Von Delft S, Morgan-Thomas A, Buck T (2019) The evolution of platform business models: Exploring competitive battles in the world of platforms. Long Range Plan, 101892, ahead for print

Zott C, Amit R (2017) Business model innovation: How to create value in a digital world. Mark Intell Rev 9(1):18–23

Value Propositions in Digital Transformation

Mariarosaria Coppola, Francesco Bifulco, Tiziana Russo Spena, and Marco Tregua

Abstract This chapter explores the role of digital technology in shaping the value propositions of cultural heritage organizations, by stressing the novelties emerging, the new activities centred around new tools, and the contribution offered by technology. In a technologies-based context, the value propositions are formed through the mutual exchange of knowledge between the actors who integrate resources into the value creation process in a digital realm. On one side, the technologies support service providers in better integrating their understanding of the offered service and what the customers can do; on the other side, the customers are supported and perform activities that increase the market value of a provider offer. Technologies have amplified the way value proposition contributes to both provider and customer co-creation. Through technologies, the service provider can better integrate its operant resources and the customer can integrate his/her operant resources while interacting with each other, for the opportunity to influence each other's outcome in the offered service. This is a process that goes back and forth between the service provider and the customer so that they can understand each other's needs and, together, create the service outcome.

M. Coppola (✉)
Italian National Commission for Listed Companies and the Stock Exchange - Corporate Governance Division, Rome, Italy
e-mail: m.coppola@consob.it

F. Bifulco
Department of Humanities, University of Naples Federico II, Naples, Italy
e-mail: fbifulco@unina.it

T. Russo Spena · M. Tregua
Department of Economics Management Institutions, University of Naples Federico II, Naples, Italy
e-mail: russospe@unina.it; marco.tregua@unina.it

T. Russo Spena, F. Bifulco (eds.), *Digital Transformation in the Cultural Heritage Sector*, Contributions to Management Science,
https://doi.org/10.1007/978-3-030-63376-9_4

1 Introduction

Cultural organizations are increasingly addressing the challenges and pressures arising from the complexity and hyper-competition of today's world.

The development of new technologies and the introduction of innovative tools are changing the way individuals experience cultural heritage, as well as the way cultural heritage companies organize and structure their value propositions and communicate them to the market. Moreover, cultural organizations started competing more intensely with one another to get new customers because of the increasing tourism trends worldwide (UNWTO 2018). The growth in competition led firms like museums to seek new solutions and leverage creativity to make their value propositions different and to outperform their competitors.

Digital technologies currently support different types of museum activities, such as gathering, preserving, exhibiting, and educating about art and collections, and they may be used to offer many new opportunities to visitors. Furthermore, the digitalization process plays an important role in involving visitors themselves in the museum's meaning-making activity and content creation and in supporting their active learning process (Dunleavy and Dede 2014). Additionally, visitors are performing their role as evaluators of their visit experience through technologies (Budge 2017; Falk and Dierking 2016). Such a role can be performed either onsite or back home, leading to new insights for curators and managers of cultural sites.

As a consequence, changes in consumer behaviours require firms to rethink their marketing strategies as well as their approaches to managing cultural firms (Weaver 2016). Marketing activities can be profoundly influenced by digitalization, thus favouring collaboration among firms, customers, and partners to co-create value in different ways. Similarly, in terms of managing a cultural firm, the role of technologies is relevant in shaping new services, monitoring activities, and planning future interventions (Ambrose and Paine 2018).

Some cultural organizations have been capitalizing on these opportunities, as mirrored by the introduction of various online services, mobile services, augmented reality in physical spaces, and so on; the results are encouraging, and firms are further investing these new technologies to continue with the research paths they have recently begun. However, this digitalization process can follow very different paths, with various aims, thus leading to the structuring of cultural value propositions that vastly differ from one another. The differences among value propositions may depend both on the need to compete and on the specific ways in which technologies have been implemented in the service offerings (Lazzeretti and Sartori 2016).

This chapter aims to explore the role of digital technology in shaping the value propositions of cultural heritage organizations, by stressing the novelties emerging, the new activities centred around new tools, and the contribution offered by technology. The perspective that this paper adopts is a business perspective; thus, we will focus on the approach firms adopted in the service offering. The core of both the theoretical development and data analysis will be a focus on the value proposition, as it represents a key construct describing the way firms address their offering to potential customers and embeds the main features of service activities and service interactions (O'Cass and Ngo 2011).

The chapter is organized as follows. First, a literature review of the concept of value proposition has been proposed to show the evolution of its conceptualization and to identify the main elements constituting it. Then, the effects of digital marketing tools in cultural firms are considered through an analysis of recent literature. The elements emerging from literature drive the investigation through three key case studies, describing the changes taking place in cultural heritage organizations through a value proposition. The results lead the authors to grasp more meaning about the ongoing changes in cultural firms' services and expand their current understanding from a theoretical perspective. Finally, future avenues of research are offered to encourage further investigation of this topic.

2 Value Propositions

While the term 'value proposition' is widely used in the literature and business practices, it has been adopted to refer to different concepts (Anderson et al. 2006). As regards the different conceptualizations deriving from different approaches, Payne et al. (2017; p. 3) argued that "it may suffer confusion with other related terms (e.g. positioning, business models, value discipline) or with precursor concepts, such as the unique selling and core benefit propositions." Table 1 in the following provides a brief summary of some of the different conceptualizations in the literature.

The value proposition concept has its roots in Lanning and Michaels' (1988) work, an internal McKinsey staff paper; according to these authors, value proposition represents a means by which the firm can describe the value promised and the costs for customers. The firm should implement three main activities to achieve success in its market: choosing the value; providing the value; and communicating the value. The firm aims to create a value proposition for customers that is superior to those offered by competitors (Lanning 1998).

More in detail, in the academic literature, the value proposition has been considered an offering to the market—addressed by the firm to customers—that plays a strategic role in achieving the competitive advantage (Webster 1994). The focus is on the supplier-crafted value for customers based on their needs and preferences. Value proposition represents the most important element of a firm's business model (Morris et al. 2005).

Creating a superior customer value proposition implies the identification of target customers, the job to be done to solve a problem or to satisfy a need of identified customers, and the offering that fulfils the customers' needs. In other words, the value proposition defines value for the customer. The value proposition should be structured based on a specific customer segment to be able to create value.

For instance, Anderson et al. (2006) offered three different approaches to the development of a value proposition: identifying all benefits a firm can offer to its

Table 1 Definition of value proposition

Definitions proposed by scholars	Source: author(s) (year)
"precise benefit or benefits at what price will be offered to what customer group, at what cost"	Lanning and Michaels (1988); p. 3
"[...] the verbal statement that matches up the firm's distinctive competencies with the needs and preferences of a carefully defined set of potential customers"	Webster (1994); p. 25
"value proposition consists of all benefits customers receive from a market offering"	Anderson et al. (2006); p. 93
"reciprocal promises of value, operating to and from suppliers and customers seeking an equitable exchange"	Ballantyne and Varey (2006); pp. 344–345
"actor's attempt to invite another actor to collaborate together on an offering that yields a positive reciprocal relationship"	Vargo and Lusch (2014)
"value propositions act as balance/aligning mechanism in the service ecosystem"	Frow et al. (2014); pp. 344–345
"value propositions as value creation promises created either by the firm independently or together with customers and other actors through resource integration based on knowledge and competencies"	Skålén et al. (2015); p. 139
"an invitation from actors to one another to engage in service"	Chandler and Lusch (2015); p. 6

Authors' elaboration

customers; detecting the favourable points of difference of its value proposition with respect to the competitors' value propositions; and focusing on specific benefits that represent key factors for the target customers. In a more recent book, Osterwalder et al. (2014) focused on the design of value propositions as a process favouring the achievement of a pattern of value creation, the leverage of the team experience, the efficacy in using ideas, and the delivery of what is more suitable for customers.

The emerging of service-dominant logic in the previous decade (Vargo and Lusch 2004) led value proposition to be thought about in a different way, namely as the replacement for both price and value delivery (Lusch and Vargo 2006). Service scholars challenged the traditional approach to recognize the interactive and multi-dimensional nature of the enjoyment of service offerings in opposition to the view that considers "value proposition" to be a simple synonym for "offering." According to this logic (Vargo and Lusch 2004), value is not an inherent property of a resource or offering, realized in exchanges. Rather, it is the outcome of interactions between the firm and the customer, realized and determined during the use of resources by the customer. As the customer defines what is valuable and determines value, the firm's role changes. The firm can only make value propositions to facilitate customers in their value creation-consumption activities (Vargo and Lusch 2004).

The interaction and relationship between the supplier and the receiver of the offering became crucial in the debate; in line with this focus, Ballantyne and Varey (2006) defined value propositions as "reciprocal promises of value, operating to and from suppliers and customers seeking an equitable exchange" (pp. 344–345).

Moreover, in a further version, Ballantyne et al. (2011) considered value proposition as a communication practice, namely a process embedding the exchange, the development of relationships, and the renewal of knowledge thanks to the interactions among parts. Relationships should be beneficial for all parties involved to survive and evolve over time; thus, value proposition as a communication process—initiated by any party of the relationship, not necessarily the firm—must make explicit all benefits promised and given up through the offering. It represents a means for firms to support and facilitate the co-creation of value not for customers but with customers (Payne et al. 2008; Frow and Payne 2011; Frow et al. 2014). Moving away from the distinction between supplier and customer, value propositions become the link through which a service system—as an arrangement of resources, people, technology, etc.—is connected to other service systems (Barile et al. 2016). The dyadic perspective (firm-customer) has been replaced by a wider conceptualization that includes multiple actors interlinked within a network or a service ecosystem (Frow and Payne 2011; Frow et al. 2014; Payne et al. 2017). To advance the multi-actor perspective in creating value propositions, Kowalkowski et al. (2012) conceptualized value proposition as formed through the reciprocal exchange of knowledge among actors; value propositions synthesize the value perceptions of actors involved, even beyond a business and a customer (Kowalkowski 2011). By employing the practice theory, the authors identified different practices of forming a value proposition—applying, assessing, adapting, and adopting—that are the core activities of the reciprocal exchange of knowledge. Additionally, value propositions have been defined in the framework of the discontinuous relationships among actors and as changeable due to the acquired awareness of actors and their changing strategies. In this line, Skålén et al. (2015) advanced the idea that value proposition is more than a simple communication tool; it results from the interweaving of three practices that form the anatomy of the value propositions: provision practices, representational practices, and management and organizational practices. Provision practices include practices (operating, problem-finding, and problem-solving) that work together to solve customers' problems; representational practices support the communication process among interacting parties, while management and organizational practices entail the networking activities of the firm to create the value proposition.

Value proposition, as proposed in service-dominant logic, was linked to the business model, due to the great similarities between the two visions (Lüftenegger et al. 2017). The authors claimed the relevant impact of the complex set of actors contributing to the shaping of value proposition and, as a consequence, of value. Secondly, Vargo and Lusch (2017) stimulated additional research in service-dominant logic to expand it towards market theory; in this contribution, the value proposition is expanded to the public domain by stressing the role of multiple actors' interventions, cooperating in shaping value propositions as solutions.

3 Granularity of Value Proposition, Personalization, and Digital Context

The literature discusses the granularity of value proposition to address its multisided level as it exists at the firm, customer segment, and individual customer levels (Barnes et al. 2009), whereas on each level, the value propositions fulfils a different purpose, for the company and the customer.

While at the firm level the value proposition provides an outside-in perspective on the mission statement and justifies the organization's existence, the customer segment level involves how value is designed for and with targeted customer segments, while adapting the value proposition to the individual customer levels means to reach each customer who can represent a significant sales volume. Traditionally, the idea of personalized value proposition has been widely discussed in the context of B2B markets, which offer opportunities to tailor the value offering to specific major customers (Anderson et al. 2006). As new technologies are starting to affirm, the possibility of personalization has been proposed as differentiating strategy also in the B2C context consisting of offering options to customize product or service (Ozuem et al. 2019). Thus, personalization has been argued for a more fine-grained approach that centres on the individual, customer level thanks to the new digital technologies. Digitized solutions strategy has been identified as a strategy aiming to reformulate a company's value proposition by integrating a combination of products, services, and data; moreover, the adoption of digital technologies does not force a firm to adopt a disruptive approach towards value proposition (Furr and Shipilov 2019), as the digitalization may be seen as a way to transform traditional value propositions and adapt them to the new context. Every aspect of marketing is affected by the rise of information-technology-based interactivity with customers, including multiple channels, i.e. computers, phones, digital devices, physical stores, etc. (Stone and Woodcock 2013). Empowered by social networks and their digital devices, consumers are increasingly dictating what they want, as well as when and where they want it. They become both critics and creators, demanding a more personalized offering and expecting to be given the opportunity to shape the products and services they consume. By taking an active part in the marketing process, customers increase their involvement with the firm's propositions, and several chances to favour additional value creation through the embedding of new technological tools can be detected (Hsu 2012). In any event, the rise of new technologies makes customers' participation more relevant, so long as customers are in the proper conditions to interact with technologies, as stressed by Standing and Mattsson (2018), who underlined that customers should be taught how to act on digital platforms to get a value proposition and, eventually, accept it.

As has been noted, the digital world is ultimately about the connection of disparate points on a network. Its domain encompasses large volumes of mostly unrelated information in many forms, and this information can be connected in infinite ways, some of which result in relevant, useful, and actionable propositions to individuals accessing the network (Ramaswamy and Ozcan 2016). At its core, personalization is the ability to manage these connections and endpoints in such a way that they become highly relevant to consumers. New technologies contribute to the higher powers of information consumption, pattern recognition, and computation that firms can use to improve customer needs, dynamically. The dynamic personalization uses existing information about user behaviour and automatically adapts content to the customer; indeed, personalization has become a new source of competition for firms, as they may offer the most suitable proposition for each customer segment due to the advantage of modularity offered by digital technologies (Ozuem et al. 2019). This requires access to a history of user behaviours, such as clicks and/or transactions, as well as a set of assumptions or rules to personalize the user's experience. Personalization increases personal relevance by allowing companies to customize products and services to the personal preferences and interests of customers on time and according to their specific needs.

Companies can integrate customer purchasing data to provide more personalized offerings and customer service or even offer customized product packages. Personalized products and experiences can provide benefits to both the business and the consumer. Offering dynamic personalization allows companies to demonstrate the value that consumers get from the use of their personal data.

4 Museum Value Proposition

Value propositions have been applied even to the museum context and with different approaches; some scholars have paid attention to the uniqueness of the value propositions and to the continuous adjustment leading to an increase in the value of a museum offer (Koster and Falk 2007), while others have investigated how innovation can change the essence of a value proposition in museums and business models (Coblence and Sabatier 2014). Still, others have framed the debate in service-dominant logic (Carù et al. 2016; Prebensen 2017). Regarding the latter, Carù et al. (2016) focused on the servicescape as both shaping value propositions and enabling value co-creation processes, while Prebensen (2017) chose a museum as a research context to depict the ties between revenue streams and the key resources used, with the origin of such ties depending on the successfulness of a value proposition.

Nowadays, museums can draw from a huge amount of resources through the use of the Internet, which allows them to communicate with millions of people adopting more innovative and less expensive methods. Furthermore, the web allows for a constant communication flow, so that customers and organizations can continuously interact.

These new digital media allow museums to implement strategies that can increase cultural knowledge by leveraging cross-mediality and viral effect and favouring word-of-mouth among consumers (González-Rodríguez et al. 2016). As regards communication flow among potential users, according to Mangold and Faulds (2009), promotion activities through social media represent a hybrid element that combines some features of traditional tools with an amplified form of word-of-mouth among users, which managers cannot control. In any event, museum managers and curators cannot ignore the huge impact that social media can have on their activities (Koontz and Mon 2014), as the digital market represents a competitive arena and a context where opportunities to further develop offerings can be achieved. A museum can interact with its audience through a large number of channels, many of which are digital. Nevertheless, communication through modern digital technology addresses not necessarily a mass audience but, rather, a wide range of different *audiences en masse*. Digital technology has become increasingly interactive and enables dialogues with visitors both online (on the web page and on social media) and onsite (at the museum). Digital developments have led to the coining of the concept 'post-museum' (Hooper-Greenhill 2000), highlighting the changing relationship between the museum and audience, with the audience entering a more participative role within the museum context.

However, digitalization regards more than communication and promotion activities. For example the most innovative museums in the world are adopting the iBeacon technology as a way to allow their visitors to interact with museum experts, while at the same time they are adopting the technology to send, to a visitor standing near a painting, a phone alert directing that visitor to interactive content relating to the artwork (Allurwar et al. 2016, Navarrete (2013). Digital technologies are changing the concept of the product, as they can augment the core product with digital services, prompt the networking of products, and change products into digital services (Kannan 2017). Upon entering the digital era, museums expanded their propositions beyond the onsite experience and the perception of the museum as an institution. In line with their mission to spread knowledge about collections, many museums today either work as, or aim to work as, media agencies, producing an extensive amount of content of various forms (Witcomb 2007).

5 Methodology and Data Collection

To better understand how digital technology impacts the value proposition of cultural heritage organizations, we adopted the case study approach, which is well-suited because of the novelty of the phenomenon (Eisenhardt and Graebner 2007) and because of its qualitative nature. In particular, a cross-case approach was chosen to capture differences within and between the cases (Yin 2013).

The cases we chose to analyse are the three museum nominees for the "best digital museum experience of the year 2017," an award that is part of the Leading Culture Destinations Awards, the Oscars for museums: Cooper Hewitt Smithsonian Design Museum of New York; the American Museum of Natural History (New York); and the British Museum of London.

Data has been gathered through multiple sources to achieve triangulation (Yin 2013), as online interviews with museum practitioners, official websites, communication reports, and different organizations' documents. Furthermore, triangulating interpretations of the data across the researchers allowed for the strengthening of data interpretations and avoiding biases and distortions in data analysis. To analyze the collected data, a framework based on the literature (Skålén et al. 2015) has been proposed, integrated with a focus on the role of technology in each interactive practice through which the value proposition takes form. The framework helped to identify the three different practices representing the anatomy of a value proposition: provision, representational, and management and organizational practices. Then, for each, an analysis of the role of digital technology is proposed to identify different kinds of value propositions.

For every case investigated, details will be offered through the sources we used; particular attention will be devoted to the perception and concrete contribution of people carrying out the digital-based activities into the three museums.

6 Findings

Three case studies will be presented in this paragraph, to stress the key features of their value proposition; while addressing these elements, particular attention will be paid to technology as a tool and as an enabler of the value proposition. Additionally, the new tools offered by up-to-date technologies will be considered to describe how the interactions among actors are taking place in the museum context and if and how the multi-actor approach, commonly stressed in recent literature, affects the activities in such a context.

6.1 Case 1: The Cooper Hewitt Smithsonian Design Museum

The Cooper Hewitt Smithsonian Design Museum is the American museum dedicated exclusively to historic and contemporary design. Closed for renovations in 2011, the museum opened again after 3 years of hard work, which transformed the old museum into a more involving space for visitors, especially younger ones. Its offering consists not only of exhibits for visitors; the museum also periodically hosts design competitions and offers a great variety of educational programs, including a master's degree program, events, hands-on workshops, talks, and family programs. The value proposition of this museum is shaped by an immersive visitor experience rooted in modern digital technologies to teach people about design, giving them the tools to become designers themselves. The main digital tool adopted by the museum to achieve this goal is a digital pen that enables a visitor to record their visit. Objects and pieces of art throughout the museum are marked with smart labels that visitors can save into a personal digital collection by using this pen; when the pen touches the label, the digital record of that object is added to the visitor's personal library. Thus, visitors can learn about the history of objects that appear on interactive tables and discover related pieces. The interactive touchscreen tables even allow the visitor to draw their own design, as simple lines can become chairs, tables, buildings, or any design object.

> We are embracing new technologies, encouraging museum audiences to be co-creators with both our collections and programs, as well as redefining how we exist as a museum resource for a digital age. 3D modelling and animation will bring objects to life. The new interactive experiences in our galleries designed with Local Projects open up the collection and allow visitors to browse and be inspired to create their own designs. The pen symbolizes the change we are making from a 'museum of looking' to a 'museum of doing'.
>
> Source: interview with Caroline Baumann, museum director

Furthermore, the interactive Gesture Match experience—based on a motion sensor—helps visitors find objects related to the visitors' body position, thereby creating a unique experience for each of them. This kind of technology searches a virtual catalogue of life-sized silhouettes in different positions and connects the visitor's posture to a similarly positioned piece of art.

As shown by the mission of the museum, presented on its official website, the Cooper Hewitt Smithsonian Design Museum aims to achieve the strong involvement of its guests.

> Our Mission—Cooper Hewitt educates, inspires, and empowers people through design. Our concept was born of the belief that design should be understood through doing, and that the desire to create and participate is universal.
>
> Source: excerpt from the official website, www.cooperhewitt.org

This implies a paradigmatic shift with respect to the previous concept of the museum experience.

> Using the Cooper Hewitt collection and exhibitions creatively, we will engage our visitors—at the museum and online—in dialogue about what matters in design. In the past, museums were all about tape and 'do not touch' signs. At Cooper Hewitt, we are encouraging the visitor to be more interactive, social, and playful.
>
> Source: interview with Caroline Baumann, museum director

Additionally, the museum has two special rooms: The Process Lab and the Immersion Room. In the first room, visitors can take part in a variety of hands-on and digital activities based on design thinking. In the Immersion Room, which is equipped with a wide collection of wallpapers, people can select a wallpaper from the museum's collection or create their own and project the patterns on the open walls surrounding the exhibit, thus stimulating their imagination.

> Using the Pen, you can select wallpapers from the Museum's permanent collection and see them projected on the walls from floor to ceiling—for a vibrant, impactful, immersive experience. You can even play designer by creating your own designs, or just stand back and watch as the wallpapers unfold across the room.
>
> Source: excerpt from the official website, www.cooperhewitt.org

The success of the new project has also been achieved due to the collaboration of different partners, as illustrated by the following excerpt from an interview with museum director Caroline Baumann.

> We were fortunate to find a wonderful partner in Eddie Opara of Pentagram. Right from the start, he understood our challenge and just how important it was—after all, this is the

nation's design museum. The entire process was very collaborative, and we involved all of our stakeholders, from the Smithsonian to our trustees and staff, in the conversation. We met regularly to hash through the issues, and I remember with great clarity the moment we hit on our current mark. We were in the top floor conference room at Pentagram and Eddie's team had generated some incredible sketches, but we were continually drawn back to the same simple yet bold logo.

Source: interview with Caroline Baumann, museum director

6.2 Case 2: The American Museum of Natural History

The American Museum of Natural History (AMNH) is the largest natural history museum in the world; since its founding, the museum has collected a huge number of specimens relating to the natural world and different human cultures.

As one of the most important scientific research institutions in the world, the American Museum of Natural History sponsors a great variety of research projects every year and has three permanent field stations: Great Gull Island, St. Catherine's Island, and the Southwestern Research Station. It has grown remarkably over the years, now including 25 impressive interconnected buildings with over 1.2 million square feet of exhibits, research tools, and libraries.

With regard to the digitalization process, the museum has launched an innovative app through which the user can explore hundreds of dinosaur fossils on his/her smartphone. The app shows a mosaic of images from the museum's dinosaur collection; zooming in on any title of the photos, the user can see what the dinosaurs once looked like, and learn about the stories of dinosaurs, and discover details about the palaeontologists who unearthed them. Furthermore, users can share comments and photos with others.

The museum has over 350 devices that can be utilized during the visit. For example the museum is equipped with a Digital Totem—an interactive monolith that introduces visitors to native cultures. Each side of the installation consists of a touchscreen that displays a map of the northwest region and a variety of pictures identifying the different topics a visitor can explore. The guest has also the opportunity to rotate and zoom in on artefacts to capture the fine details that are invisible when an object is enclosed in a glass bowl.

Another interesting section of the museum is the Digital Universe, developed by the American Museum of Natural History's Hayden Planetarium by gathering data from several organizations worldwide to create one of the most accurate 3-D atlases of the universe.

Our mission is to bring the frontier of astrophysical research to the public via exhibitory, books, public programs, and online resources.

Source: excerpt from the official website, www.amnh.org

The Digital Universe is distributed to planetariums, science centres, and museums worldwide and is also available to download (a free version is available on the official website of the museum) thanks to several partnerships with planetarium technology companies. The free version can be experienced through "Partiview." This is a program, created by the Virtual Director Group at the National Center for Supercomputing Applications (NCSA) at the University of Illinois, that visualizes and animates three-dimensional particle data. By using this digital tool, the user can navigate 3-D data as if he/she were flying. If a user needs help, the museum offers support via e-mail.

> The Hayden Planetarium mainly serves its Digital Universe users via e-mail help lines. While we are not particularly staffed for this level of service, we do try to answer all requests that are sent, and we enjoy hearing from you.
>
> Source: excerpt from the official website, www.amnh.org

In its first Digital Universe Flight School, the museum has trained the younger generations to master the Digital Universe Atlas. The museum's educators and astrophysicists have teamed up to help students design their own personalized journeys through the cosmos.

> Mission statement of the Hayden Planetarium—The office will conduct, interpret, and bring frontier astrophysics research into the educational offerings of the American Museum of Natural History. In particular, the Office of the Director will enable the Space Show, Science Bulletins, and the various educational outreach projects of the Museum's National Center for Science Literacy Education and Technology to keep abreast of the latest discoveries in astrophysics. This effort includes, but is not limited to, establishing strategic collaborations with colleagues as well as creating partnerships with academic canters, societies, institutions, and laboratories.
>
> Source: excerpt from the official website, www.amnh.org

With regard to social networks, this institution has an official account on Twitter and an official page on Facebook through which, every day, it shares photos of the least-known animal species, thereby providing more knowledge and details about them to its followers. Additionally, the museum's official account on YouTube takes the user behind the scenes of the museum's exhibits and provides news and information about scientific research, further exhibitions, education, and programs that the museum offers.

> Social media tools and strategies] has revolutionized the way that museums are communicating with their audiences. When used properly, it is an inexpensive and accessible way for museums to engage with people. They not only give museums new ways to do traditional functions like marketing and gathering feedback but open up other new opportunities.
>
> Source: excerpt from Elizabeth E. Merritt, founding director of the American Association of Museums Center

6.3 Case 3: The British Museum

The British Museum is a public institution that is located in London and dedicated to human history, art, and culture. The museum first opened to the public in 1759 and has one of the world's largest collections of artefacts.

In 2009, the British Museum started a collaboration with Samsung to launch a new project related to digital technologies applied to education programs. The companies created the Samsung Digital Discovery Centre, a technological hub for young people to learn about art and human history and interact with the museum's collection.

> The Museum is delighted to continue our long-standing partnership with Samsung. Samsung's world-leading technology enables us to be at the forefront of digital education, with a programme that is enhanced year on year. Families and schoolchildren of all ages have found these superb digital tools irresistible, and for us they have become indispensable in opening up and encouraging active engagement with our vast and varied collection.
>
> Source: Interview with Neil MacGregor, director of the British Museum

> Thanks to the partnership the Museum has been able to offer more Augmented Reality learning than any other UK museum, offering a range of different styles of AR mobile activities for phones and tablets. The AR mobile program Passport to the Afterlife, which runs on Samsung Galaxy Nexus phones in the ancient Egypt galleries, has been cited in academic dissertations and presented at major conferences in the US and UK. The partnership has also enabled some unusual collaborations, including with well-known UK fashion designers such as Tatty Devine and Fred Butler to create a series of dynamic workshops for 13-18 years old.
>
> Source: Excerpt from the official website, www.britishmuseum.org

The museum even offers virtual tours of its galleries that enable people across the world to access its art.

> We're thrilled to reveal this new Virtual Reality tour of our Egyptian galleries! Working with Oculus, we've developed a first-of-its-kind interactive 360 experience that you can access from any device. This is best viewed using the Facebook app and to make the most of the experience—and be fully immersed—launch it on a Samsung Gear VR headset. Explore galleries of ancient sculpture and Egyptian mummies, putting the Museum at your fingertips from anywhere in the world!
>
> Source: official British Museum Facebook page

As stated by the Head of Digital and Publishing of the British Museum, virtual reality can support the physical experience and expand the enjoyment of an artwork.

> Virtual reality is the next frontier for museums. Though nothing can replace the experience of visiting a museum, and learning about an object through looking, this adds a whole new element to that experience—opening up a kind of intimate study previously reserved only for specialist curators.
>
> Source: excerpt from an interview with Chris Michaels, Head of Digital and Publishing, British Museum

Furthermore, the museum is developing a new technology to avoid congestion in its most crowded galleries. This technology works to attract visitors to lesser-known items by choosing less popular pieces of art based on the tastes and preferences of museum visitors.

> When you look into the future, digital will play a much bigger role when it comes to making people engage with the collections and taking people through it [...] You will be able to understand much more precisely what people are looking for, where their special interest is, how much time they have, do they come with kids or without kids [...] You will then be able to answer with a tailor-made suggestion as to where to go and perhaps take them to two or

three other places they did not recognise [...] To make them see what they want to see, and then make them see yet another thing.

Source: interview with Neil MacGregor, director of the British Museum

In the document illustrating the museum's strategy for the coming years, the cultural organization shows its need for additional competencies and skills to sustain the digitalization process and compete in a changing world.

For the British Museum to take its proper place in the digital world requires access to external expertise. To achieve the desired reach, we need sustained partnerships with technology companies and digital publishers.

Source: excerpt from Towards 2020—The British Museum Strategy

The museum even took part in a project on Twitter, called "#AskACurator," which allowed users to ask museum staff about their interests.

About the use of social media, the following excerpt is from an interview with Neil MacGregor, director of the British Museum.

We've got to get mobile right because that's what brings and connects the audience outside to the audience inside the museum. Half of our audience now looks at our website on their mobile phones. They're all carrying mobile phones as they walk through the door. And, what connects that experience together? Social media—everyday thousands and thousands of pictures get taken here and put onto Facebook, Instagram, Twitter, so it's a part of the life of the place.

Source: interview with Neil MacGregor, director of the British Museum

Additionally, the museum has an active programme of lectures, podcasts, and audio activities that are published on SoundCloud, thus favouring the experience even outside the context of the museum and enabling re-analysis of the content that the museum offers. In this way, further creation of knowledge and new experiences can be achieved.

7 Discussion

By adopting a conceptual framework based on the work of Skålén et al. (2015), this research analyzed the value propositions of three world-famous museums. The main contribution of this chapter is answering the call for research by Vargo and Lusch (2017); more in detail, the study addresses the role of technology for the enactment of each practice shaping value propositions in line with the theoretical approach by Skålén et al. (2015). Value propositions are formed by combining three practices, so value propositions differ, although they are all technology-based.

Tables 2, 3 and 4 summarize the results of the data analysis with reference to the three practices proposed by Skålén et al. (2015) and observed in relation to the three museums investigated.

The first case analyzed, the *Cooper Hewitt Smithsonian Design Museum*, shows a visitor-centric approach. Provision practices reveal the strong empowerment of the

Table 2 Provision practices

Aggregated practices of the value proposition	Definition	Exemplars	Digital marketing activities	Role of technology
Provision practices	Assisting the core customer value creation and addressing customers' needs and problems	*Smithsonian*—"Using the Pen, you can select wallpapers from the Museum's permanent collection and see them projected on the walls from floor to ceiling—for a vibrant, impactful, immersive experience. You can even play designer by creating your own designs, or just stand back and watch as the wallpapers unfold across the room"	The visitor is involved in user-generated content creation	The technology enables customers' activities. It is a tool that allows the customers to live experiences personalized to each of them
		AMNH—"The Hayden Planetarium mainly serves its Digital Universe users via e-mail helplines. While we are not particularly staffed for this level of service, we do try to answer all requests that are sent, and we enjoy hearing from you"	The digital tools are used in a traditional way, as they represent one of many channels through which the firm helps its customers and solves their problems. Furthermore, they are used to augment the product	The technology expands customer experiences, as they are augmented through digital devices that provide more information
		British Museum—"We offer Special Education Needs (SEN) sessions at the Samsung Centre, in which the participants discover a particular theme by using the interactive e-board and handling objects. The participants get to	The digital tools favour the enjoyment of a part of the offering	The technology supports only determined customer activities like those related to the educational programs; it also offers a completely digital experience to users, as it allows for a virtual tour

(continued)

Table 2 (continued)

Aggregated practices of the value proposition	Definition	Exemplars	Digital marketing activities	Role of technology
		explore the galleries and use digital cameras to collect pictures of objects"		of some exhibitions

Authors' elaboration

visitor, who, through the use of technology, can select and create an experience more suitable to his/her needs and preferences.

The museum value proposition requires a very active role of the visitor, who can discover more by "learning by doing" rather than simply acting as a passive spectator. The technology in this kind of value proposition represents an important tool that allows people to be more interactive and actively take part in shaping their experiences, with more chances to personalize the offerings and take part in the shaping of the value proposition (Ozuem et al. 2019). Thus, not only should the firm adapt to digitalization and be designed in a suitable way but also the value co-creation processes must be adapted to digitalization. Thus, technology assumes a crucial role, especially in the enactment of provision practices that support the creation of value for customers, as it revolutionizes the way they enjoy art—namely by doing. Technology represents a tool that revolutionizes the offerings themselves.

However, digital technology also impacts representational practices, as it prompts a constant bidirectional flow of information between the museum and its customers; this mutuality has been observed in the interactions and in the benefits perceived by a firm and the customers (Vargo and Lusch 2017), while little attention was previously paid to knowledge exchange as an outcome of the co-creation of the value proposition. In any event, knowledge is not just renewed in the interaction (Ballantyne et al. 2011); it is a concrete outcome of arranging a value proposition. Social media tools allow the visitor to participate in the life of the museum and express comments and preferences. Visitors—or, simply, users—can discuss the contents, to share and even create them, thereby becoming co-creators of content, as proposed by Pulh and Mencarelli (2015) when dealing with the consequence of empowered consumers.

On the other hand, technology plays a marginal role in the management and organizational practices. These practices, in the case of the Cooper Hewitt Smithsonian Design Museum, involve a great variety of stakeholders to obtain technological support in organizing the activities and sharing resources with other partners, thereby helping to organize the museum's offering. The value proposition in this case is technology-enabled, as digitalization has allowed the museum to create a whole new offering. Consequently, technology enables and depicts the effects of a multi-actor approach to the value proposition, even as something emergent instead of something extrinsically planned in the business model (Lüftenegger et al. 2017).

Table 3 Representational practices

Aggregated practices of value proposition	Definition	Exemplars	Digital marketing activities	The role of technology
Representational practices	Describes the activities of the value proposition and their fulfilment, creates the structure of the value proposition, and allows for the communication of value proposition to customers or the co-creation of the value proposition with customers	*Smithsonian*—"Cross-Platform Publishing sits at the nexus of Digital and Emerging Media, Communications, Curatorial, Education, Exhibitions, the Director's Office, as well as Development departments and the Shop helping to originate, develop, manage, and publish almost all forms of content at Cooper Hewitt"	The promotion activities use digital channels to achieve a broad number of users	The museum uses a website to offer a lot of information about its programs and exhibitions as well as the YouTube channel and the official Facebook page of the museum
		AMNH—"Our mission is to bring the frontier of astrophysical research to the public via exhibitory, books, public programs, and on-line resources"	The main digital activities are promotion and communication, although they activate a unidirectional communication flow—from the firm to customers	The representational practices are enacted through the support of digital media such as the website
		British Museum—"The Museum needs to rethink completely how it transmits information about the collection, and how it engages its visitors with the objects. New technology allows new ways of visiting the galleries: stories and images, enquiries and interactions, individual and	The chance to experience the offering of the museum is proposed even through at-a-distance technologies	Social media play a crucial role by prompting bidirectional communication among the museum and its visitors or web users

(continued)

Table 3 (continued)

Aggregated practices of value proposition	Definition	Exemplars	Digital marketing activities	The role of technology
		group explorations all need to be crafted and promoted. And those who can never visit may now be enabled to experience, learn and enjoy"		

Authors' elaboration

The second case, the American Museum of Natural History, has shown how technology amplifies customer experiences by providing richer information and additional opportunities. It is also used by the firm to support the customer and address his/her problems. Promotion and communication activities are carried out mainly through digital media; however, this is a traditional kind of communication that activates a unidirectional flow from the firm to its customers considered as a whole. Social media are useful for promoting some activities and raising awareness of the offering rather than collecting suggestions or even content. Thus, we can state that the usage of digital media not only creates effects through uncontrolled processes or hard-to-control processes in the form of electronic word-of-mouth (Hausmann 2012), but also favours an aware involvement of customers in firms' processes.

Likewise, the museum offers web users an interesting blog where the most important curators, heads of product design, and insiders publish articles containing the latest news about the design world. Nevertheless, the blog leaves little space for ordinary people, who can share the content of articles only on social media. At the same time, it enables networking activities that are useful in organizing and managing the value proposition.

Technology—acting as an enabler of connections and relationships through online resources such as the web site and the digitized collections—can reach partners all over the world and create links that break down traditional borders. Likewise, the online resource can be experienced by a great number of users who do not need to be physically present with the offering, in line with the proposal by Hsu (2012). In this case, technology amplifies the value proposition.

The core product is augmented with digital services, and part of the offering is digitized. This evidence is in line with the recent conceptualization by Payne et al. (2017), focusing on the customer value proposition as a tool favouring an organization's ability to set the right context to propose and then achieve superior value. The digitalization, in fact, offers new opportunities to discover the museum's offering in a more in-depth way and to reach a larger number of people. The only constraint on this consideration is given by the usability of new technologies, namely the skills

Table 4 Management and organizational practices

Aggregated practices of the value proposition	Definition	Exemplars	Digital marketing activities	The role of technology
Management and organizational practices	Organizes the work of providing and representing value propositions and is used to hire staff that can provide and communicate service; it is also related to how firms involve other actors to create, deliver, or negotiate value propositions	*Smithsonian*—"We were fortunate to find a wonderful partner in Eddie Opera of Pentagram. Right from the start, he understood our challenge and just how important it was—after all, this is the nation's design museum. The entire process was very collaborative, and we involved all of our stakeholders, from the Smithsonian to our trustees and staff, in the conversation"	A multi-actor approach to service design was adopted to shape new value propositions	The museum has activated a great variety of collaborations to acquire the needed resources and skills with regard to the digitization
		AMNH—"Some key projects and milestones in our journey are: to digitize major parts of our collection and make it openly available to public and scientific audiences worldwide; to create a new Museum website and apps to share our expertise and collection and engage virtual communities such as NHM members, citizens, scientists, and amateur naturalists"	The distribution of the firm's offerings also uses digital channels, thereby expanding the number of users	The technology enables networking activities that are useful in organizing and managing the value proposition

(continued)

Table 4 (continued)

Aggregated practices of the value proposition	Definition	Exemplars	Digital marketing activities	The role of technology
		British Museum—"New technologies allow the Enlightenment ideal to be given a quite new reality. It should be possible to make the collection accessible, explorable, and enjoyable, not just for those who visit, but to everybody with a computer or a mobile device. It can become the private collection of the whole world"	The distribution of the firm's offerings also uses digital channels, thereby expanding the number of users	The technology offers new channels to make artwork accessible

Authors' elaboration

required of every user; as stressed by Standing and Mattsson (2018), the technology-based value proposition may perform its role in full if users are in suitable conditions to act.

In the third case, i.e. the British Museum, technology supports only part of the visitor experience—that dedicated to specific activities such as learning. The technology provides new content delivery methods, but the offerings and content remain mainly unchanged. Even in this case, although the communication is carried out mainly on social media, it is traditional and creates few opportunities for visitors and users to take part in the museum's processes. This value proposition is not based on changing the content offered to users but is useful in stressing the role of multiple actors in defining value proposition as solutions (Vargo and Lusch 2017); in this manner, the key factors can be identified (Anderson et al. 2006) and offered to targeted customers.

8 Conclusion

The main contribution of this chapter is that it creates an understanding of the role of technology in the shaping of the value proposition.

As discussed, according to Skålén et al. (2015), three aggregate practices are relevant to the composition and operationalization of value proposition(s). Our study portrayed these practices in the cultural heritage contexts and discussed how technologies support them to optimize the composition and execution of value propositions.

Specifically, it is possible to detect the duality of the role that technology plays in each of the three practices and, consequently, on the value proposition (see Table 5).

The provision practice mainly affects the service offering, as the content of the value proposition can be changed through customer involvement via technology. It can be amplified because the multi-actor approach depicts new ways of contributing to the definition of a value proposition, and new methods of delivering content can be offered by technology. When developing value propositions, it is important to understand customers' needs (Vargo and Lusch 2004), and if service providers simply ask customers what they want, they risk being backward-looking and obtaining only the spoken desires and not the actual underlying customer needs. To understand customers' latent needs, managers must immerse themselves in customers to understand the problems and underlying needs during the customers' whole service experience. Introducing an element of co-creation impacts the value proposition design strategy and will require a new data process that gives both firms and consumers the opportunities to expand and explore their involvement and co-creation.

The representational practice depicts how technology can support customers' involvement and, consequently, shape a multi-actor context; in this way, key attention is paid to the core relationship between a firm and the consumers, though other actors' contributions are taken into account, even in the communication process. Technologies improve the value propositions as communication practice

Table 5 The roles of technology in the value proposition

Practice	Role of technology	Value proposition
Provision	Improves the offering	Technology-enabled
Representational	Enhances involvement	
Management and organization	Encourages relationships through digital resources and new digital skills	
Provision	Amplifies the offering	Technology-amplified
Representational	Promotes the creation of new channels and the integration among digital and physical context	
Management and organization	Acts as connector	

Authors' elaboration

with the potential to integrate exchange activities, relationship development, and knowledge renewal. Ballantyne and Varey (2006) point out that there can be no satisfying relationship development unless the involved participants reciprocally determine their own sense of what is of value and communicate it to their counterparts.

Finally, management and organization practices are shaping new relationships because of technology. Thus, the key interactions supporting a value proposition are being complemented by new ones; technology represents the tool that favours connection among actors, and it shapes new channels hosting the multi-actor interactions. Furthermore, the company's customer value proposition should be built on the competencies and resources that the company can utilize more effectively than its competitors—competencies and resources that are unique and that result in competitive advantage.

In a technologies-based context, the value propositions are formed through the mutual exchange of knowledge between the actors who integrate resources to the value creation process in a digital realm. On the one hand, the technologies support service providers in better integrating their understanding of the offered service and what the customers can do; on the other hand, the customers are supported and perform activities that increase the market value of a provider offer. As the results show, the visitors—through the technologies—co-create the service, but also for other customers. By spreading the word about the application and the service obtained from it in their social network, they support other customers in service engagement and experience. In addition, technologies amplify the way that value proposition contributes to both provider and customer co-creation. Through technologies, the service provider better integrates his/her operant resources and the customer integrates his/her operant resources while interacting with each other, for the opportunity to influence each other's outcome in terms of the offered service. This process goes back and forth between the service provider and the customer so that each can obtain an understanding of the other's needs and that, together, they can create the service outcome.

In sum, technologies provide the basis for moving from a provider-centric initiation of value propositions to be assessed by the customer in use, to an emphasis on reciprocity, where providers and customers can interchangeably initiate or participate in value propositions. In one instance, customers initiate an inquiry with providers participating in a response. In another instance, customers start, with suppliers enquiring as to their ability to deliver. The technologies amplify this by challenging the traditional provider-dominant view of initiators and participants with a view of open-ended, discovery-oriented, and inherently relational perspectives (Frow et al. 2014).

References

Allurwar N, Nawale B, Patel S (2016) Beacon for proximity target marketing. Int J Eng Comput Sci 5(5)
Ambrose T, Paine C (2018) Museum basics: the international handbook. Routledge, London
Anderson JC, Narus JA, Van Rossum W (2006) Customer value propositions in business markets. Harv Bus Rev 84(3):91–99
Ballantyne D, Varey RJ (2006) Creating value-in-use through marketing interaction: the exchange logic of relating, communicating and knowing. Market Theory 6(3):335–348
Ballantyne D, Frow P, Varey RJ, Payne A (2011) Value propositions as communication practice: taking a wider view. Ind Market Manag 40(2):202–210
Barile S, Lusch R, Reynoso J, Saviano M, Spohrer J (2016) Systems, networks, and ecosystems in service research. J Serv Manag 27(4):652–674
Barnes C, Blake H, Pinder D (2009) Creating and delivering your value proposition: managing customer experience for profit. Kogan Page, London
Budge K (2017) Objects in focus: museum visitors and Instagram. Curator Museum J 60(1):67–85
Carù A, Colm L, Cova B (2016) Innovating services through experiences: an investigation of servicescape's pivotal role. In: Toivonen M (ed) Service innovation. Springer, Tokyo, pp 149–170
Chandler JD, Lusch RF (2015) Service systems: a broadened framework and research agenda on value propositions, engagement, and service experience. J Serv Res 18(1):6–22
Coblence E, Sabatier V (2014) Articulating growth and cultural innovation in art museums: the Louvre's business model revision. Int Stud Manag Organ 44(4):9–25
Dunleavy M, Dede C (2014) Augmented reality teaching and learning. In: Spector M, Merrill MD, Elen J, Bishop MJ (eds) Handbook of research on educational communications and technology. Springer, New York, pp 735–745
Eisenhardt KM, Graebner ME (2007) Theory building from cases: opportunities and challenges. Acad Manag J 50(1):25–32
Falk JH, Dierking LD (2016) The museum experience revisited. Routledge, London
Frow P, Payne A (2011) A stakeholder perspective of the value proposition concept. Eur J Market 45(1/2):223–240
Frow P, McColl-Kennedy JR, Hilton T, Davidson A, Payne A, Brozovic D (2014) Value propositions A service ecosystems perspective. Market Theory 14(3):327–351
Furr N, Shipilov A (2019) Digital doesn't have to be disruptive: the best results can come from adaptation rather than reinvention. Harv Bus Rev 97(4):94–104
González-Rodríguez MR, Martínez-Torres R, Toral S (2016) Post-visit and pre-visit tourist destination image through eWOM sentiment analysis and perceived helpfulness. Int J Contemp Hospit Manag 28(11):2609–2627
Hausmann A (2012) The importance of word of mouth for museums: an analytical framework. Int J Arts Manag 14(3):32–43
Hooper-Greenhill E (2000) Changing values in the art museum: rethinking communication and learning. Int J Herit Stud 6(1):9–31
Hsu TY (2012) A unified content and service management model for digital museums. Int J Humanit Arts Comput 6(1-2):87–99
Kannan PK (2017) Digital marketing: a framework, review and research agenda. Int J Res in Market 34(1):22–45
Koontz C, Mon L (2014) Marketing and social media: a guide for libraries, archives, and museums. Rowman & Littlefield, London
Koster EH, Falk JH (2007) Maximizing the external value of museums. Curator Museum J 50 (2):191–196
Kowalkowski C (2011) Dynamics of value propositions: insights from service-dominant logic. Eur J Market 45(1/2):277–294

Kowalkowski C, Persson Ridell O, Röndell JG, Sörhammar D (2012) The co-creative practice of forming a value proposition. J Market Manag 28(13–14):1553–1570
Lanning M (1998) Delivering profitable value. Perseus Publishing, New York
Lanning MJ, Michaels EG (1988) A business is a value delivery system. McKinsey Staff Paper 41 (July)
Lazzeretti L, Sartori A (2016) Digitization of cultural heritage and business model innovation: the case of the Uffizi Gallery in Florence. Il capitale culturale. Stud Value Cult Herit 14:945–970
Lüftenegger E, Comuzzi M, Grefen PW (2017) Designing a tool for service-dominant strategies using action design research. Serv Bus 11(1):161–189
Lusch RF, Vargo SL (2006) Service-dominant logic: reactions, reflections and refinements. Market Theory 6(3):281–288
Mangold WG, Faulds DJ (2009) Social media: the new hybrid element of the promotion mix. Bus Horiz 52(4):357–365
Morris M, Schindehutte M, Allen J (2005) The entrepreneur's business model: toward a unified perspective. J Bus Res 58:726–735
Navarrete (2013) Digital cultural heritage. In: Rizzo I, Mignosa A (eds) Handbook on the economics of cultural heritage. Edward Elgar, Cheltenham, pp 251–271
O'Cass A, Ngo LV (2011) Examining the firm's value creation process: a managerial perspective of the firm's value offering strategy and performance. Br J Manag 22(4):646–671
Osterwalder A, Pigneur Y, Bernarda G, Smith A (2014) Value proposition design: how to create products and services customers want. Wiley, New York
Ozuem W, Howell KE, Lancaster G (2019) The impact of digital books on marketing communications. J Retail Consum Serv 50:131–137
Payne AF, Storbacka K, Frow P (2008) Managing the co-creation of value. J Acad Market Sci 36 (1):83–96
Payne A, Frow P, Eggert A (2017) The customer value proposition: evolution, development, and application in marketing. J Acad Market Sci 1–23
Prebensen NK (2017) Innovation potentials through value proposals: a case study of a museum in Northern Norway. In: Prebensen NK, Chen JS, Uysal MS (eds) Co-creation in tourist experiences. Routledge, London, pp 64–75
Pulh M, Mencarelli R (2015) Web 2.0: is the museum-visitor relationship being redefined ? Int J Arts Manag 18(1):43–51
Ramaswamy V, Ozcan K (2016) Brand value co-creation in a digitalized world: an integrative framework and research implications. Int J Res Market 33(1):93–106
Skålén P, Gummerus J, von Koskull C, Magnusson P (2015) Exploring value propositions and service innovation: a service-dominant logic study. J Acad Market Sci 43(2):137–158
Standing C, Mattsson J (2018) "Fake it until you make it": business model conceptualization in digital entrepreneurship. J Strat Market 26(5):385–399
Stone M, Woodcock N (2013) Social intelligence in customer engagement. J Strat Market 21 (5):394–401
UNWTO (2018) Tourism demand in 2017: trends and facts. Retrieved from http://media.unwto.org/press-release/2018-04-23/strong-outbound-tourism-demand-both-traditional-and-emerging-markets-2017
Vargo SL, Lusch RF (2004) Evolving to a new dominant logic for marketing. J Market 68(1):1–17
Vargo SL, Lusch RF (2014) Inversions of service-dominant logic. Mark Theory 14(3):239–248
Vargo SL, Lusch RF (2017) Service-dominant logic 2025. Int J Res Market 34(1):46–67
Weaver S (2016) Creating great visitor experiences: a guide for museums, parks, zoos, gardens & libraries. Routledge, London
Webster FE Jr (1994) Defining the new marketing concept. Market Manag 2(4):22–31
Witcomb A (2007) The materiality of virtual technologies: a new approach to thinking about the impact of multimedia in museums. In: Cameron F, Kenderdine S (eds) Theorizing digital cultural heritage. MIT, Cambridge, MA, pp 35–48
Yin RK (2013) Case study research: design and methods. Sage, New York

Part II
Customers' Insights, Engagement and Analytics

Customer Insights and Consumer Profiling

Tiziana Russo Spena, Anna D'Auria, and Francesco Bifulco

Abstract This chapter addresses the analysis of the new approach to segmentation and consumer profiling. Specifically, it addresses the need to know how companies can detect the role of segmentation within the wider process of actioning customer insights. The growing use of analytics means that companies are getting better at knowing what consumers want (and do not want) and are adapting their operations and offerings to respond accordingly. Depending on the degree of personalization offered, dynamic data and analytics tools are critical in matching the right consumer to the right outcomes. True personalization requires cultural businesses to rethink their consumer insights process as well as their analysis and segmentation approaches.

1 Introduction

Market segmentation is both an important part of business management and an active area of contemporary research that has been constantly under intensive investigation (McDonald and Dunbar 2012). The development of market segmentation theory has been partially contingent on the availability of marketing data, advances in analytical techniques, and the progress of segmentation methodology (Karsten et al. 2005). All the traditional segmentation methods rely on the identification or creation of a set of descriptive variables from which the differences among customers are identified (Beane and Ennis 1987; Calvet et al. 2016). This information is of paramount importance to gain advantages over competitors as well as

---

T. Russo Spena (✉) · A. D'Auria
Department of Economics Management Institutions, University of Naples Federico II, Naples, Italy
e-mail: tiziana.russospena@unina.it; anna.dauria@unina.it

F. Bifulco
Department of Humanities, University of Naples Federico II, Naples, Italy
e-mail: fbifulco@unina.it

T. Russo Spena, F. Bifulco (eds.), *Digital Transformation in the Cultural Heritage Sector*, Contributions to Management Science,
https://doi.org/10.1007/978-3-030-63376-9_5

enhance customer relationship management, through the design of an effective marketing strategy. As a result, a variety of strategies with varying degrees of a priori customer knowledge necessities are identified for the successful application of targeting and marketing operative choices (Kotler and Armstrong 2018). Through the proliferation of digital and database technologies, the data and information related to customers increase in abundance these days. New channels, including social networks, digital media, and devices, have created an explosion of data, which means that managing this data has become more complex. The priority for many businesses in the new digital era is to connect the dots between multiple platforms and devices so that a more comprehensive view of their consumer profiles can be developed. Gathering information about the customer base and the ability to process that information into predictions about future requirements requires that companies use new methods and tools to target the market. Data mining breaks from traditional paradigms and explores the discovery of knowledge without the pre-established hypothesis (Agard and Kusiak 2004).

Businesses started using a new consumer segmentation approach based on data about consumer behaviour to better target those consumers (Assael 2005; Camilleri 2018; Hjort et al. 2013). The single view of the consumer through all the different touchpoints allows the business to personalize the experience further. When consumers started buying goods online, they shared not only more of their personal information but also their purchasing history. Digital marketing and online touchpoint shopping offered businesses advantages over traditional physical touchpoints or traditional channels, including the ability to target consumers with personalized offers based on their online shopping and browsing data. Companies have access to a multitude of touchpoints, social networks, customer relationship management (CRM) systems, cookies on websites, or in-store loyalty schemes (van de Sanden et al. 2019; Woodcock et al. 2011), which collectively provide much richer insights into consumer behaviours. Depending on the maturity and depth of their consumer data, more mature businesses are going to combine contextual data from unstructured data sources, such as social media or other behavioural data, with existing personal consumer data to engage with consumers in the most relevant way possible, and ideally in real time. Similarly, other businesses, whose data collection is less advanced, have started to better track and measure an individual's purchasing journey across their separate repositories of transactional data.

Thus, it becomes apparent that the traditional clustering methods appear to be less cost- and time-efficient (Tuma et al. 2011), which might lead to some deficiencies. Particularly in the case of identifying high-profitable consumers, the segmentation results might not be robust (Witten and Tibshirani 2010). As a consequence, an efficient and accurate market segmentation methodology to handle high-dimensional and also sparse datasets is highly required (Zhou et al. 2020).

In this new digital context, all businesses, including cultural heritage businesses, must do more with their customer data. Besides investing in the technologies to personalize customized offerings, a cultural heritage business must also consider its analytics capabilities to acquire and process data that will enable the business to better address marketing decisions. In situations in which the customer database is huge, a new approach and tools to better manage the increased amount of data on customers and make decisions regarding who and how to better serve, represent new challenges that must be addressed.

This chapter aims to go in-depth into the analysis of a new approach to segmentation and consumer profiling. Specifically, it addresses the need to know how companies can detect the role of segmentation within the wider process of actioning customer insights (Sinkula et al. 1997). The growing use of analytics means that companies are getting better at knowing what consumers want—and do not want—and are adapting their operations and offerings to respond accordingly. Depending on the degree of personalization offered, dynamic data and analytic tools are critical in matching the right consumer to the right outcomes. True personalization requires cultural businesses to rethink their consumer insights process as well as their analysis and segmentation approaches.

The chapter is organized as follows: First, literature contributions on market segmentation will be discussed, as market segmentation remains one of the most applied techniques when companies perform a market analysis to identify their target. Following, the focus will be on hypersegmentation, user profiling, and customer insights, and then a specific section discusses consumer profiling in the cultural heritage sector. Finally, the increasing role of mobile data and artificial intelligence in the cultural sector will be described, with some representative examples mentioned. The chapter will end with the authors' discussion and conclusion on both theoretical and empirical evidence.

2 Market Segmentation in the "Data Era"

Market segmentation is still regarded as essential for marketing strategy. Segmentation significantly contributes to the understanding of the characteristics of the corresponding market, the prediction of customers' behaviour, the detection and exploration of new market opportunities, and the identification of groups worth pursuing (Dolnicar et al. 2018; Huerta-Muñoz et al. 2017). The importance of good market segmentation was first recognized and introduced in the academic literature by Smith (1956), who emphasized, among other things, that market segmentation "*represents a rational and more precise adjustment (than product differentiation) of product and marketing effort to consumer or user requirements*" (Smith 1956; p. 5). In addition, he pointed out that market segmentation and product differentiation are completely different, even though they may look alike. This helps in target customer analysis, based on which customer attraction and retention strategies are framed.

Many other authors define segmentation bases as sets of variables (or characteristics) that are used to divide potential customers into several homogeneous groups (Aghdaie et al. 2014). Traditional marketing strategies are then based on segments instead of individuals, which are ideally separated into clusters to identify similar behaviour expectations and needs. The literature contains many different segmentation methods depending on the availability of several attributes (Karsten et al. 2005). Key attribute segmentation—based on the identification of product features or service characteristics that have different levels of relevance for some group of customers—has been opposed to the behaviour model segmentation relies on the availability of variables or other information that adequately describes the customer behaviour (MaGee 2008; Camilleri 2018). The result is that the marketers' segmentation choice consists to have to decide the attributes or features to include as variables and the weight to be applied to each. As many researchers emphasize elsewhere, there are also some unobservable (hidden) variables (Stavroglou et al. 2019), such as benefits, cultural characteristics, and sentiments that could influence the effectiveness of the chosen segmentation basis. Ranging from simple a priori to complex analysis, nearly every method shares the common trait that clusters (good or bad) are created. Indeed, no methods can guarantee that effective segments are created, and different methods often create different cluster results for no discernible reason (Huang et al. 2010). However, common to the different methods is the assumption that, once identified, the customer segments would not undergo any changes over time, which is not the case in the real world, and no possibility of the migration pattern of the customers from one group to another is assumed.

In recent decades, what has become more apparent is that the analysis of customer needs, behaviour, or expectations relies more on dynamic data, collected throughout the entire buying process, i.e. before, during, and after purchase (Chen et al. 2012). Information technology and the related phenomena of big data and the use of predictive analytics modelling, create new opportunities for companies to elaborate a more compelling customer segmentation process (Verdenhofs and Tambovceva 2019).

Customer data and their elaboration based on big data and algorithms help marketers better segment customers into more refined groups and also help predict customers' behaviour. Some studies conducted on dynamic customer segmentation are in the area of traditional customer relationship management systems that basically work with data gathered from offline channels. Furthermore, some researchers on online user behaviour have started to affirm that due to the large heterogeneity of consumer tastes and preferences available through online user interactions (Keane and Wasi 2016; Osharin and Verbus 2018), the potential of segmentation is immense, ranging from tailoring promotions and ads to delivering better product and brand recommendations. As a result of updating customer knowledge with the new data, the segmentation process undergoes specific changes that are reflected in the form of new dynamic clusters, the elimination of old clusters, and the creation of new clusters. However, the search in the field of customer segmentation through multiple data collection via different channels both online and offline is still in its infancy. There is a need to explore the utilization of data for the segmentation of customers using a more integrated approach that can collect and elaborate on data to extract behaviours and needs. This requires careful consideration not only of how the data should be processed so that it reflects the behaviour, but also of suitable inputs to feed these data into actions and insights. As noted, big data approaches differ from traditional data mining. Big data approaches can follow the flow of information and analyze data in real time. They require advanced and unique storage, management, analysis, and visualization of information technologies (Chen et al. 2012). They allow companies to create dynamic customer profiles by capturing customer attributes in real time and to move from a mass segmentation approach to segmenting right down to the individual level of customer needs.

3 Hypersegmentation: Build One Consumer Profile in Digital Marketing

In the digital context, segmentation is seen as part of the conjunction with customer profiling; however, there are reasons for a distinction from the customer profiling that is to describe types (persona) of customers. Normally, different types of information are combined in customer profiling, such as demographics, as well as behavioral data or information about lifestyle. Customer profiling helps to create an understanding of customers, to identify the best prospects based on certain attributes, or to improve services and increase customer satisfaction (Fan et al. 2005; Hassan and Tabasum 2018). According to some scholars, the new opportunities of hypersegmentation are now possible due to the means of moving towards the definition of ever more narrow market segments and the so-called "segments of one", i.e. segment that is organized based on customers' unique and individualized behaviours and needs (Dibb 2001, 2005).

Digital technology enables companies to identify customers' needs based on the specific contexts, events, and triggers—including unusual occurrences in customers' lives or transactions that impact their purchase behaviour. These technologies support companies with the most actionable forms of insights, providing actionable opportunities for cross-selling, up-selling, and retention offers, which result in high reported conversion rates (Bailey et al. 2009; Delen and Ram 2018). Thus, customer profiling is used not only for segmentation but also for other purposes, including marketing communications, offering development, and financial planning (Dunk 2004; Fan et al. 2005; Hassan and Tabasum 2018).

3.1 User Profiling

In the online context, the profile of the customer, i.e., the user profile, has been characterized by a more personalized, interactive, and dynamic approach (Lops et al. 2011). Modern techniques are highly influenced by new technologies and digital tools, shaping the behavior and preferences, and thereby the profile, of the online customer (or, better, user), which is now characterized by a more personalized, interactive, and dynamic approach.

The first studies on consumer and user profiling were related mainly to engineering and computer science (Lainé-Cruzel et al. 1996; Shivakumar et al. 1997), based merely on quantitative data, as described by Krulwich (1997), who stated that a "*user's profile consists simply of the data that the user has specified. These data are compared to those of other users to find overlaps in interests between users, and each user is recommended new items from the data of other users with overlapping interests*" (1997; p. 37). In 1997, Korfhage distinguished between a simple and an extended version of the user profile; the first one is obtained through the observation of the user, while the second one comprises more detailed information provided directly by the individual (Korfhage 1997, in Triantaphyllou and Felici 2006). More recently, new aspects have been taken into account, in particular unquantifiable information. For example: "*user-profiling involve[s] the interpretation of the whole set of previous user interactions, which are compared with each item not yet evaluated, in order to measure their similarity and recommend the most similar items*" (Lops et al., 2011 in Saia et al. 2014; p. 1); "*[a] profile is a description of someone containing the most important or interesting facts about him or her*" (Schiaffino and Amandi 2009; p. 193); and "*user profiles represent cognitive skills, intellectual abilities, intentions, learning styles, preferences and interactions with the system. (...) These values may be final or change over time*" (Nada and Fouad 2011; p. 152). Finally, Amoretti et al. (2017) extended the profile of the single user to others acting nearby, stating that user profiling takes into account not only a user's individual behaviour but also the behaviour of other, similar users. However, consumer profiling as a technique is not a recent concept because, as suggested by Dangi and Malik (2017), "*personalisation as [a] phenomenon is probably as old as trade flow itself*" (2017; p. 125), although only recently have marketing scholars started paying attention to this concept. One of the first scientific contributions on this topic was provided by Surprenant and Solomon (1987), who stated, "*The relative efficiency of personalisation is determined by the nature of the service rendered and [the] consumer's expectations about personalisation*" (Surprenant and Solomon, in Dangi and Malik 2017; p. 127). With reference to the direct connection between the user's profiling and personalization, an interesting perspective is the one by Sridevi and Umarani (2013), according to whom, a "*user profile is a record of user specific data*" (Sridevi and Umarani, in Dangi and Malik 2017; p. 129).

Regarding how to get information, Adomavicius et al. (2011) distinguished between information obtained *explicitly, implicitly,* or *inferring*. In the first case, users provide information voluntarily—for example, by filling out a web form to access a web page or get a smartphone app. In the second and third cases, information can be obtained through the observation of consumer behaviour or from pre-existent data. More recently, scholars focused on the relevance of digital devices and new technologies in user profiling processes (Boeck et al. 2011; Levesque et al. 2015; Viviani et al. 2010); the cross-fertilization between new technologies and profiling theories led to new approaches that transformed how consumers are profiled. With special reference to digital marketing, the development of a new role for consumers—leading marketers to new and more focused strategies—is due mainly to the ICTs, as people are even more informed and able to share information and experiences, affecting firms' and other consumers' behaviour and decisions. For example, social media and online forums afford consumers the ability to research products that are most suitable to their specific needs. New research shows the importance of analyzing online conversations; such insights are pertinent to broad situation analysis, providing a gauge of how well consumer segments are being served by one's own brand as well as competitors' brands (Hill et al. 2017; Law and Ng 2016).

In conclusion, most scholars show that companies are even more oriented towards a user-centric approach, to categorize customers and to create ad hoc services for each target (Aghababaei and Makrehchi 2017; Trusov et al. 2016; Uncles et al. 2012; Viviani et al. 2010), moving from targetization to personalization.

3.2 *Buyer Personas: Moving from One to a Group of Who Matters*

The term "buyer persona" has recently become the new marketing mantra, especially in the professional context tied to the new digital opportunities and personalization challenges.

It has been used to identify examples of archetypes of real buyers that allow marketers to craft strategies to promote products or services to the market. The distinction between buyer and customer is critical (Homburg et al. 2002; Wynstra et al. 2015) because marketers assume all too often that customer experience tells the full story. It is also described as a representation of the goals, attitudes, and behaviours of specific groups of customers who may engage and relate to products, services, or brands in a similar way (Table 1).

In this regard, Rinjani and Dellyana (2017) recalled the definitions of both customer persona and buyer persona, stating that the two concepts are often used as synonyms; in detail, they cited Scott (2007), according to whom the function of

Table 1 Persona versus segment

Persona	Segment
Research driven	Clearly identified groupings that can be measured
Used to design experiences	Used to execute and measure
Representative of an individual customer. He/she is relatable and real	Aggregated, impersonal description of a group
Must be described in detail and may belong to one of different segments	Evaluated based on marketing accessibility
Company's objectives are to humanize and connect	Company's objectives are to analyze and seize an opportunity

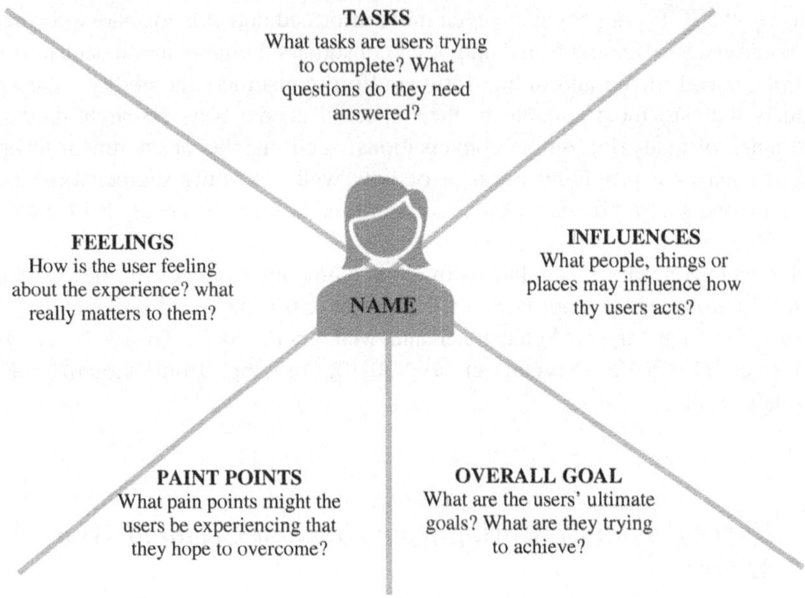

Fig. 1 The elements of buyer persona. Source: Authors' elaboration

the buyer persona towards a company "*is to create a strategy for its promotion and marketing for its products or service to the specific group and type of people that has been concluded*" (Scott 2007, in Rinjani and Dellyanan, 2017; p. 101), while De Jong (2016) defined customer persona as an "*example or archetypes that represent a specific group and type of people*" (De Jong 2016 in Rinjani and Dellyana 2017; p. 101).

The buyer persona goes a critical step further to reveal the story behind the business. Ciunci (2016) distinguished between the terms "core buyer persona", concerning the buyer in his own environment, and the "product persona connection", revealing the buyer's attitudes towards the product and company.

The buyer persona gives marketing confidence regarding what really matters for his/her buyers. Information regarding the use or the task the customer is trying to address through the product, the people, and information that can influence his/her choices, the feelings he/she experience during their journey, and the triggers they could encounter. The overall goal of the customer provides a comprehensive understanding of the main aim that he/she is trying to achieve (Fig. 1).

For these reasons, the buyer persona approach is based on designing buyer journeys for customer prospects (Lieberman 2019) by categorizing them into semi-fictional representations of the ideal customer based on market research and real data about existing customers, known as personas. It is a technique through which businesses can better relate to their key buyers and deliver better-tuned marketing content and messaging. It has also been noted that any buyer personas are starting points for marketing and are not definitive results.

However, the buyer persona approach does not exclude the need for companies to engage in segmentation (Mekonnen and London 2018). In a hyper-personalized and interactive context, segmentation not only is a process of deriving desirable (micro-) customer segments from a mass (heterogeneous, macro-) market but could also be the opposite, i.e. a process of building up micro-segments based on transaction likelihoods to form maps of customer groups at greater aggregate levels. Companies will not only manage their interactions with consumers and tailor offerings to selected customer groups on an individual basis but will also measure the likelihood of customers taking up new offerings using customer analytic data and propensity modelling, which, when combined with segmentation programmes, will enable the measurement of customer lifetime value and the dynamic optimization of market segments. In the area of market segmentation, the link between propensity modelling, customer analytics, and the determination of optimal customer segments over time is particularly worthy of further research, given the lack of understanding of dynamism in market segmentation programmes (Verdenhofs and Tambovceva 2019).

4 Customer Insights

The main objective of customer segmentation is to understand the customer base and gain customer insights that will enable the design and development of differentiated marketing strategies.

Customer insights as a term have come into vogue in both academic and practitioner discourse (Wills and Williams 2004; Wills and Webb 2007) to reflect the multiple informational sources in existence about customers, ranging from market research to transactional data mining, as well as data from marketplace experimentation and third-party sources (Slater and Narver 2000). The few empirical studies reviewing customer insights in practice (Wills and Webb 2007) concur that customer insights arise from "multiple data sources", yet there is a paucity of evidence on the forms of insights that companies are generating and from where (Forsyth et al. 2006). Hirschowitz (2001) regards segmentation as a subset of customer insights, citing such segmentation bases as socio-demographic, geo-demographic, and value-based as customer insights examples. However, customer insights are not just a new name for market segmentation, or they encompass separate sets of activities and processes. Customer insights are made up of carefully evaluated information about current and potential customers (Wieneke and Lehrer 2016) (Table 2). This involved the provision, simplification, and understanding of large unstructured customer data sets including external data, i.e. demographics, consumer confidence, macro market trends, third-party data (e.g. news stories), social-media discussions, sociocultural trends through online chatter identification of other specific customers in the market, and recommender systems to identify likely future events (e.g. areas of potential growth). They come from a combination of quantitative and qualitative research and data analysis. As Verdenhofs and

Table 2 Sources of insights

CRM database	The data include: (1) personal details of a customer, i.e. their names, email addresses, Skype addresses, ages, and titles; (2) all the interactions made with the customer including the last time you talked, the last time they submitted feedback, and the last time they requested to receive a newsletter; (3) the purchases histories of the customers; (4) customers' levels of engagement, e.g. the last time they got in touch with the company or the last time they visited the company website
Social listening	The data include what the customer is asking for, or what the customer is complaining about, as well as what the customer wants to know about your product and how the customer rates or reviews the product
Company website	The data include where visitors come from, what keywords they used to find you, what pages they visited, and how long they spent on those pages
Customer feedback survey	Customer satisfaction surveys, focus group etc.

Tambovceva (2019) stated, by drilling down into the demographic and psychographic distinctions, the organizations are able to understand and hone better the unique segments of their customer base. Companies need to know who they are speaking to and serving best and customer insights provide clarity about who exactly their customers are. Customers—and, above all, the marketing insights—are identified as the more reasoned thoughts and conclusions based on the analysis of data and information established from market research, surveys, and so forth. Companies can get insights from company reports or the analysis of websites; however, customer conversations reveal information that would have gone unnoticed otherwise. Website analytics tools can help companies discover more about customer engagement through the company's website. Metrics like time on site, event tracking, goal tracking (i.e. regularly reading a blog, downloading or watching videos), and customer paths can reveal how visitors are using companies' websites and how engaged they are over specific time periods. This data can be filtered down from the overall website to specific pages. Social media platforms have similar analytical tools available through the administration sections. Companies are able to view data about interactions such as comments, likes, shares, clicks, and follows. Each social channel is slightly different in terms of how it is named and reported the metrics, but they all generally focus on the same types of data. Analyzing these numbers can help companies discover what followers are interested in and what kind of messaging seems to connect best with them so that the companies can use this when responding to future posts or interactions, comments, reviews, likes, shares, clicks, follows, app uses, downloads etc. Customer surveys or email messaging platforms provide valuable information through data and metrics like open rate and click-through rate. These numbers can be used similarly to social media numbers, helping companies improve messaging, callouts, subjects, and headlines.

After all, data alone does not mean anything if meaning, direction, and goals are not taken from it. Findings related to customer insights must be transformed into an actionable decision process and inform the company's marketing initiatives.

Consumer insights provide a deeper understanding of customers, which leads to marketing on a more direct and personal level. Businesses today must gather such consumer insights to implement effective marketing strategies. These strategies can apply to how products and services are presented to consumers as well as to the development of the products and services themselves. Consumer insights can also help companies identify new problems that the company can solve with additional product or service offerings. According to some authors, the potential power of customer insights is increasingly based on individualized customer analytics and propensity modelling, which helps determine the likelihood of the uptake of specific propositions (Wieneke and Lehrer 2016). Events and triggers informing companies about how to deal with customers individually are considered to be particularly effective with the goal of improving profitability and customer retention.

Once the foundational aspects of data insights, human resources, and software are present, firms must still work to develop a data orientation within their broader culture. For some, such cultural shifts will require a completely different approach to decision-making, from top-down to bottom-up and long-range planning to short-term reactions (Merendino et al. 2018). This entails both philosophical shifts and more pragmatic considerations. At a macro level, business orientations must shift towards a culture of continual improvement through testing and learning. This includes adopting a data-driven approach to mining historical data for clues on paths forward, as well as to evolving market and customer processes to emphasize this constant mining of existing data. This requires a renewed marketing approach to better identify possible business opportunities, understand the output, and act upon findings. Garnering buy-in and sharing ideas and successes can also be helpful.

5 Consumer Profiling in Cultural Heritage

The studies in consumer profiling in cultural heritage are quite recent, and most of them take into account new technologies as tools to identify customer behaviour and preferences, although the number of contributions on the theme is still quite low. The first contributions were published in the early 2000s, mainly in computer science disciplines (Bonfigli et al. 2004; Cabri et al. 2001; Liiv et al. 2009;). In fact, recently, digital devices—i.e. tablets, smartphones, and applications—have been increasingly included in the cultural domain, aimed at joining different and various ways of conveying cultural heritage. Mobile devices are a constant part of everyday life, and most people are very familiar with them; therefore, they are properly considered the most suitable way to create a direct interaction between users and the attraction (Cuomo et al. 2015).

Scholars' contributions highlight the fact that the employment of digital devices in cultural heritage has yet to be exploited; many companies use applications allowing them to provide personalized services or content, but most of them still use these tools only to spread information from existing databases. According to scholars such as Lo Bue et al. (2015), the real challenge for companies is the following: "*How to adapt it to the personal preferences, as well as to the current context (location, social, temporal etc.) of the visitor and, most importantly, how to narrate it and create a coherent, continuous experience over time*" (Lo Bue et al. 2015; p. 2). Therefore, companies must be able to transform the information obtained in the appropriate messages or communications through a suitable language (texts, images, videos, audio etc.), detecting consumers' preferences (Katz et al. 2006) and performing a segmentation to identify the best way to satisfy the selected target. In this regard, an interesting contribution was provided by Brida et al. (2013), who, in their study, performed a segmentation analysis, identifying two sets of clusters based on tourists' behaviour taking part to a cultural event; in detail, they referred to "motivations clusters" and "expenditures clusters" (Brida et al. 2013). However, further advancements move scholars, managers, and practitioners towards the personalization of cultural services, as cultural heritage offers many opportunities. It is then important to identify a visitor's preferences to let him/her enjoy a personalized experience and propose services to the visitor in the most suitable way. In this regard, in the following sub-paragraphs, theoretical and empirical evidence will be discussed to highlight the relevance of new technologies and digital tools in different cultural services.

5.1 Mobile Data and Consumer Profiling

Although technologies in the cultural sector are still used mainly to spread information, mobile devices are being largely employed in museums and archaeological sites (Filip et al. 2015; Lin et al. 2014). However, the degree of diffusion of digital devices in cultural heritage usually does not correspond to the fast evolution of new technologies; many opportunities can still be exploited. For example, Lo Bue et al. (2015) proposed a framework aimed at creating a visitor model through the collection and analysis of visitors' preferences and behaviour and based on the opportunity to achieve free information. In detail, "*visitor model preferences are exploited using a graph similarity approach in order to identify personalized opportunities for visitors by filtering relevant Cultural Objects*" (Lo Bue et al. 2015, p. 2). Such information can be collected from catalogues or websites (internal information) or imported from available open data related to cultural attractions (external information). One form of evidence is the Russian Linked Culture Cloud. This initiative is very representative, as the goal is to create a database on Russian cultural heritage available to anyone and built through end-user applications and the engagement of visitors and experts. The information collected comes from museums, galleries, archives, libraries, and other local institutions that are able to get, modify, and share information and data.

The following box discusses an example related to the concepts described above.

Exhibit 1: The Metropolitan Museum of Art

Recently, The Metropolitan Museum of Art in New York conducted an analysis aimed at profiling users of the official website, due to the museum's huge and increasing number of visitors. The starting point of the investigation was the following questions: "Who exactly are these users? What motivates them to come to our website? What are their needs and expectations when they browse the collection? Where are they coming from?" In detail, the analysis was performed to observe the target of users frequently visiting the website, in order to improve the quality of the content and provide even more satisfying services, thereby enhancing the users' experience.

To accomplish this goal, the analysts adopted various methodologies and tools, such as Google Analytics, heat maps, target segmentation, and an online survey. Google Analytics and heat maps were employed to observe how long users spent viewing one or more pages of the website, which section they preferred, and how they reached the website to visit the online collection (i.e. directly via Google.com or by clicking on a link from another website or social media). Meanwhile, surveys were useful for obtaining information to shape users' profiles and detect their motivation when visiting the website. In this regard, most visitors did so for their jobs—as researchers or teachers—or to improve their competences, as well as to find inspiration for their own creative work.

The results obtained through Google Analytics and the surveys (more than 1200 answers were collected) led to the defining of six core user segments, namely, professional researchers, student researchers, personal-interest information seekers, inspiration seekers, casual browsers, and visit planners.

Professional researchers are frequent users who come to the online collection mainly directly from search engines or through metmuseum.org. As experts in art, they look for specific information. For this reason, they use advanced search functionalities and the zoom options to see details of the artwork.

Students are mainly art students. Their motivations are quite similar to those of the researchers, as they visit the website directly through the search engine and to find the content useful for their studies.

Personal-interest information seekers are users who have an interest in art that is not connected to their professions or jobs; they enter the website directly from the search engine and also through mobile devices; in many cases, they visit the website during their visit to access a higher quantity of, and more detailed, information.

Inspiration seekers are people in search of inspiration, for recreation or their profession, (i.e. artists and creative art professionals such as photographers and designers).

(continued)

Exhibit 1: The Metropolitan Museum of Art (continued)

Casual browsers are users who, similar to the previous group, search for inspiration or visual experience without a specific purpose, or just for recreation.

Finally, visit planners are users who are planning to visit the museum; in some cases, they visit the online collection directly from the museum to find out what they can see.

As anticipated, through target segmentation, as well as the observation of users' preferences, analysts aimed to enhance users' online experience, providing content fitting their inclinations and interests, including through a new design or layout, or improving the interaction between the users and the cultural institution.

Once the information has been collected, it is possible to compare and match that information with consumers' preferences to better satisfy their expectations and offer a complete visit experience thanks to the technological facilities (Kuflik et al. 2017). Customer insights collection can also support managers in improving economic results thanks to users' engagement, for example through apps and websites encouraging followers or visitors to share information and posts or express their likes. In addition, to acquire useful data, consumers' feedback—for example through social networks' platforms—is as important as their interests. It is also useful to better define the offering on the basis of their implicit or explicit suggestions.

The following box discusses an example related to the concepts described above.

Exhibit 2: The Hi.Stories

Hi.Stories is an innovative start-up, begun in April 2017. The company deals with digital innovations for cultural heritage through gaming initiatives and the creation of 3D reconstructions, eco-sustainable 3D prints, and applications for museum display, as well as the use of the territory, thereby shaping personalized and customized services.

In general, the main aim of Hi.Stories is to be a local reference for territorial enhancement through digital technologies. In this regard, one must mention the partnership with the FAI—the National Trust of Italy for arts and nature—and the fact that the project involves schools to help students understand how technology and culture can dialogue. In particular, young high school students are involved in the development of thematic and cultural itineraries to be developed and made interactive through the support of Hi.Stories software and machinery applications. Therefore, the target on which they choose to focus is composed mainly of young people, who are more inclined to use digital tools such as applications, and with the aim of helping them understand that cultural content and technological innovation play equally important roles

(continued)

Exhibit 2: The Hi.Stories (continued)
when it comes to digital skills for the museum and cultural sector. At the same time, these tools are useful in identifying customer preferences and behaviour.

In this regard, when shaping services, Hi.Stories takes into account the General Data Protection Regulation of 2016, according to which, when registering for services, only information such as an individual's username, password, and registration email should be required. The request for additional personal data (i.e. age, sex, geographical origin) would allow companies to develop remarketing practices; however, companies must consider the privacy issues as stated by the aforementioned General Data Protection Regulation.

The statistical analysis data, managed by platforms like Google Play and the App Store, provide the company with statistical information useful for understanding and interpreting users' behaviour to shape satisfying services. The results are doubly beneficial, as users are provided with appropriate and satisfying services contributing to the local territorial valorization, which is one of the main goals of Hi.Stories.

5.2 *Artificial Intelligence and Consumer Profiling*

Advances in the field of big data collection provide cultural firm marketers with the ability to collect and aggregate vast amounts of information, with the ultimate aim of turning data into insights or actionable strategy. According to Marshall (2018), "*These same technologies can also allow museums to gather useful data about visitors to their exhibitions, including analysis [of] which aspects of the exhibition attract the most interest, how long visitors interact with specific parts of the exhibition, the flow of visitors through the exhibition, and whether or not visitors are returning for multiple visits. This sort of data can be particularly useful to museums that are not externally funded and thus need to optimise their exhibits to attract as many visitors and as often as possible*" (Marshall 2018; p. 16). Therefore, the ability to collect, select, and manage data is even more important for companies interested in finding the most suitable way to satisfy consumers. Artificial intelligence is said to greatly assist cultural firms in this process (Nourani et al. 2018; Pan 2016;) by drawing conclusions from unstructured data about causes and effects within extremely large data sets. With the ability to detect and extrapolate upon patterns, technologies can help marketers identify opportunities and act upon them in real time. From here, Artificial intelligence (AI) and Machine Learning (ML) functionality transform useful and relevant data into information. This information, when blended with context, expertise, and intuition, becomes knowledge. AI techniques, including social listening, can glean information about markets and consumers, particularly in terms of satisfaction, purchasing patterns, and product demand. They emerge as a successful solution for updating customer segments with new information (Marshall 2018). For example, as soon as a new customer completes a purchase, that customer is automatically added to his/her respective segments based on the buying patterns. Then marketing campaigns are triggered immediately.

With reference to artificial intelligence systems in cultural heritage, an interesting contribution is provided by Fontanella et al. (2020), who stated that cultural heritage is one of the fields impacted by artificial intelligence, as new solutions to collect and manage data are increasingly employed.

The following box describes an example related to the concepts indicated above.

Exhibit 3: American Museum of Natural History (AMNH)

The American Museum of Natural History (AMNH) was founded in 1869 and is currently the largest natural history museum in the world. The museum is located in New York City and welcomes approximately five million visitors annually.

Despite the huge number of visitors, to improve the visiting experience, the museum pays particular attention to visitors' comments, online reviews through social media platforms, and suggestions obtained through a survey that the museum sends to each visitor 2 days after a visit, using the email addresses that visitors provide when purchasing tickets.

Apart from multiple-choice questions such as "How likely are you to recommend the American Museum of Natural History?", inviting respondents to select a numerical value between 1 and 10, there are questions which generate a qualitative response that is considered highly useful in shaping the visitors' profiles; for example "What is the most important reason for your score?"

The data are processed using Natural Language Processing (NLP) and a sentiment analysis service through an IBM platform. For example, the sentiment analysis reports on a specific set of words, or entities to observe with words are more frequent in the open-ended survey questions.

This analysis is performed every 6 months, in line with the notable number of persons visiting the museum.

Similar tools are Google Cloud and Natural Language Processing API, allowing for performing an analysis used to evaluate reviews shared on the TripAdvisor platform.

The results of the above-mentioned analysis are compared to a general sentiment score—ranging from –1 (very negative) to +1 (very positive)—generated for the top seven museums (by attendance) in the United States, namely, the National Air and Space Museum and the National Gallery of Art (generating the highest score), the American Museum of Natural History, the Metropolitan Museum of Art, the National Museum of American History, the National Museum of Natural History, and the 9/11 Memorial Museum.

(continued)

Exhibit 3: American Museum of Natural History (AMNH) (continued)

The case study highlights how relevant it can be for cultural organizations to analyze and detect information about visitors to improve their commercial services. It also highlights the usefulness of tools such as IBM Watson or Google Cloud Natural Language Processing in managing large amounts of qualitative data and extracting insights on visitor preferences and expectations, as well as aspects of the visitor experience and their perceptions.

Marketing in the cultural heritage sector aims to develop an understanding of the specific markets in which companies operate and the consumers they target, monitoring their behaviour to track the success of their activities in terms of key metrics. Web analytics and traditional market research (customer satisfaction) are often engaged, with AI providing a vast array of opportunities beyond customer satisfaction (Al-Otaibi et al. 2018; Zara et al. 2012). For instance, voice-of-customer programs allow companies to move beyond interview-based data to also incorporate large amounts of unstructured customer data. In this context, data can be analyzed, and feedback provided in real time, allowing decisions and actions to be taken immediately.

With reference to web analytics in cultural heritage, a study carried out by Voorbij (2010) on cultural heritage institutions in The Netherlands showed that gathering web statistics is quite common and Google Analytics is the most popular method. In addition, from the study, it emerged that web analytics also showed that new technologies can coexist with physical services, as "*Virtual visits do not only compensate [for] the decline in physical visits, but also lead to better-prepared visitors. Thus, the quantity of physical visits may decrease, while the quality improves*" (Voorbij 2010; p. 278).

The following box describes an example related to the concepts discussed above.

Exhibit 4: The National Gallery of London

The National Gallery of London was founded in 1824 and today boasts a collection of more than 2300 pieces of art, with more than five million visitors each year. In line with this, one of the main challenges of the museum's management is predicting the attendance of temporary exhibitions to properly receive customers and ensure that the physical capacity of an exhibition space is suitable for the number of expected visitors, as well as creating a more enjoyable experience and improving the Gallery's reputation. In particular, this aspect is relevant with reference to obtaining funding.

To accomplish this aim, the Data and Insights team at the National Gallery developed predictive models to forecast the potential attendance about 12–18 months before an exhibition opens. Previous investigations put into evidence the most useful variables for creating a reliable forecasting model (viz. if an

(continued)

Exhibit 4: The National Gallery of London (continued)
exhibition is thematic or monographic; which is the movement and period of the art presented in the exhibition; how famous the artist is; the likelihood that the UK public will pay for an exhibition focused on that artist; and the costs of the exhibition).

The forecast is considered the foundation of the plans defined to achieve the intended results. In fact, as the model is based on historical data from similar previous exhibitions, it represents a tool for planning future events and initiatives.

The results of such an investigation can influence ticket prices, exhibition locations, exhibition calendars, exhibition run times, and marketing activities, chosen to attract visitors and increase the quality of their visiting experience, as well as to induce them to repeat their visits to the gallery.

It must be considered that the insights obtained should be interpreted considering the mission of the museum as an institution and considering its social impact on the community. In this regard, apart from the number of customers, aspects such as the valorization of different cultures are also considered key elements in the work of The National Gallery, as financial revenue is only one part of a complex operating context.

It is clear that the development of models to provide visitors with satisfying experiences and accomplish the social role of the cultural organization is very useful and can take place quickly once the organization identifies how to obtain data and information about consumers' behaviour. Also, the models improve the visibility of the museum and its competitiveness.

In conclusion, forecasting future customers' behaviour trends can positively influence workers' and managers' attitudes and provide useful insights with which to make strategic decisions.

6 Discussion

Although new methods and marketing strategies have been introduced in the last years, segmentation—namely, the action of dividing customers into like-minded groups—remains one of the most applied techniques to define the target and identify how to shape satisfying products and services. While in the traditional approach firms used to define a target on which to focus, today, the new role of consumer—that is even more informed and for whom expectations are even higher—represents a real challenge for traditional marketing strategists, as segmenting and targeting the market is no longer enough. This requires marketers to re-examine their business processes and marketing strategies in order to recognize and fulfil each customer's needs (Dangi and Malik 2017).

Managers' and analysts' goals are strived to define the profile of the categories of customers served by the company. To describe their profile, companies can count on different types of information: implicit, if deduced from the behaviour of the customer before, during, and after joining the services, or explicit, if derived from the direct and conscious participation of the customer during the communication process and during and after their enjoyment of the service).

The proposition of a tailor-made offer, as well as the identification of the most suitable communication channels and messages, can be the best way to attract customers' interests and learn their expectations and preferences. Indeed, while segmentation continues to be vital for marketing planning, organizations are now aware of the need to develop individualized customer interactions. In line with this, the scientific debate has recently focused on the relevance of new technologies and digital tools in shaping marketing strategies to communicate with and satisfy consumers, and, in particular, in consumer profiling processes (Levesque et al. 2015; Viviani et al. 2010).

One of the main problems affecting managers who collect information about customers is the variability of the information collected, including information that often is not comparable and that cannot be categorized, with special reference to data obtained implicitly. In this scenario, digital instruments can be very helpful in interpreting and analyzing the information obtained.

The cross-fertilization between new technologies and profiling theories led to the spread of a set of new approaches that transformed how consumers and users are observed, and that created the opportunity to optimize customer segments using propensity modelling data derived from CRM systems which, when clustered, can determine the most likely customers for specific offering. This is an invaluable piece of information for determining the effectiveness of segmentation approaches when the two are combined.

In this regard, in developing an AI foundation, firms must consider account privacy and regulation issues, as nowadays consumers are more concerned about the way companies use personal data in marketing strategies. Indeed, the use of customer data for both personalized marketing and development of customized products and services will require a new data governance process and framework that gives consumers control over how their data are used.

It must be noted that the application of tools and systems such as artificial intelligence requires firms to have robust systems capable of tracking relevant data in real time. They must also be able to store data for historical analysis because the data requirements for AI are quite high. While collecting data may seem easy, it is important to note that many IT systems are not designed for data pulls. For instance, many advertising agencies' systems are designed to track an individual client's performance, not to extract data from campaigns. Similarly, many businesses suffer from data silos. Many systems do not use a common tracking ID number, or worse, they arrange data in fundamentally different ways, requiring custom software to merge data sets. While some forms of ML (e.g. reinforcement) can operate without training data sets, accessing historical data sets is valuable.

References

Adomavicius G, Mobasher B, Ricci F, Tuzhilin A (2011) Context-aware recommender systems. AI Mag 32(3):67–80

Agard B, Kusiak A (2004) Data mining for subassembly selection. J Manuf Sci Eng 126 (3):627–631

Aghababaei S, Makrehchi M (2017) Activity-based Twitter sampling for content-based and user-centric prediction models. Hum Centric Comput Inform Sci 7(1):3

Aghdaie M, Fami Tafreshi P, Behzadian M (2014) Customer-oriented benefit segmentation: an integrated approach. Int J Bus Innovat Res 8(2):168–189

Al-Otaibi S, Alnassar A, Alshahrani A, Al-Mubarak A, Albugami S, Almutiri N, Albugami A (2018) Customer satisfaction measurement using sentiment analysis. Int J Adv Comput Sci Appl 9(2):106–117

Amoretti M, Belli L, Zanichelli F (2017) UTravel: smart mobility with a novel user profiling and recommendation approach. Pervasive Mobile Comput 38:474–489

Assael H (2005) Consumer behavior: a strategic approach. Indian Dreamtech Press

Bailey C, Baines PR, Wilson H, Clark M (2009) Segmentation and customer insight in contemporary services marketing practice: why grouping customers is no longer enough. J Market Manag 25(3-4):227–252

Beane TP, Ennis DM (1987) Market segmentation: a review. Eur J Market 21(5):20–42

Boeck H, Roy J, Durif F, Grégoire M (2011) The effect of perceived intrusion on consumers' attitude towards using an RFID-based marketing program. Proc Comput Sci 5:841–848

Bonfigli ME, Cabri G, Leonardi L, Zambonelli F (2004) Virtual visits to cultural heritage supported by web-agents. Inf Softw Technol 46(3):173–184

Brida JG, Disegna M, Scuderi R (2013) Visitors of two types of museums: a segmentation study. Expert Syst Appl 40(6):2224–2232

Cabri G, Leonardi L, Zabonelli F (2001) Web-assisted visits to cultural heritage. In: Proceedings tenth IEEE international workshop on enabling technologies: infrastructure for collaborative enterprises. WET ICE 2001. IEEE, pp 356–361

Calvet L, Ferrer A, Gomes MI, Juan AA, Masip D (2016) Combining statistical learning with metaheuristics for the multi-depot vehicle routing problem with market segmentation. Comput Ind Eng 94:93–104

Camilleri MA (2018) Travel marketing, tourism economics and the airline product. Springer, Cham

Chen D, Sain SL, Guo K (2012) Data mining for the online retail industry: a case study of RFM model-based customer segmentation using data mining. Database Market Cust Strat Manag 19 (3):197–208

Ciunci C (2016) Marketing in the trenches: 25 real-world marketing tips to achieve dramatic business growth. Lulu.com

Cuomo S, De Michele P, Galletti A, Ponti G (2015) Visiting styles in an art exhibition supported by a digital fruition system. In: 2015 11th international conference on signal-image technology and internet-based systems (SITIS). IEEE, pp 775–781

Dangi H, Malik A (2017) Personalisation in marketing: an exploratory study. Int J Internet Market Advert 11(2):124–136

Delen D, Ram S (2018) Research challenges and opportunities in business analytics. J Bus Analytics 1(1):2–12

Dibb S (2001) New millennium, new segments: moving towards the segment of one? J Strat Market 9(3):193–213

Dibb S (2005) Market segmentation: implementation barriers and how to overcome them. Market Rev 5(1):13–30

Dolnicar S, Grün B, Leisch F (2018) Market segmentation analysis: understanding it, doing it, and making it useful. Springer, London

Dunk AS (2004) Product life cycle cost analysis: the impact of customer profiling, competitive advantage, and quality of IS information. Manag Account Res 15(4):401–414
Fan W, Gordon MD, Pathak P (2005) Effective profiling of consumer information retrieval needs: a unified framework and empirical comparison. Decis Support Syst 40(2):213–233
Filip FG, Ciurea C, Dragomirescu H, Ivan I (2015) Cultural heritage and modern information and communication technologies. Technol Econ Dev Econ 21(3):441–459
Fontanella F, Colace F, Molinara M, Di Freca AS, Stanco F (2020) Pattern recognition and artificial intelligence techniques for cultural heritage. Elsevier, London
Forsyth JE, Galante N, Guild T (2006) Capitalizing on customer insights. McKinsey Q 3:42–53
Hassan MMTM, Tabasum M (2018) Customer profiling and segmentation in retail banks using data mining techniques. Int J Adv Res Comput Sci 9(4):24–29
Hill SR, Troshani I, Chandrasekar D (2017) Signalling effects of vlogger popularity on online consumers. J Comput Inf Syst 60(1):76–84
Hirschowitz A (2001) Closing the CRM loop: the 21st century marketer's challenge: transforming customer insight into customer value. J Target Meas Anal Market 10(2):168–178
Hjort K, Lantz B, Ericsson D, Gattorna J (2013) Customer segmentation based on buying and returning behaviour. Int J Phys Distrib Logist Manag 43(10):852–865
Homburg C, Krohmer H, Cannon JP, Kiedaisch I (2002) Customer satisfaction in transnational buyer–supplier relationships. J Int Market 10(4):1–29
Huang Y, Niu B, Gao Y, Fu L, Li W (2010) CD-HIT Suite: a web server for clustering and comparing biological sequences. Bioinformatics 26(5):680–682
Huerta-Muñoz DL, Ríos-Mercado RZ, Ruiz R (2017) An iterated greedy heuristic for a market segmentation problem with multiple attributes. Eur J Oper Res 261(1):75–87
Karsten S, Tomczak T, Herrmann A (2005) Development of a taxonomy of strategic market segmentation: a framework for bridging the implementation gap between normative segmentation and business practice. J Strat Market 13(3):151–173
Katz S, Kahanov Y, Kashtan N, Kuflik T, Graziola I, Rocchi C et al (2006) Preparing personalized multimedia presentations for a mobile museum visitors' guide—a methodological approach. In: Trant J, Bearman D (eds) Museums and the Web 2006. Archives & Museum Informatics, Toronto. Available at http://www.archimuse.com/mw2006/papers/katz/katz.html
Keane MP, Wasi N (2016) How to model consumer heterogeneity? Lessons from three case studies on SP and RP data. Res Econ 70(2):197–231
Kotler P, Armstrong G (2018) Principles of marketing. Pearson, New York
Krulwich B (1997) Lifestyle finder: intelligent user profiling using large-scale demographic data. AI Mag 18(2):37–37
Kuflik T, Lo Bue A, Stock O, Wecker AJ (2017) When will cultural heritage content creation get to the digital age? In: Adjunct publication of the 25th conference on user modeling, adaptation and personalization, pp 335–336
Lainé-Cruzel S, Lafouge T, Lardy JP, Abdallah NB (1996) Improving information retrieval by combining user profile and document segmentation. Inf Process Manag 32(3):305–315
Law M, Ng M (2016) Age and gender differences: understanding mature online users with the online purchase intention model. J Global Scholars Market Sci 26(3):248–269
Levesque N, Boeck H, Durif F, Levesque A (2015) The impact of proximity marketing on consumer reaction and firm performance: a conceptual and integrative model. In: Twenty-first Americas conference on information systems. Puerto Rico, pp 1–8
Lieberman M (2019) How 'the new customer buyer's journey' is reshaping the way you strategically manage your brand. J Brand Strat 8(1):76–85
Liiv I, Tammet T, Ruotsalo T, Kuusik A (2009) Personalized context-aware recommendations in SMARTMUSEUM: combining semantics with statistics. In: 2009 third international conference on advances in semantic processing. IEEE, pp 50–55
Lin JQP, Din H, Wu S (2014) IT-enabled innovative services as a museum strategy: experience of the National Palace Museum Taipei Taiwan. In: Digital heritage and culture: strategy and implementation. World Scientific, pp 3–20

Lo Bue AL, Wecker AJ, Kuflik T, Machì A, Stock O (2015). Providing personalized cultural heritage information for the smart region—a proposed methodology. In: UMAP workshops

Lops P, De Gemmis M, Semeraro G (2011) Content-based recommender systems: state of the art and trends, In recommender systems handbook. Springer, Boston, MA, pp 73–105

MaGee S (2008) How to identify a target market and prepare a customer profile. Edward Lowe Foundation. Available at https://edwardlowe.org/erc

Marshall MT (2018) Interacting with heritage: on the use and potential of IoT within the cultural heritage sector. In 2018 fifth international conference on internet of things: systems, management and security. IEEE, pp 15–22

McDonald M, Dunbar I (2012) Market segmentation: how to do it and how to profit from it. Wiley, Chichester

Mekonnen A, London GSM (2018) Digital marketing strategy for affinity marketing. In: Digital marketing and consumer engagement: concepts, methodologies, tools, and applications: concepts, methodologies, tools, and applications. IGI Global, Hershey, PA, pp 87–104

Merendino A, Dibb S, Meadows M, Quinn L, Wilson D, Simkin L, Canhoto A (2018) Big data, big decisions: the impact of big data on board level decision-making. J Bus Res 93:67–78

Nada YA, Fouad KM (2011) An approach to improve the representation of the user model in the web-based systems. IJACSA Int J Adv Comput Sci Appl 2(12):152–160

Nourani V, Elkiran G, Abba SI (2018) Wastewater treatment plant performance analysis using artificial intelligence—an ensemble approach. Water Sci Technol 78(10):2064–2076

Osharin A, Verbus V (2018) Heterogeneity of consumer preferences and trade patterns in a monopolistically competitive setting. J Econ 125(3):211–237

Pan Y (2016) Heading toward artificial intelligence 2.0. Engineering 2(4):409–413

Rinjani ANS, Dellyana D (2017) Integrated marketing communication for GRAN. J Innovat Bus Entrepren 2(1):100–111

Saia R, Boratto L, Carta S (2014) Semantic coherence-based user profile modeling in the recommender systems context. In: KDIR, pp 154–161

Schiaffino S, Amandi A (2009) Intelligent user profiling. In: Bramer M (ed) Artificial intelligence an international perspective. Springer, Berlin, pp 193–216

Scott DM (2007) The new rules of marketing and PR: how to use news releases, blogs, podcasting, viral marketing & online media to reach buyers directly. Wiley, Hoboken, NJ

Shivakumar N, Jannink J, Widom J (1997) Per-user profile replication in mobile environments: algorithms, analysis, and simulation results. Mobile Netw Appl 2(2):129–140

Sinkula JM, Baker WE, Noordewier T (1997) A framework for market-based organizational learning: linking values, knowledge, and behaviour. J Acad Market Sci 25(4):305–318

Slater SF, Narver JC (2000) The positive effect of a market orientation on business profitability: a balanced replication. J Bus Res 48(1):69–73

Smith WR (1956) Product differentiation and market segmentation as alternative marketing strategies. J Market 21(1):3–8

Sridevi K, Umarani R (2013) Web personalization approaches: a survey. Int J Adv Res Comput Commun Eng 2(3):1533–1539

Stavroglou SK, Pantelous AA, Stanley HE, Zuev KM (2019) Hidden interactions in financial markets. Proc Natl Acad Sci USA 116(22):10646–10651

Surprenant CF, Solomon MR (1987) Predictability and personalization in the service encounter. J Market 51(2):86–96

Triantaphyllou E, Felici G (2006) Data mining and knowledge discovery approaches based on rule induction techniques (vol 6). Springer

Trusov M, Ma L, Jamal Z (2016) Crumbs of the cookie: user profiling in customer-base analysis and behavioral targeting. Market Sci 35(3):405–426

Tuma MN, Decker R, Scholz SW (2011) A survey of the challenges and pitfalls of cluster analysis application in market segmentation. Int J Market Res 53(3):391–414

ction

of customer experience and customer engagement have been widely
ne marketing and business literature (Brodie et al. 2011; Kumar et al.
and Wilson 2010; Verhoef et al. 2009) and this research is still
day to identify and evaluate the impacts of digital technologies on
gagement and experience (Demangeot and Broderick 2016; Eigenraam
Maslowska et al. 2016; Parise et al. 2016).
nvolved in these studies are focused mainly on the retail setting, and the
of digital technologies in a particular research context such as cultural
ill missing. Traditionally, the role of the museum has been to preserve
cultural heritage objects and give people access to experience them. The
of various kinds of digital technologies has changed the role of the
well as how visitors enjoy and experience their cultural heritage journey
and Bergamasco 2010; Petrelli et al. 2013; Tallon and Walker 2008).
ular, museums have been analyzed by looking at how they can use online
d social media to create value (Capriotti et al. 2016; Padilla-Meléndez
uila-Obra 2013) and trying to understand how the visiting experience
Minkiewicz et al. 2014). Recent contributions are starting to identify the
ourney in the cultural heritage—a sort of "visitor journey," with the
of before-during-after-the-visit phases (Antón et al. 2018). Augmented
ual reality, and context-aware exhibition guides are some examples of the
potential of the new forms of immersive experiences proposed by cultural
rganizations to engage their customers. As exhibition opportunities and
aces broaden, the challenges and the need for new management logics
ltural heritage represents a particular setting of inquiry; digitization
a serious issue as materiality, authenticity, or "aura," cannot be transferred
ital" (Petrelli et al. 2013; p. 58). Nevertheless, due to current advances in
y, visitors are not more only the audience but represent an active part of
meaning and content-making (Tallon and Walker 2008), thereby fostering
s of visitor engagement.
studies have focused on how digital technologies can influence visitors'
ent throughout the journey. This chapter aims to analyze the impact of
chnologies on customer engagement, namely, visitor engagement, proposed
ral organizations. To achieve this aim, the chapter starts with a literature
n the concept of customer engagement, looking for the consequence of the
igital technologies in marketing and business literature and its application in
-based service experiences. Then, the research process is explained with the
n of the case studies and the data collection. The chapter continues with an
tion of the achieved results. Finally, the discussion and conclusions are
ed.

Uncles M, Kennedy R, Nenycz-Thiel M, Singh J, Kwok S (2012) In 25 years, across 50 categories, user profiles for directly competing brands seldom differ: affirming Andrew Ehrenberg's principles. J Advert Res 52(2):252–261

van de Sanden S, Willems K, Brengman M (2019) In-store location-based marketing with beacons: from inflated expectations to smart use in retailing. J Market Manag 35(15–16):1514–1541

Verdenhofs A, Tambovceva T (2019) Evolution of customer segmentation in the era of big data. Market Manag Innovat 1:238–243

Viviani M, Bennani N, Egyed-Zsigmond E (2010) A survey on user modeling in multi-application environments. In: Third international conference on advances in human-oriented and personalized mechanisms, technologies and services (CENTRIC). IEEE, pp 111–116

Voorbij H (2010) The use of web statistics in cultural heritage institutions. Perform Meas Metrics 11(3):266–279

Wieneke A, Lehrer C (2016) Generating and exploiting customer insights from social media data. Electron Market 26(3):245–268

Wills S, Webb S (2007) Measuring the value of insight—it can and must be done. Int J Market Res 49(2):155–165

Wills S, Williams P (2004) Insight as a strategic asset—the opportunity and the stark reality. Int J Market Res 46(4):393–410

Witten DM, Tibshirani R (2010) A framework for feature selection in clustering. J Am Stat Assoc 105(490):713–726

Woodcock N, Green A, Starkey M (2011) Social CRM as a business strategy. J Database Market Custom Strat Manag 18(1):50–64

Wynstra F, Spring M, Schoenherr T (2015) Service triads: a research agenda for buyer–supplier–customer triads in business services. J Oper Manag 35:1–20

Zara IA, Velicu BC, Munthiu MC, Tuta M (2012) Using analytics for understanding the consumer online. Seria Stiinte Economice Timisoara 18:791

Zhou J, Zhai L, Pantelous AA (2020) Market segmentation using high-dimensional sparse consumers data. Expert Syst Appl 145:113136

Digital Engagement and
Experience

Cristina Caterina Amitrano, Tiziana Ru

Abstract This chapter aims to analyze the
customer engagement strategy, namely visit
organizations. The analysis of customer engag
lights the contribution of new forms of tou
reached through interactive websites, new gui
media. In particular, the analysis of different ca
impacts of digital technologies along the custon
ment before, during, and after the visit. The vis
static process but as a dynamic constructed p
involves multiple touchpoints, both online and
interactions that affect visitors' emotions and
visitor's journey is profoundly changed by what v
journey, what the emotions lead to, what the in
social interactions—both online and offline—and
activities the other visitors perform at the touchpo

C. C. Amitrano (✉)
PoliS-Lombardia, Milan, Italy
e-mail: cristina.amitrano.bds@edu.polis.lombardia.it

T. Russo Spena
Department of Economics Management Institutions, University
Italy
e-mail: russospe@unina.it

F. Bifulco
Department of Humanities, University of Naples Federico II, Nap
e-mail: fbifulco@unina.it

T. Russo Spena, F. Bifulco (eds.), *Digital Transformation in the C*
Sector, Contributions to Management Science,
https://doi.org/10.1007/978-3-030-63376-9_6

1 Introdu

The concepts
analyzed in t
2010; Molle
conducted t
customer en
et al. 2018;
Scholars
importance
heritage is
and storage
introductio
museums a
(Carrozzin
In partic
websites a
and del Á
happens (
customer
delineatio
reality, vi
disruptive
heritage
virtual sp
arise. C
"become
to the di
technolo
creating
new kin
Few
engage
digital t
by cult
review
use of
cultura
selecti
explan
presen

Uncles M, Kennedy R, Nenycz-Thiel M, Singh J, Kwok S (2012) In 25 years, across 50 categories, user profiles for directly competing brands seldom differ: affirming Andrew Ehrenberg's principles. J Advert Res 52(2):252–261

van de Sanden S, Willems K, Brengman M (2019) In-store location-based marketing with beacons: from inflated expectations to smart use in retailing. J Market Manag 35(15–16):1514–1541

Verdenhofs A, Tambovceva T (2019) Evolution of customer segmentation in the era of big data. Market Manag Innovat 1:238–243

Viviani M, Bennani N, Egyed-Zsigmond E (2010) A survey on user modeling in multi-application environments. In: Third international conference on advances in human-oriented and personalized mechanisms, technologies and services (CENTRIC). IEEE, pp 111–116

Voorbij H (2010) The use of web statistics in cultural heritage institutions. Perform Meas Metrics 11(3):266–279

Wieneke A, Lehrer C (2016) Generating and exploiting customer insights from social media data. Electron Market 26(3):245–268

Wills S, Webb S (2007) Measuring the value of insight—it can and must be done. Int J Market Res 49(2):155–165

Wills S, Williams P (2004) Insight as a strategic asset—the opportunity and the stark reality. Int J Market Res 46(4):393–410

Witten DM, Tibshirani R (2010) A framework for feature selection in clustering. J Am Stat Assoc 105(490):713–726

Woodcock N, Green A, Starkey M (2011) Social CRM as a business strategy. J Database Market Custom Strat Manag 18(1):50–64

Wynstra F, Spring M, Schoenherr T (2015) Service triads: a research agenda for buyer–supplier–customer triads in business services. J Oper Manag 35:1–20

Zara IA, Velicu BC, Munthiu MC, Tuta M (2012) Using analytics for understanding the consumer online. Seria Stiinte Economice Timisoara 18:791

Zhou J, Zhai L, Pantelous AA (2020) Market segmentation using high-dimensional sparse consumers data. Expert Syst Appl 145:113136 [illegible] 2012 [illegible]

[illegible]

[illegible]

[illegible]

[illegible]

[illegible]

[illegible]

[illegible]

Digital Engagement and Customer Experience

Cristina Caterina Amitrano, Tiziana Russo Spena, and Francesco Bifulco

Abstract This chapter aims to analyze the impact of digital technologies on the customer engagement strategy, namely visitor engagement, proposed by cultural organizations. The analysis of customer engagement and digital technologies highlights the contribution of new forms of touchpoints and engagement strategies reached through interactive websites, new guide devices, mobile apps, and social media. In particular, the analysis of different case studies helps identify the different impacts of digital technologies along the customer journey, namely, digital engagement before, during, and after the visit. The visitor's engagement emerges not as a static process but as a dynamic constructed process performed by customers. It involves multiple touchpoints, both online and offline, and several activities and interactions that affect visitors' emotions and behaviours and experience. The visitor's journey is profoundly changed by what visitors discover while is on his/her journey, what the emotions lead to, what the insights the customers gain during social interactions—both online and offline—and even by the consequences of the activities the other visitors perform at the touchpoints.

C. C. Amitrano (✉)
PoliS-Lombardia, Milan, Italy
e-mail: cristina.amitrano.bds@edu.polis.lombardia.it

T. Russo Spena
Department of Economics Management Institutions, University of Naples Federico II, Naples, Italy
e-mail: russospe@unina.it

F. Bifulco
Department of Humanities, University of Naples Federico II, Naples, Italy
e-mail: fbifulco@unina.it

T. Russo Spena, F. Bifulco (eds.), *Digital Transformation in the Cultural Heritage Sector*, Contributions to Management Science,
https://doi.org/10.1007/978-3-030-63376-9_6

1 Introduction

The concepts of customer experience and customer engagement have been widely analyzed in the marketing and business literature (Brodie et al. 2011; Kumar et al. 2010; Mollen and Wilson 2010; Verhoef et al. 2009) and this research is still conducted today to identify and evaluate the impacts of digital technologies on customer engagement and experience (Demangeot and Broderick 2016; Eigenraam et al. 2018; Maslowska et al. 2016; Parise et al. 2016).

Scholars involved in these studies are focused mainly on the retail setting, and the importance of digital technologies in a particular research context such as cultural heritage is still missing. Traditionally, the role of the museum has been to preserve and storage cultural heritage objects and give people access to experience them. The introduction of various kinds of digital technologies has changed the role of the museums as well as how visitors enjoy and experience their cultural heritage journey (Carrozzino and Bergamasco 2010; Petrelli et al. 2013; Tallon and Walker 2008).

In particular, museums have been analyzed by looking at how they can use online websites and social media to create value (Capriotti et al. 2016; Padilla-Meléndez and del Águila-Obra 2013) and trying to understand how the visiting experience happens (Minkiewicz et al. 2014). Recent contributions are starting to identify the customer journey in the cultural heritage—a sort of "visitor journey," with the delineation of before-during-after-the-visit phases (Antón et al. 2018). Augmented reality, virtual reality, and context-aware exhibition guides are some examples of the disruptive potential of the new forms of immersive experiences proposed by cultural heritage organizations to engage their customers. As exhibition opportunities and virtual spaces broaden, the challenges and the need for new management logics arise. Cultural heritage represents a particular setting of inquiry; digitization "becomes a serious issue as materiality, authenticity, or "aura," cannot be transferred to the digital" (Petrelli et al. 2013; p. 58). Nevertheless, due to current advances in technology, visitors are not more only the audience but represent an active part of creating meaning and content-making (Tallon and Walker 2008), thereby fostering new kinds of visitor engagement.

Few studies have focused on how digital technologies can influence visitors' engagement throughout the journey. This chapter aims to analyze the impact of digital technologies on customer engagement, namely, visitor engagement, proposed by cultural organizations. To achieve this aim, the chapter starts with a literature review on the concept of customer engagement, looking for the consequence of the use of digital technologies in marketing and business literature and its application in cultural-based service experiences. Then, the research process is explained with the selection of the case studies and the data collection. The chapter continues with an explanation of the achieved results. Finally, the discussion and conclusions are presented.

2 Customer Engagement

Customer engagement is a multidimensional concept that has attracted much interest in several disciplines such as psychology, sociology, and organizational behaviour (Bowden 2009; Brodie et al. 2011, 2013). In marketing and business literature, some studies analyze this construct mainly in terms of customer behaviour towards the firm (Kumar et al. 2010), while others conceptualize it as a psychological state (Mollen and Wilson 2010). Despite this, there is a general consensus that customer engagement entails a customer's behavioural response to an organization that involves active participation through value co-creating activities and contributions (Brodie et al. 2011, 2013) and extends beyond purchases and transactions (Gentile et al. 2007; van Doorn et al. 2010).

Further contributions started searching for the link between customer engagement and customer experience that "encompasses the *total* experience, including the search, purchase, consumption, and after-sale phases of the experience" (Verhoef et al. 2009; p. 32). Customer engagement has been defined as "a psychological state that occurs by interactive, co-creative customer experiences with a focal agent/object (e.g. a brand, product, etc.) in focal service relationships" (Brodie et al. 2011; p. 260). It goes beyond involvement, as engagement requires an active role of the customer (Mollen and Wilson 2010) and its participation in co-creating experiences. It represents the specific resource contributions, such as time, energy, and efforts that consumers invest in relationships and it results in the customers' behavioural manifestation towards the brand or firm that goes beyond transactions (Verhoef et al. 2009). The inherent proactive behaviour of customers in the concept of engagement is related to customers' measurable—direct and indirect—contributions to the firm, while customer experience is "an outcome of the firm's actions and may not include the actions of the customer towards the firm (...) customer engagement is a measure of the customers' actions towards the firm" (Pansari and Kumar 2017; p. 296).

Moreover, some scholars have tried to identify different elements composing customers' engagement. An integrated framework developed by Demangeot and Broderick (2016) identified four main components: (1) the interaction engagement concerning the degree of closeness of firms' value proposition to meet customers' expectations, (2) the activity engagement when customers start to become involved in specific actions, (3) the behavioural engagement related to customers' intentions to interact and have a relationship with a firm, and (4) the communication engagement that encourages customers to recommend the firm and continue the interactions. The first two dimensions—interaction and activity engagement—are those that prompt customers' behaviours to act and start a relationship with a firm; this relationship and the sharing of comments and recommendations are defined as behavioural and communication engagement, respectively.

The typical dyadic view of customer engagement as a co-creation process (Kunz et al. 2017) has been recently challenged with the proposition of the concept of multi-actor engagement to highlight how the process of engagement evolves and spreads among multiple actors (Brodie et al. 2019; Li et al. 2017; Jaakkola and Alexander 2014; Storbacka et al. 2016). Engagement goes beyond the transactional exchange (Alexander et al. 2018) and incorporates a social-interactive dimension, as it is determined by connections with other actors (Brodie et al. 2019; Chandler and Lusch 2015). Studies on brand communities indicate that a community's characteristics affect customers' intentions to engage (Dessart et al. 2015). Engagement involves inherently interactive processes such as "sharing," "advocating," and "socializing" that influence one another's value outcomes and the development of the community (Brodie et al. 2013).

It has also been demonstrated that customer engagement affects value co-creation by virtue of customers' diverse resource contributions towards the focal firm and other stakeholders that modify and/or augment the offering. Furthermore, customer engagement affects other stakeholders' perceptions, preferences, expectations, or actions towards the firm or its offering (Brodie et al. 2013; Jaakkola and Alexander 2014). In this view, more recently, some scholars have suggested replacing the term customer engagement with the new term actor engagement (Alexander et al. 2018; Brodie et al. 2019; Storbacka et al. 2016). This term not only stresses the focus on embracing the broader network relationships among versatile actors in the service ecosystems; it also considers the dynamic and iterative process that reflects actors' dispositions to invest resources in their interactions with other connected actors in a service ecosystem.

3 Digital Engagement and Experience

Digital technologies spur many businesses to rethink how they serve customers in new, faster, and better ways. They help firms improve their value proposition, deepen customer relationships, and increase engagement (Maslowska et al. 2016). Additionally, digital technologies enable the development of communities that strengthen the relationship between customers and a brand (Wirtz et al. 2013). Early literature has emphasized the centrality of flow construct in the digital experience (Novak et al. 2000). Flow regards an immersive state experienced during the online navigation favoured by the interactivity and other elements such as higher skills and perceived control by users. Flow theory is extensively adopted in online experience research and customers' online behaviour has recently gained scholars' attention, in particular defining digital engagement practices (Eigenraam et al. 2018). Customers become proactive and more empowered and the timing and the context of their experiences expand, as they can access an offering anywhere and at any time.

A great part of the literature focuses on the brand online research with firms' investments in online communities in order to create a stronger relationship with their customers (Baldus et al. 2015). Other studies also have focused on the role of the Internet in the shopping experience and on the main features of digital tools enabling customers' online purchase decisions (Van der Heijden et al. 2003).

However, the growing importance of digital technologies and the increasing amount of data created by customers through the use of digital platforms and mobile apps has gained the attention of many scholars, underlining the positive impacts of customer engagement to both parties with value creation and feedback loops of dynamic interactions (Lemon and Verhoef 2016; Voorhees et al. 2017). A more comprehensive approach is claimed in order to explore the digital customer experience, compelling an open-ended experience enabled by multiple devices and connected touchpoints (Kranzbühler et al. 2017). In this view, customer experience emerges in a more dynamic way and implies a multilevel analysis of customers' life worlds (Hollebeek et al. 2019). The customer experience is conceptualized as a journey with a company over time, "during the purchase cycle across multiple touchpoints," while customer engagement—that is, as part of the overall customer experience—"constitutes specific touchpoints along the customer journey" (Lemon and Verhoef 2016; p. 74). In the digital era, the customer journey concerns both real and virtual contexts and comprises a sequence of phases, several relationships, multiple channels, and touchpoints (De Keyser et al. 2015; Halvorsrud et al. 2016; Lemon and Verhoef 2016) including partner-owned, customer-owned, social, and independent touchpoints (Lemon and Verhoef 2016). The interdependencies between the phases are relevant (Voorhees et al. 2017) and in each of them, the customer can be engaged through different channels and touchpoints (Barwitz and Maas 2018).

Some scholars have further highlighted digital customers' behavioural manifestations that go beyond the purchase or purchase-related activities: they have identified five digital engagement practices: (1) for fun, (2) for learning, and (3) for giving feedback to a brand, as well as where customers; (4) talk about a brand or (5) work for a brand as behaviours that "reveal customer engagement with a brand and can be undertaken on digital media and platforms" (Eigenraam et al. 2018; p. 104).

The analysis of digital engagement has also been conducted in specific business sectors; as stated by Islam and Rahman (2016), the main studies have looked at services like hospitality and tourism, telecom, and healthcare. In particular, in the tourism sector, Cabiddu et al. (2014) identified three kinds of customer engagement prompted by the use of social media—persistent engagement, customized engagement, and triggered engagement—that range from an ongoing form of dialogue and interaction with the company to the engagement fostered proactively by the company in the crucial events of the customer by leveraging social graphing instruments. Throughout the years, the role of social media has continued to attract scholars' attention as they influence consumers' decisions and engagement in relationships with brands (Harrigan et al. 2018).

3.1 Engagement Platforms and Practices

The above-mentioned contributions highlight how scholars' attention is increasingly focused on digital platforms as digital contexts that facilitate and stimulate business to customer, customer to customer, and customer to business interactions (Table 1).

The digital engagement platform—both brand community and social media—allows firms to conduct and be part of interactions with customers and actors all in one place (Brodie et al. 2013; Baldus et al. 2015).

In particular, Breidbach et al. (2014) have emphasized the crucial role that platforms play in customers' engagement, proposing the concept of engagement platforms as physical or virtual touchpoints designed to provide structural support

Table 1 Engagement platforms and practices

Author/s	Concept	Definition
Brodie et al. (2013)	Engagement in the virtual brand community	"interactive experiences between consumers and the brand, and/or other members of the community"
Breidbach et al. (2014)	Engagement platforms	"as physical or virtual touch points designed to provide structural support for the exchange and integration of resources, and thereby cocreation of value between actors in a service ecosystem"
Baldus et al. (2015)	Online brand community engagement	"is the compelling, intrinsic motivations to continue interacting with an online brand community"
Storbacka et al. (2016)	Engagement platforms	"it is, environments containing artifacts, interfaces, processes and people–facilitate actor engagement by providing access to engagement opportunities. Through engagement platforms, actors can engage with a focal firm (e.g., in the course of a customer relationship) or with other actors (e.g., a community of actors engaging around a specific subject of their interest)"
Kunz et al. (2017)	Customer engagement and Big Data	"a dualistic perspective of engagement on both the firm's expectations and activities, as well as the customer's experiences and goals (...) Big Data analytics allows firms to measure both firm and consumer value in real-time and allows companies the opportunity to understand the customer through multidimensional profiles and dynamic adjustments of their marketing instruments, targets and budgets"
Eigenraam et al. (2018)	Digital customer engagement practices	"as consumers' online, behavioural manifestations of brand engagement that go beyond purchase (...) as manifestations of consumers' motivational states of brand engagement (i.e., the intrapersonal dynamics of brand engagement), namely cognitive (i.e., how much consumers think about a brand), emotional (i.e., what people feel about a brand), and behavioural brand engagement (i.e., how much energy, effort and time consumers spend on using a brand)"

Authors' elaboration

for the exchange and integration of resources. The focus is also on the role of such platforms in enabling co-creation processes involving multiple actors. Engagement platforms are defined as essential intermediaries in the engagement process because they facilitate and orchestrate connections among multiple actors in the service ecosystem (Breidbach et al. 2014; Storbacka et al. 2016).

Baldus et al. (2015) have analyzed the role of the brand community as a place where firms can talk to customers and listen to them, allowing them to focus on what the actors are interested in and need. Digital engagement is more about getting into a conversation than just selling or come-to-customer interactions. The community also provides a staging area for everything customers saying and every interaction, which can then be re-used and re-appropriated whenever customers want and for whatever purpose.

According to some scholars, there is a need to adopt a more comprehensive approach in order to explore the unified digital experience (Eigenraam et al. 2018), enabled by multiple devices and multiple potential touchpoints. This kind of experience facilitates customer engagement, by involving cognitive, emotional, and behavioural aspects (Marbach et al. 2016) and taking into account also the role of social communities (Trevinal and Stenger 2014). In such evolving contexts, engagement is depicted as a multidimensional and multilevel construct including affective, physical, cognitive, sensorial, social, symbolic, and temporal dimensions of customer interactions in the service system (Eigenraam et al. 2018). These different dimensions are linked to the customization and ease of use of new technologies, as well as their increasing connectedness (Brodie et al. 2019).

4 Digital Technologies and the Visiting Experience

Digital opportunities have also been exploited by cultural organizations, starting from the development of the Internet, which allowed museums to propose interactive websites and the use of social media as tools to communicate with customers (Capriotti et al. 2016; Padilla-Meléndez and del Águila-Obra 2013), and extending to the recent evolution of digital technologies that provide visitors with a new form of interactivity that has revolutionized the traditional logics and scenario (Petrelli et al. 2013).

The new technology overcomes spatial and temporal constraints, enriches the experience context by layering multisensory elements, and favours customization of the visiting experience (Tallon and Walker 2008). In this regard, it prompts the interactivity of the experience by allowing visitors—through some digital devices—to choose what the exhibit presents when they need it (Haywood and Cairns 2006). Furthermore, current advances in the development of digital technologies enable the enjoyment of experiences by real users as well as remote Internet users (Carrozzino and Bergamasco 2010). Thus, the need arises to take into account different phenomena.

In the cultural heritage setting, digital technologies redefine the role of visitors, as they enable interaction with the heritage content and peer-to-peer relationships; thus, the cultural heritage can be experienced in a non-linear way and edited collaboratively (Affleck and Kvan 2008). However, various scholars (Sung et al. 2010) have highlighted the potential pitfalls of some advanced digital devices that can shift the visitors' attention from the exhibits and constrain social interactions in the physical visit, thereby reducing the appreciation of the cultural heritage goods.

Despite this potential dark side of technologies, the competition of cultural heritage organizations with retail, leisure, and entertainment industries can be faced through the use of digital technologies, which enable the adoption of innovative approaches to co-creation experiences to engage actual visitors and attract potential audiences. In particular, Minkiewicz et al. (2014) have analyzed the concept of co-creation during the visiting experience, making a specific distinction between co-creation of the experience as a first element and the co-created value as a derived outcome of the experience itself. Further, they have identified that visitors co-create their experiences through three main elements: co-production, engagement, and personalization. The latter is the only one that has been related to technology by Minkiewicz et al. (2014), but the role of digital technologies has also been recognized as a stimulus to interaction and immersion, so we can consider it to be a feature crossing the entire service experience.

More recently, the analysis of the co-creation of the visiting experience has been deepened by Antón et al. (2018), who have tried to enlarge the previous studies from a temporal perspective, looking before and after the visit and not only during the visit itself. In the first stage, co-creation is related to visitor knowledge, involvement, and planning before the visit. In the second stage, visitors co-create in situ by participating in the museums' activities and interacting with staff or other visitors. In the third stage, co-creation occurs when visitors intensify their experiences through further participation in the museum's activities and social networks and by giving their opinion in blogs and other social networks. These three stages are equally influenced by digital technologies, as the searching for information and the planning of a visit are facilitated thanks to internet technologies and social networks. The co-creation of the visiting experience and visitors' interactions are enhanced by virtual and augmented reality technologies and mobile applications, and the sharing of opinions and impressions is encouraged by the ease of use of social network and website platforms.

5 Research Process

The research proposes a qualitative approach design, as this is more suitable when one is dealing with new and complex phenomena. We have conducted multiple exploratory case study research (Eisenhardt 1989; Yin 2014) with two main steps.

We selected three cases among ten museums that have already been analyzed as case studies in previous research on digital technologies in cultural institutions

Table 2 Features of the selected case studies

Name	Louvre museum	Museum del Prado	Rijksmuseum
Location	Paris (FR)	Madrid (ES)	Amsterdam (NL)
Type of museum	National	National	National
Collection	Anthropology Garden Archaeology Historic Building/Site Art—History	Art	Art—History
Social media channels	Facebook, Twitter, Instagram, Pinterest, YouTube, Daily Motion	Facebook, Twitter, Instagram, Pinterest, YouTube	Facebook, Twitter, Instagram, Pinterest, YouTube
N. reviews on TripAdvisor[a]	89,129	48,695	39,510

[a]Last access: September 2019

(Symbola Foundation 2017). The selection was conducted based on the following common features (Table 2): they are all European national museums, their collections are based mainly on art, they have official accounts on the most used social media channels, they have more than 30,000 reviews on TripAdvisor, and they are among the top eight museums in the global reputation ranking (van Riel and Heijndijk 2017).

As a first step, we analyzed secondary data from the selected museums' official websites and social networks, as well as from previous research and studies (Symbola Foundation 2017; van Riel and Heijndijk 2017) to identify how museums enhance their actual and potential visitors' knowledge, involvement (before the visit) and participation (during the visiting experience) using digital technologies.

In the second stage of the research, following Kozinets' (2002) suggestions, we analyzed the comments left on the TripAdvisor platform by users who have visited the selected museums, to verify how the visiting experience is shared and which opinions and impressions are encouraged by museums' use of digital technologies. As noted by some scholars (Yang and Fang 2004), while the online comments of customers do not completely reflect their experiences, they represent useful means of highlighting the experience dimensions and their link to the customer engagement. In detail, as other researchers suggest (O'Connor 2008), we selected the five most recent reviews for each case study. We have both chosen the reviews with the highest scores (i.e. five stars), to gain the opinions of the most involved and engaged visitors, and focused on the experience through the digital technologies, thus using "app" and "interactive" as keywords.

Further, we analyzed the collected data using the three phases identified in the framework developed by Antón et al. (2018) on the co-creation of the visiting experience to identify the impact of digital technologies on the particular kind of customer experience in museums.

6 Findings

The research has allowed for the identification of digital engagement along the visitor journey, using the various digital technologies implemented by the three cultural organizations chosen as case studies, namely, official websites, mobile applications, digital guides or games, and social media accounts. The analysis of these technologies and their impact on digital engagement has been conducted using the three phases or steps proposed in the literature by Antón et al. (2018): before, during, and after the visit.

6.1 *Digital Engagement Before the Visit*

As highlighted in the literature (Capriotti et al. 2016; Padilla-Meléndez and del Águila-Obra 2013) our results show that firms can attract potential customers through the use of digital technologies, which cultural organizations exploit to help potential or actual visitors gain knowledge and information, start their involvement, and assist in the planning of the visit (Table 3). The Louvre Museum has developed an official website with information not only about its collection but also about activities, tours, exhibitions, and events in order to attract potential visitors and enable planning. Further, a "learning about art" feature has been added to the website's main menu so that users can prepare themselves to learn about what art is and what are the main characteristics they will see during their visiting experience; particular attention is paid to children through video and tales about the museum, as well as to the need to start an educational process for digital tools, as new digital competencies must be developed to enable people to better understand art and

Table 3 Features of digital technologies that the three museums used to attract customer

Museum	Features of the official website
Louvre Museum	– Desktop layout – Information on collections, tours, exhibitions, events – Section on learning art – Video and tales for children – Online tickets
Museum del Prado	– Responsive layout – Information on collections, tours, exhibitions, events – Section on learning art – Interactive itinerary – Personalization of the future visit – Online tickets
Rijksmuseum	– Responsive layout – Information on collections, tours, exhibitions, events – Section with digitalized collection – Online tickets

Authors' elaboration

culture. Finally, on both the website and the official Facebook page, potential visitors can easily buy their tickets.

The Museum del Prado is particularly aware of the importance of digital technologies and the ongoing transformation of visitors from physical to virtual. This awareness can be highlighted through the analysis of the layout and the features of the official website. Firstly, it has been developed with a responsive layout to allow users to navigate from a desktop computer as well as through mobile devices, especially smartphones. Secondly, it is focused on the masterpieces of the museum's collection that are the main elements within the website, so that virtual visitors can see the treasures preserved inside the museum. In addition, the website contains other important elements, such as a page with all the initiatives and events, and all the information about the history of the museum and how to visit it. Moreover, visitors can buy tickets directly on the official website and, through the "MyPrado" option, available upon the creation of an account, create their own itinerary of works to see or suggest to other users.

Starting from the challenges in attracting audiences, but above all to find the easiest way to share collections and be connected to a wide range of users, the Rijksmuseum has used digital technologies to provide its collection free through the Rijksstudio on its official website. There, users can browse the entire collection or create their own Rijksstudio with the selection of masterpieces. The website has been developed to have a responsive layout and a basic menu that helps users easily find what they are searching for. There are three main items regarding information about (1) ongoing events and how to plan the visit, (2) the digitalized collection "Rijksstudio", and (3) the history of the museum. Beyond these possibilities offered to users, the Rijksmuseum helps actual and potential visitors gain quick access to the museum, as they can easily buy tickets online to skip the ticket counter and book a tour in advance.

6.2 Digital Engagement During the Visit

The enhancement of customer engagement in a cultural experience through digital technologies can help museums co-create value with their visitors (Minkiewicz et al. 2014). The visiting experience can be improved thanks to visitors' participation in interactive activities, interactions with other visitors or museum staff, and the use of mobile applications or other digital tools (Table 4).

Since the beginning of the twenty-first century, the Louvre has tried to stimulate visitors' engagement through digital technologies. In 2013, a new type of audio guide was developed in collaboration with Nintendo: the Louvre-Nintendo 3DS™ XL Audio Guide. It has the function of the classic audio guide with commentaries and interviews, but it also offers 3D photos, reconstruction, and high-definition images. In 2016, these efforts were reinforced with the development of the app "My Visit to the Louvre", available in six languages and full of 3D reconstructions, with suggested itineraries and a geo-localisation map.

Table 4 Types of digital technologies

Museum	Digital technologies
Louvre Museum	– Audio guide (in collaboration with Nintendo) – Mobile app
Museum del Prado	– Three types of mobile apps (masterpieces, main artist, new exhibition space)
Rijksmuseum	– Mobile app – Digital game (for family)

Authors' elaboration

Starting with the update of the official website, the Museum del Prado has also developed new tools to enhance the visiting experience, namely, three kinds of mobile apps. Two of them are created around high-definition images of the museum's 14 masterpieces and those by the painter Bosch; they allow the visitor to zoom in on details invisible to the naked eye, to activate the infrared or X-ray functions, and to crop a particular detail and share it directly via social media. The third app has been developed in connection with the presentation of new exhibition space and helps visitors learn about pieces of the collection that can be enlarged and visualized in 360 degrees by sliding their fingers on the screens of their mobile devices.

In the Rijksmuseum, interactions among visitors have been improved thanks to the development of a digital game dedicated to families, which invites visitors to solve eight mysteries during their visit. Moreover, the museum uses digital technologies to improve the visiting experience through the Rijksmuseum app for mobile devices; it offers themed tours with different multimedia content such as audio clips, animations of works' details, and extra information. The interactions, in particular those through social networks, are further enabled through the provision of free Wi-Fi within the entire museum. The Rijksmuseum is also experimenting with virtual reality and beacon technologies to enable participation in the visiting experience without distraction from other visitors.

6.3 Digital Engagement After the Visit

The importance of the museum-visitor relationships after the "core" service experience (Antón et al. 2018) is enhanced through digital technologies when visitors continue to participate in the museum's activities following the visiting experience and use social networks (e.g. TripAdvisor) to share their opinions and impressions about the technologies they used during their visits, as well as their lived interactions (Table 5).

Visitors are digitally engaged thanks to digital platforms on which they interact virtually and share their experience with potential visitors and the wider online community. Their engagement can be analyzed through two different activities

Table 5 Visitors' comments and suggestions on the digital technologies

	Louvre Museum	Museum del Prado	Rijksmuseum
Suggestions to use mobile app	"The maps weren't very accurate or helpful in terms of how far away things were (...). My husband downloaded the Louvre app to his phone whilst we were there, which we found really helpful. Found most of it well-organised." (level 6 contributor) "(...) download the Louvre app and use it to find your favourite pieces. The Louvre is HUGE with lots of rooms and staircases and it's easy to get lost. The app does a great job of giving you turn by turn directions to the works you want to see." (level 4 contributor)	"I downloaded the app (...) able to choose which paintings to look at as I had only 2 hours to spend here. The app had different itineraries to choose from such as Recommended Visit (150 mins) that lists 50 paintings and a Do Not Miss section (45 mins) that lists 10 paintings." (level 5 contributor)	"Don't forget to download the app to your phone so you will have a free audio guide, which in the museum costs [an] extra 5 euros!! Just bring your earphones with you! Free wi-fi is available, which works great, so you can get online to use the app." (level 5 contributor) "(...) a fun and interactive app. This museum's approach to guiding via a free app is commendable. It's easy to use and can satisfy people who want just the basic information." (level 5 contributor)
Suggestions to use interactive guide devices	"We hired the Louvre's guides which are stored on Nintendo 3DS XL. Our kids are technology dependent, and the interactive guides were absolutely BRILLIANT. It kept them engaged and entertained whilst providing the information we needed (audio and video) on the various exhibits whilst also indicating our location thus making it extremely easy to follow the interactive maps from one exhibit to another." (level 4 contributor) "I would recommend paying the extra 5 Euros for the Interactive guide devices. That is how we were able to find those 'hidden gems' and understand/learn what we were looking at." (level 5 contributor)	"It is very worth . . . paying the €4 for the guided audio, which is very practical and informative. When you see a number near an artwork, press the number and then hit play. You will have good overall information about what you are seeing." (level 5 contributor)	"(...) kids tour. This involved a tablet and headset each where you have to follow the trail. You start with taking a photo of yourself in a certain position and then you have to look around and find the next place to go (...). They also get you to study the painting by asking individual team members to discover a certain thing about it. It also tells you interesting facts (...). It leads you down back stairways to less visited parts (...) is very interactive. The kids loved it." (level 6 contributor)

Authors' elaboration from TripAdvisor

conducted in the digital environment: the suggestion to use mobile applications offered by the museums and the recommendation to try the interactive guide devices.

As anticipated above, the results collected in the table can be synthesized into two main categories of visitors' suggestions to other online users—actual or future visitors—concerning digital technologies.

First, visitors highlight the helpful support of a mobile app that prevents them from feeling left alone or lost inside a museum, to plan a visit in a specific span of time, to save money by not renting the audio guide inside the museum, and to experience a funny and interactive visit. Second, visitors appreciate and suggest the use of other digital technologies available in the museums, such as the audio guide with tablet and headset, as these technologies are considered useful with the different recommended tours (i.e. for families, with games for children), geo-localisation, and interactive maps.

This peer-to-peer advice is an example of how digital engagement is intrinsically a social activity, as digital technologies—from mobile apps to interactive guides, from websites to social media—enhance customers' socialization.

7 Discussion

This chapter goes in-depth into the analysis of customer engagement and digital technologies and how cultural organizations are stimulating digital engagement through interactive websites, guide devices, mobile apps, and social media. In particular, the analysis of the case studies has enabled the identification of the different impacts of digital technologies along the customer journey, namely, digital engagement before, during, and after the visit.

The three cases investigated show as organizations widely use digital technologies to help their potential visitors or their actual and potential visitors collect information about exhibitions, opening hours, and services and events, and book or buy tickets. Further, the experience before the visit is enhanced through users' involvement in exploring the digitalized collection (Rijksmuseum) and creating a personalized itinerary (Museum del Prado).

This pre-visit experience is later enhanced through the use of a wider range of digital technologies during the real visiting experience, when customer engagement takes place inside the museums. All the analyzed museums have developed new ways to engage their visitors and help them have an unforgettable experience, in particular through mobile applications. The ease of choosing a tour and being oriented inside the museums' collections, the possibility of deepening the information and seeing the works' details, and the opportunity to interact with friends and other people through the sharing of the experience on social networks accounts are the main goals that the three museums have achieved through the development of the different mobile apps. Moreover, the Louvre Museum and the Rijksmuseum have made efforts to engage families with children through interactive audio guides that either seem like a videogame (Louvre) or have been conceived as a game to be played during the visit (Rijksmuseum).

The experience continues after the visit thanks to visitors' sharing of opinions and suggestions on social networks. The three museums have created official accounts on the major social networks, and an analysis of one of these—i.e. TripAdvisor—has shown how visitors perceive the use of digital technologies as something to recommend as an enabler for a more engaging and interactive visiting experience. These results confirm what has been stated in the literature on digital customer engagement (Eigenraam et al. 2018) in a cultural heritage context of analysis: the main visitors' digital engagement practices after the visit are those categorized as "talking about the brand," aimed at helping other customers and recommending the brand to a friend.

The positive impacts that digital technologies have on customer experience and customer engagement (Demangeot and Broderick 2016; Eigenraam et al. 2018; Kunz et al. 2017; Maslowska et al. 2016) have been studied in the literature, but the analysis of how the different technologies can be integrated is still in its infancy. This chapter highlights how digital technologies can improve museums' value proposition, enrich the visitor experience, and favour visitors' engagement all along the "visitor journey," namely, before-during-after the visit (Antón et al. 2018; Minkiewicz et al. 2014; Padilla-Meléndez and del Águila-Obra 2013).

In line with recent contributions detecting engagement as a multidimensional construct (Brodie et al. 2019; Kranzbühler et al. 2017), our results show as the visitor's engagement emerges not as a static process but as a dynamic constructed process performed by customers. The experiential journey of visitors involves multiple touchpoints, both online and offline, and several activities and interactions that affect visitors' emotions and behaviours. The touchpoints are mutually influencing, as the interactions taking place in physical places are affected by and affect the online interactions. Touchpoints mirror the opportunity visitors have to customize their experience resulting in the outcome of a behavioural, emotional, and social dimension of experience.

The intended journey is profoundly changed by what visitors discover while is on their journey, what the emotions lead to, what the insights the visitors gain during social interactions—both online and offline—and even by the consequences of the activities, the other visitors perform at the touchpoints. Consequently, the multiple dimensions of engagement at physical and digital place become integrated during the journey (Lemon and Verhoef 2016; Bolton et al. 2018), and the visitor's journey is turned into a personalized and dynamic experience.

Today, museums and cultural organizations face many challenges in attracting customers' attention, as the competition is higher within the wide entertainment industry. The understanding of how digital technologies—especially mobile apps and digital platforms—can be used to enhance customer engagement is unavoidable and undelayable. The analysis of the different impacts of digital technologies on the visitor journey is an important issue for both academics and practitioners; further research can go in-depth in the analysis and propose a new integrated framework to stimulate digital engagement in the cultural heritage sector.

References

Affleck J, Kvan T (2008) A virtual community as the context for discursive interpretation: a role in cultural heritage engagement. Int J Herit Stud 14(3):268–280

Alexander MJ, Jaakkola E, Hollebeek LD (2018) Zooming out: actor engagement beyond the dyadic. J Serv Manag 29(3):333–351

Antón C, Camarero C, Garrido MJ (2018) Exploring the experience value of museum visitors as a co-creation process. Curr Issue Tour 21(12):1406–1425

Baldus BJ, Voorhees C, Calantone R (2015) Online brand community engagement: scale development and validation. J Bus Res 68(5):978–985

Barwitz N, Maas P (2018) Understanding the omnichannel customer journey: determinants of interaction choice. J Interact Market 43:116–133

Bowden JLH (2009) The process of customer engagement: a conceptual framework. J Market Theory Pract 17(1):63–74

Breidbach CF, Brodie RJ, Hollebeek L (2014) Beyond virtuality: from engagement platforms to engagement ecosystems. Manag Serv Qual 24(6):592–611

Brodie RJ, Hollebeek LD, Jurić B, Ilić A (2011) Customer engagement: conceptual domain, fundamental propositions, and implications for research. J Serv Res 14(3):252–271

Brodie RJ, Ilic A, Juric B, Hollebeek L (2013) Consumer engagement in a virtual brand community: an exploratory analysis. J Bus Res 66(1):105–114

Brodie RJ, Fehrer JA, Jaakkola E, Conduit J (2019) Actor engagement in networks: defining the conceptual domain. J Serv Res 22(2):173–188

Bolton RN, McColl-Kennedy JR, Cheung L, Gallan A, Orsingher C, Witell L, Zaki M (2018) Customer experience challenges: bringing together digital, physical and social realms. J Serv Manag 29(5):776–808

Cabiddu F, De Carlo M, Piccoli G (2014) Social media affordances: enabling customer engagement. Ann Tour Res 48:175–192

Capriotti P, Carretón C, Castillo A (2016) Testing the level of interactivity of institutional websites: from museums 1.0 to museums 2.0. Int J Inf Manag 36(1):97–104

Carrozzino M, Bergamasco M (2010) Beyond virtual museums: experiencing immersive virtual reality in real museums. J Cult Herit 1(4):452–458

Chandler JD, Lusch RF (2015) Service systems: a broadened framework and research agenda on value propositions, engagement, and service experience. J Serv Res 18(1):6–22

De Keyser A, Lemon KN, Klaus P, Keiningham TL (2015) A framework for understanding and managing the customer experience. Market Sci Inst Working Paper Ser 85(1):15–121

Demangeot C, Broderick AJ (2016) Engaging customers during a website visit: a model of website customer engagement. Int J Retail Distrib Manag 44(8):814–839

Dessart L, Veloutsou C, Morgan-Thomas A (2015) Consumer engagement in online brand communities: a social media perspective. J Prod Brand Manag 24(1):28–42

Eigenraam AW, Eelen J, Van Lin A, Verlegh PW (2018) A consumer-based taxonomy of digital customer engagement practices. J Interact Market 44:102–121

Eisenhardt K (1989) Building theories from case study research. Acad Manag Rev 14(4):532–550

Gentile C, Spiller N, Noci G (2007) How to sustain the customer experience: an overview of experience components that co-create value with the customer. Eur Manag J 25(5):395–410

Halvorsrud R, Kvale K, Følstad A (2016) Improving service quality through customer journey analysis. J Serv Theory Pract 26(6):840–867

Harrigan P, Evers U, Miles MP, Daly T (2018) Customer engagement and the relationship between involvement, engagement, self-brand connection and brand usage intent. J Bus Res 88:388–396

Haywood N, Cairns P (2006) Engagement with an interactive museum exhibit. In McEwan T, Gulliksen J, Benyon D (eds) People and computers XIX—the bigger picture. Springer, London, pp 113–129

Hollebeek LD, Islam JU, Macky K, Taguchi T, Costley C, Smith D (2019) Personality-based consumer engagement styles: conceptualization, research propositions and implications. In

Hollebeek LD, Sprott D (eds) Handbook of research on customer engagement. Edward Elgar, London, pp 224–244
Islam JU, Rahman Z (2016) The transpiring journey of customer engagement research in marketing: a systematic review of the past decade. Manag Decis 54(8):2008–2034
Jaakkola E, Alexander M (2014) The role of customer engagement behavior in value co-creation: a service system perspective. J Serv Res 17(3):247–261
Kozinets RV (2002) The field behind the screen: using netnography for marketing research in online communities. J Market Res 39(1):61–72
Kranzbühler AM, Kleijnen MH, Morgan RE, Teerling M (2017) The multilevel nature of customer experience research: an integrative review and research agenda. Int J Manag Rev 20(2):433–456
Kumar V, Aksoy L, Donkers B, Venkatesan R, Wiesel T, Tillmanns S (2010) Undervalued or overvalued customers: capturing total customer engagement value. J Serv Res 13(3):297–310
Kunz W, Kunz W, Aksoy L, Aksoy L, Bart Y, Bart Y et al (2017) Customer engagement in a big data world. J Serv Market 31(2):161–171
Lemon KN, Verhoef PC (2016) Understanding customer experience throughout the customer journey. J Market 80(6):69–96
Li LP, Juric B, Brodie RJ (2017) Dynamic multi-actor engagement in networks: the case of united breaks guitars. J Serv Theory Pract 27(4):738–760
Marbach J, Lages CR, Nunan D (2016) Who are you and what do you value? Investigating the role of personality traits and customer-perceived value in online customer engagement. J Market Manag 32(5–6):502–525
Maslowska E, Malthouse EC, Collinger T (2016) The customer engagement ecosystem. J Market Manag 32(5–6):469–501
Minkiewicz J, Evans J, Bridson K (2014) How do consumers co-create their experiences? An exploration in the heritage sector. J Market Manag 30(1–2):30–59
Mollen A, Wilson H (2010) Engagement, telepresence and interactivity in online consumer experience: reconciling scholastic and managerial perspectives. J Bus Res 63(9):919–925
Novak TP, Hoffman DL, Yung YF (2000) Measuring the customer experience in online environments: a structural modeling approach. Mar Sci 19(1):22–42
O'Connor P (2008) User-generated content and travel: a case study on Tripadvisor. com. In: O'Connor PP, Höpken W, Gretzel U (eds) Information and communication technologies in tourism. Springer, Wien, pp 47–58
Padilla-Meléndez A, del Águila-Obra AR (2013) Web and social media usage by museums: online value creation. Int J Inf Manag 33(5):892–898
Pansari A, Kumar V (2017) Customer engagement: the construct, antecedents, and consequences. J Acad Market Sci 45(3):294–311
Parise S, Guinan PJ, Kafka R (2016) Solving the crisis of immediacy: how digital technology can transform the customer experience. Bus Horiz 59(4):411–420
Petrelli D, Ciolfi L, van Dijk D, Hornecker E, Not E, Schmidt A (2013) Integrating material and digital: a new way for cultural heritage. Interact New Vis Hum Comput Interact 20(4):58–63
Storbacka K, Brodie RJ, Böhmann T, Maglio PP, Nenonen S (2016) Actor engagement as a microfoundation for value co-creation. J Bus Res 69(8):3008–3017
Sung YT, Hou HT, Liu CK, Chang KE (2010) Mobile guide system using problem-solving strategy for museum learning: a sequential learning behavioural pattern analysis. J Comput Assist Learn 26(2):106–115
Symbola Foundation (2017) Museum of the Future. Mu.SA Project. Retrieved at http://www.project-musa.eu/wp-content/uploads/2017/03/MuSA-Museum-of-the-future.pdf
Tallon L, Walker K (2008) Digital technologies and the museum experience: handheld guides and other media. Rowman, Altamira
Trevinal AM, Stenger T (2014) Toward a conceptualization of the online shopping experience. J Retail Consum Serv 21(3):314–326
Van der Heijden H, Verhagen T, Creemers M (2003) Understanding online purchase intentions: contributions from technology and trust perspectives. Eur J Inf Syst 12(1):41–48

van Doorn J, Lemon KN, Mittal V, Nass S, Pick D, Pirner P, Verhoef PC (2010) Customer engagement behavior: theoretical foundations and research directions. J Serv Res 13 (3):253–266

Voorhees CM, Fombelle PW, Gregoire Y, Bone S, Gustafsson A, Sousa R, Walkowiak T (2017) Service encounters, experiences and the customer journey: defining the field and a call to expand our lens. J Bus Res 79:269–280

van Riel CBM, Heijndijk P (2017) Why people love art museums. Rotterdam School of Management. Erasmus University. Retrieved at http://api.rsm.nl/files/index/get/id/b2d8c8f0-870e-11e7-91c6-299a8ddd9fd0

Verhoef PC, Lemon KN, Parasuraman A, Roggeveen A, Tsiros M, Schlesinger LA (2009) Customer experience creation: determinants, dynamics and management strategies. J Retail 85(1):31–41

Wirtz J, den Ambtman A, Bloemer J, Horváth C, Ramaseshan B, van de Klundert J et al (2013) Managing brands and customer engagement in online brand communities. J Serv Manag 24 (3):223–244

Yang Z, Fang X (2004) Online service quality dimensions and their relationships with satisfaction: a content analysis of customer reviews of securities brokerage services. Int J Serv Ind Manag 15 (3):302–326

Yin RK (2014) Case study research: design and methods. Sage, Thousand Oaks, CA

Business Intelligence and Social Media Analytics

Tiziana Russo Spena, Marco Tregua, Angelo Ranieri, and Francesco Bifulco

Abstract In this chapter, the business intelligence and social media analytics (SMA) are brought into focus to address the strategies, methods, and technologies for managing the data analysis processes. The overall goal is to identify differences in categories, tools, and techniques concerning the development of various analytics processes as well as their application and obtained results in cultural heritage businesses. The focus is on business intelligence and social media analytics to partnering business activities towards the achievement of better results from different perspectives, such as efficiency, interactivity with customers, improvement of internal processes, and a wiser decision-making process based on information. To clarify the theoretical and practical implications on the field, several examples of results achieved by firms that have implemented business intelligence and social media analytics in their daily activities are illustrated.

1 Introduction

Nowadays, the business intelligence (BI) approach implies the collection and analysis of big data. Business intelligence applications are not yet widespread, but specialists have stated that they will soon dominate the advances of the organizations in the coming years (Power and Heavin 2017). Currently, less than half of data are taken care of through BI tools, due to three main factors: BI vendors are about to offer their own platforms, several software programmes are in development, but their

T. Russo Spena (✉) · M. Tregua · A. Ranieri
Department of Economics Management Institutions, University of Naples Federico II, Naples, Italy
e-mail: tiziana.russospena@unina.it; marco.tregua@unina.it; angelo.ranieri2@unina.it

F. Bifulco
Department of Humanities, University of Naples Federico II, Naples, Italy
e-mail: fbifulco@unina.it

T. Russo Spena, F. Bifulco (eds.), *Digital Transformation in the Cultural Heritage Sector*, Contributions to Management Science,
https://doi.org/10.1007/978-3-030-63376-9_7

prices are lowering due to competition, and in 3–5 years BI will be a common and tactical instrument.

"Big data" refers to an unstructured, complex, and extremely large data set that requires sophisticated tools to store, manage, and analyze (Chen et al. 2012). Additionally, due to the growth of digital devices, big data evolve at high speeds and demand real-time analytics (Gandomi and Haider 2015). Huge volumes of data, fast applications, and versatility in different domains are some of the reasons why big data are developing so significantly in the business domain, especially in digital marketing (Balusamy et al. 2017). The usage of big data and the further development of business intelligence practice to favour innovation, efficiency, and new managerial practices are increasingly being thought of as a strategic lever (Grover et al. 2018). As a consequence, analyses can be based on the extensive usage of statistical instruments levering big data, mainly because of the recently recognized advantages stemming from the common efforts of businesses, consultants, and service providers (Wang et al. 2018). To sum up, it has already been stated that marketing analytics involves data collection, management, and analysis and represents a "technology-enabled and model-supported approach to harness customer and market data to enhance marketing decision making" (Lilien 2011; p. 5).

As noted by George et al. (2014), big data management and analysis represent new challenges in management research that should be addressed to review current processes and practices. Insights have recently been offered by scholars (Moe et al. 2017), but additional research is still needed, especially as it concerns the shaping of new business models (Brandt et al. 2017) and the adaptation of some of the methodological tools used to investigate social media and its content (Abbasi et al. 2018).

One of the industries recently affected by the usage of big data and business intelligence is the services industry; the great involvement of service providers, the soft aspects featuring services, and the significant amount of attention paid by the most relevant actors are elements leading to the usage of these new instruments in relation to services, including advances in providing health care services for both firms and patients (Wang et al. 2018) as well as improvements in efficiency in service firms from banking to retailing (Dezi et al. 2018).

In addition, the use of social media has grown significantly over the years and its spread has changed the way people interact, communicate, and express their opinions (Arora et al. 2019). Social media has been described as one of the most important channels for managing customer relationships, analyzing their behaviour, and carrying out predictive analyses. Customers' information can be collected and analyzed through social media platforms as, by definition, they are Internet-based applications that prompt the creation and sharing of content (Kaplan and Haenlein 2010; Roblek et al. 2013). The result is that a large amount of user-generated content represents a great opportunity to obtain knowledge about how customers feel, behave, and interact.

Nevertheless, the real opportunity for the cultural heritage sector is that social media enables the analysis of cultural service provision and dynamics in new ways and, as places of data and information collection and production, can be useful not only in evaluating the outcomes of certain business strategies (Montalvo 2011) but also in supporting relationship marketing efforts (Noone et al. 2011). This is also what emerges from recent research works in management studies, which indicate that social media performance is positively related to marketing performance (Tafesse and Wien 2018) and, therefore, plays a significant role in the decision-making regarding the activities to perform.

As a consequence, this chapter provides an analysis of the novel topics related to business, namely, business intelligence and social media analytics. Indeed, the increasing amount of content created on social media platforms is calling for sophisticated analysis that separates relevant from non-relevant content and data.

Specifically, this chapter focuses on business intelligence and social media analytics (SMA) to address the challenge through the development of strategies, methods, and technologies to manage data analysis processes. The overall goal is to identify differences in categories, tools, and techniques concerning the development of these analytics processes as well as their application and obtained results in cultural heritage businesses. The focus is on business intelligence and social media analytics to partnering business activities towards the achievement of better results from different perspectives, such as efficiency, interactivity with customers, improvement of internal processes, and a wiser decision-making process based on information.

More in detail, a focus on business intelligence and social media analytics is firstly proposed with reference to recent business and management literature to operationalize some of the new theoretical content and to better frame the aim of this chapter. To clarify the theoretical and practical implications on the field, several examples of results achieved by firms that have implemented business intelligence and social media analytics in their daily activities are illustrated. Finally, conclusions complete this chapter, together with proposals for further research.

2 Business Intelligence

The activity of collecting data and information is often associated with the meaning of "business intelligence", as the activity is aimed at leveraging data to support decision-making and perform business processes based on data elaboration and knowledge management (Negash and Gray 2008). Many definitions were proposed to better depict what business intelligence is, and different perspectives have been adopted. For instance, some scholars focused on the role of business intelligence in furthering the adoption of innovation launched by SMEs (Puklavec et al. 2018) or as a support to competition and to set up long-term strategies (George et al. 2018). Others focused on the ongoing changes in some industries, from hospitality and tourism (Mariani et al. 2018) to health care (Gastaldi et al. 2018). Ultimately, authors are focusing on different elements, like the features of a business intelligence system, the advantages that can be achieved, the most relevant outcome and the ways to combine them with insights from big data, and the actions that business intelligence can impact.

To better clarify what business intelligence means and how its main features can affect firms, we propose a summary (Tables 1 and 2) presenting some of the most relevant definitions of business intelligence proposed in the last 20 years by scholars from different fields of science. These definitions have been categorized into two main groups including four categories. The first two categories stressed the role of technologies as a tool or supporting processes (Table 1), the last two emphasize the processual dimension (Table 2).

The first group embeds the definitions oriented towards describing business intelligence as a set of technologies, like applications, used to gather and combine data. The support of mathematics or IT advanced tools as platforms are crucial in the most recent definitions to better shape a tool levering data to favour decision-making. Indeed, Wu et al. (2007) described the applications to act on data, from collection to analysis, while Vercellis (2011) highlighted the mathematical models favouring information retrieval. More recently, the grouping of tools became even wider, when Hung and Chen (2020) paid attention to the bundle of business intelligence tools and ERP systems to get full benefits. In summary, these contributions describe the technicalities shaping business intelligence as a set of technologies and solutions to gather and analyze data. These actions are instrumental to the decision-making process, as it is recalled in some of the definitions of this group and as it is more evident in the next one.

Decision-making is frequently recalled in the definitions highlighted in the second group; data collected and analyzed represent the evidence to be transformed into information to support complex decisions. Already in 1998, Revelli stated that business intelligence has the objective of reducing uncertainty in decision-making about strategy. So, business intelligence is the instrument favouring businesses, their managers, and other business areas, as it represents an integrated infrastructure to support management, as claimed by Baars and Kemper (2008). The most commonly supported decision-making processes pertain to strategy, but other activities are not set aside, as Rouhani et al. (2012) recalled sales, customer analysis, and other business conditions. In recent years, the implementation of business intelligence assumed a supportive role in the iterative processes of decision-making (Ali et al. 2019). Therefore, while authors focused on different nuances of what a firm can achieve through business intelligence, it can be claimed that business intelligence represents all-embedding support of managerial tasks at different levels.

Dealing with information is not the only part of the decision-making process, as other uses also emerge. Indeed, the third group of definitions considers business intelligence as a means of combining and describing information in a more useful way as compared to raw data. Siegel (2000) clarified the relevance of turning data into actionable knowledge; namely, the proposed business intelligence as a way to collect data, combine data, and generate knowledge useful for problem solving. From a more direct perspective, Green (2007) described business intelligence as business information. Therefore, it is not an entity but, rather, consists of the information itself. With more attention paid to technical features, Tešendić and

Table 1 Overview of business intelligence definitions: a focus on technologies as tools

Author(s)	Definition proposed	BI main content
Michalewicz et al. (2006)	"a broad category of application programs and technologies for gathering, storing, analysing, and providing access to data".	A set of technologies
Wu et al. (2007)	"term used to describe applications and technologies which are used to gather, provide access to and analyse data and information about the organization, to help make better business decisions".	
Glaser and Stone (2008)	"IT platform and tools used to gather, provide access to, and analyse data about organization operations and activities. The platform is composed of a set of information technologies that are often represented as tack-one technology set on top of another".	
Ranjan (2009)	"is a broad category of applications and technologies for gathering, providing access to, and analysing data for the purpose of helping enterprise users make better business decisions".	
Vercellis (2011)	"a set of mathematical models and analysis methodologies that systematically exploit the available data to retrieve information and knowledge useful in supporting complex decision-making processes".	
Eriksson and Ferwerda (2019)	"Business intelligence (BI) systems are software applications that are used to gather and process data and to deliver the processed data in [an] understandable way to the end users".	
Hung and Chen (2020)	In today's business environment, BI systems are frequently bundled together or built with a good connection to existing ERP systems. Businesses implementing BI alone may not receive its full benefit if the necessary support structure and a fit of it to its problem domain are not in place.	
Revelli (1998)	"is the process of collection, treatment and diffusion of information that has as an objective, the reduction of uncertainty in the making of all strategic decision[s]".	A support for decision-making
Pirttimäki and Hannula (2003)	"is often used to refer to both information technology-based systems and actual business information management processes".	
Azvine et al. (2006)	"is all about capturing, accessing, understanding, analysing and converting one of the fundamental and most precious assets of the company, represented by the raw data, into active information in order to improve business".	
Baars and Kemper (2008)	"is now commonly understood to encompass all components of an integrated management support infrastructure".	
Nelson (2010)	"a management strategy used to create a more structured and effective approach to decision making".	

(continued)

Table 1 (continued)

Author(s)	Definition proposed	BI main content
Rouhani et al. (2012)	"is an instrument of analysis providing automated decision-making about business conditions, sales, customer demand and product preference and so on".	
Ali et al. (2019)	BI institutionalization may positively contribute to a managerial role in using BI application repetitively for the decision-making iteration in businesses.	

Sources: Authors' elaboration

Table 2 Overview of business intelligence definitions: a process view

Author(s)	Definition proposed	BI main content
Siegel (2000)	"is the legal, ethical collection of data and information that is analysed and transformed into actionable knowledge for use in strategic planning and problem solving".	A way to express information
Davies (2002)	"as the result of acquisition, interpretation, collation, assessment, and exploitation of information".	
Green (2007)	"is not a single entity; it is decomposed into business information".	
Tešendić and Krstićev (2019)	Business intelligence (BI) refers to methodologies, analytical tools, and applications used for data analysis of business information.	
Mansell and Ruhode (2019)	Business intelligence tools play an important role for businesses across all industries for their data and information management solutions. By harnessing the capabilities of business intelligence, companies are able to predict and better meet customer needs.	
Lönnqvist and Pirttimäki (2006)	"refers to a managerial philosophy and a tool used to help organizations manage and refine business information with the objective of making more effective business decisions".	A process
Negash and Gray (2008)	"refers to the process of extracting, transforming, managing and analyzing business data, in order to support decision making".	
Shollo and Kautz (2010)	"is both a process and a product. As a process [. . .] is the set of legal and ethical methods an organization uses to harness information [. . .]. As a product [. . .] is information about competitors' activities from public and private sources".	
Ahmed et al. (2019)	A business value creation process for BI exists and [...] it is divided into three subprocesses: the BI conversion process, BI use process, and BI competitive process. [...] The use of BI has become necessary for organizations to compete effectually.	
Schulz et al. (2020)	Recent developments in business intelligence have not only led to the availability of more and more heterogeneous data but also to more and more heterogeneous user groups accessing them.	

Source: Authors' elaboration

Krstićev (2019) recently described business intelligence as the methodologies for acting on data and getting business information. Therefore, all authors agreed on considering information as the element composing business intelligence and enabling its transformation into knowledge to better exploit such a tool.

Finally, the fourth category is the expression of business intelligence as a process, namely, as the actions to be performed to act on data and to make them useful for an actor. The processual view is complex and combines conceptual and practical views; indeed, while Lönnqvist and Pirttimäki (2006) described business intelligence as a managerial philosophy, Negash and Gray (2008) paid more attention to the practical implementation of business intelligence by referring to the extraction, transformation, management, and analysis of business data. Another all-embedding perspective was adopted by Shollo and Kautz (2010) as they referred to business intelligence as a product and a process, both centred on information. The trend in research on business intelligence recently led to consideration, with more attention, of its implementation, as in Ahmed et al. (2019), who described it as a process composed of three subprocesses, namely, conversion, use, and competitive. What emerged from the literature is a shift towards business intelligence implementation due to its being more concretely adopted in recent days and the fact that the activities on which it is based are sometimes seen as a sequence; in some other cases, they are concurrent (Guedea-Noriega and García-Sánchez 2019).

All these categories are oriented mainly to one of the four key elements emerging from the review, but they should not be intended as stand-alone blocks, as the collection of data representing business intelligence is frequently the expression of information supporting decision-making through articulated processes. Thus, the four goals of business intelligence can be combined and are not mutually exclusive, as Sathiyamoorthi (2020; p. 1) argued: "business intelligence is the way in which a company can use data to improve business and operational efficiency whereas data analytics involves improving ways of making intelligence out of that data before acting on it". Similarly, Yusof et al. (2019) combined decision-making and the processual view and leaned on Vizgaitytė and Skyrius (2012), who had claimed that business intelligence offers the capability "to gain insights and perform better in decision-making by using a particular set of technologies and tools" (p. 148). Additionally, Yusof et al. (2019) stated that BI has become a relevant complement to customer relationship management and that its implementation "will improve the efficiency of organizations, hence increase productivity and revenue" (p. 499).

3 Social Media and Big Data Analytics

Social media analytics (SMA) is an integral part of the business intelligence process that involves the compilation, analysis, and interpretation of behavioural customer data to derive business insights for better marketing decisions (Wedel and Kannan 2016; Leung et al. 2013) and to enhance competitive advantage (Akter et al. 2016; Ribarsky et al. 2014). Organizations must generate business intelligence to identify new challenges and opportunities; social media analytics enables companies to achieve the intelligence needed (Hu et al. 2019) by gaining immediate access to a huge amount of data useful for producing social media intelligence. Indeed, as supported by Lee (2018), social media intelligence is achieved by "combining knowledge generated from traditional business intelligence activities and knowledge gained from social media analytics" (p. 207).

However, to better clarify the different definitions and topics discussed, while business intelligence is the ability to make meaningful use of a large amount of data, also known as big data, social media analytics is composed of significant tools for obtaining and analyzing various personal and individual data of stakeholders from social media (Dinter and Lorenz 2012) as sources for business intelligence.

In business literature, scholars propose different definitions of social media analytics taking into account the different uses and objectives for organizations. The analysis of literature led to the description of social media analytics either through their tools and capabilities or as a process based on different phases. These views do not contrast with each other, but they do adopt two different perspectives as described below: the first based on social media analytics features and the second centred on a processual view.

Regarding the first view, some authors (He et al. 2015) focused on tools and the analytic capabilities that define social media analytics as the use of "advanced informatics tools and analytics techniques to collect, monitor, and analyze social media data to extract useful patterns and intelligence" (He et al. 2015; p. 802). Other authors (Wittwer et al. 2016) adopted the approach proposed by Sussin (2015) to provide an overarching definition identifying SMA as "an umbrella term that includes a number of specialized techniques, such as social filtering, social network analysis, social conversation quantification, engagement tracking, social channel analysis, sentiment analysis and paid social media measurement" (p. 1). All in all, the main purpose of the authors describing social media analytics via their tools and analytics capabilities is to offer the qualitative description and analysis of the available social content.

Concerning the second perspective (namely, the processual view), the social media analytics process is data centric and implies three different phases: data capturing, data understanding, and findings presentation (Fan and Gordon 2014). It also relies on multiple social media platforms that can differ from each other according to the types of purpose and ways of interacting. Microblogging (as on Twitter), social networking (as on Facebook), and video sharing (as on YouTube) are some of the most popular social media methods used to share opinions, create content, establish relationships, exchange ideas (Grover et al. 2018; Li and Xie 2020), and especially empower users by providing the possibility to make their voices heard (Koontz and Mon 2014; Li and Xie 2020). Previous contributions show that most authors considered social media analytics as a process shaped by various steps, centred on data analysis and aimed at improving decision-making; while they agree on the aforementioned features, they do not use the same naming and the same details for each step (Andryani et al. 2019; Ayodeji and Kumar 2019; Brooker et al. 2016; Stieglitz et al. 2018; Suseno et al. 2018). Three steps seem to summarize and share what scholars have proposed when adopting a processual view, in line with what Fan and Gordon (2014) proposed.

First, data capturing is a preprocessing phase, due to the possibilities of social media that generate a large amount of content. However, before the generated data can be analyzed, they must be discovered, collected, and prepared. For this reason, the process of data capturing, also known as text mining, includes the cleaning and refining of text useful in transforming raw data into a usable and understandable format (Balan and Rege 2017; Batrinca and Treleaven 2015). Usually, a huge array of information is called "big data", which can originate from different sources such as cloud applications, software, social influencers, data warehouse appliances, the public, network technologies, legacy documents, business applications, meteorological data, sensor data, and social media (Jeble et al. 2018). It is of great importance at this time to ensure the quality of data generated and, therefore, to retrieve all possible information and store the results.

Second, data interpretation and understanding are another critical phase as far as the content-based analysis is required. Among the content-based analyses, text analysis is the most common and creates the possibility of automatically gathering meaningful information. Additionally, regarding social media, text analysis is regarded as the analysis of the lexicon used in posts, comments, and even photos (Misirlis and Vlachopoulou 2018). Apart from text analysis, the other techniques are mentioned by Akter et al. (2016), who identified a possible framework of six dimensions used to create and/or co-create value via social media analytics: opinion mining or sentiment analysis, topic modelling, engagement analysis, predictive analysis, social network analysis, and trend analysis. Scholars as Pang and Lee (2008) agree that sentiment analysis represents the most adopted technique for analyzing opinions, feelings, and subjective evaluation in text. Sentiment analysis consists of the study of positive or negative feelings, opinions, and sentiments in the users' texts (Pang and Lee 2004). This kind of analysis draws on "computational linguistics, natural language processing and other methods of text analytics to automatically extract user sentiments or opinions" (Fan and Gordon 2014; p. 77), which include "machine learning techniques" (Li and Wu 2010). In practice, the methods range from simple word count to semantic methods; however, no technique is free from limitations, especially when less-satisfied customers are the more active ones on social media. Recently, predictive analysis has also shown promising results in social media analytics. Based on statistical models and other empirical methods (Shmueli and Koppius 2011), it is a technique used for predicting new processes and future outcomes (Lassen et al. 2017) from unstructured data and, in this way, contributes to the achievement of business intelligence. In this context, artificial intelligence and its upcoming capabilities, such as natural language processing (NLP) and computer vision (CV), enable the processing and use of textual, visual, metadata, and other types of social media data (Gayo-Avello et al. 2013) in a new way.

Finally, the last step, known by different terms, such as findings presentation or data visualization, consists of presenting the results with novel interactive visual displays by offering interesting new features, enabling the full monitoring of all

Table 3 Overview of objectives, tools, and techniques of social media analytics

Steps	Data capturing	Data interpretation and understanding	Data visualization
Relation with social media	Data as a source	Data as a context of analysis	Data as an outcome
Objectives	Retrieve all possible information and select it based on different attributes	Analyze the information retrieved to obtain different useful results such as models, trends, and patterns	Present the results of analysis with a representation of the data
Tools & techniques	Data cleaning Data selection	Opinion mining Sentiment analysis Topic modelling engagement analysis Predictive analysis Social network analysis Trend analysis	Visual reporting Visual modelling Visual mapping Dynamic modelling
Main contributions	Batrinca and Treleaven (2015); Balan and Rege (2017)	Akter et al. (2016); Fan and Gordon (2014); He et al. (2015); Li and Wu (2010); Misirlis and Vlachopoulou (2018); Pang and Lee (2004, 2008)	Aparicio and Costa (2015); Schreck and Keim (2012).

Source: Authors' elaboration

activities, and also helping organizations make decisions on time (Aparicio and Costa 2015). In particular, visualization involves generating useful visual representations of data, such as diagrams and graphs. Therefore, as supported by Schreck and Keim (2012), referring to social media analytics, organizations would benefit from applying this methodology to large and complex generated data.

In Table 3, a categorization of objectives, tools, techniques, and related contributions is proposed.

4 Business Intelligence in Cultural Heritage Sector

As shown above, several definitions were proposed to describe what business intelligence is and how it supports the activities of firms. In the cultural heritage sector, some advances were proposed because of the support to be offered to visitors when they sought a monument in a destination, during a guided tour, or when providing insights about an artwork when inside an exhibition. Others were brought about by firms to steer their decision-making towards better results. In any case, the changes taking place in cultural-heritage-based services are based on the usage of data collected, business insights, sensors, geo-localization systems, and cloud servers.

The changes taking place are particularly relevant and affect not only visitors but also organizations (Bearman and Geber 2008). There is a need for firms to implement new instruments to challenge competitors, adapt to the new scenarios, and get the opportunities represented by the emerging digital heritage. The interplay among data, decision-making, strategy, and operations become complex and assumed an increased urgency in the management practices (Rouhani et al. 2012). A strategy cannot be assumed in conditions of low awareness, so using data is a way to make business intelligence concrete support to firms' activities. Recent research highlighted this goal but stressed the need to further deal with some features such as interactivity (Ali et al. 2019) and its implementation in real business contexts (Ahmed et al. 2019).

Exhibit 1: Norman Rockwell Museum—Stockbridge

The Norman Rockwell Museum in Stockbridge (US) is probably not as famous as the MoMA, Louvre, Tate Gallery, or Museo Reina Sofía, but throughout the years it has achieved impressive performance in terms of sales. Indeed, already in 2012, the non-profit organization managing this museum sold US$1.5 million in products through the on-site retail and US $120,000 through the e-commerce business. Prints, books, and souvenirs are the top sellers of this museum, which is located in the Massachusetts countryside and which hosts more than 500 original works authored by Rockwell, along with personal items, photographs, and other documents.

The management of the museum analyzed customers' profiles and started getting worried about their age, as word-of-mouth through souvenirs given to children and grandchildren was not enough to assure future sales. Therefore, the management of the museum decided to partner with a company dealing with data analysis through business intelligence. The analysis of historical data, predictive models, and data from the whole cultural industry led to the setting up of various campaigns to expand sales, interest, and potential sales. The management chose to implement four campaigns among the ones proposed, and in 3 months the results were astonishing: The second time purchasing rate increased by 150%, revenue increased by about 50% in a year and by up to 77% during the campaigns, and the expected increase in revenue was exceeded by 16%.

The ingredients for such a successful recipe stand on the precision in aiming at the right target; indeed, the firm partnering with the museum stated that there is a 1:4 ratio, namely, for every increase in precision in setting the target, the revenue increase is 4. The identification of buying and behavioural patterns from buyers favoured the definition of product recommendations, cross-sales, and the right offerings in terms of content and time. Additionally, while the business intelligence information was run on wide bunches of data, the solutions were proposed to every single customer in the most customized way possible. Therefore, assuming decisions in the interaction with customers and getting them interested in the offerings were easy tasks thanks to the

(continued)

Exhibit 1: Norman Rockwell Museum—Stockbridge (continued)
power of data and the elaboration performed via the business intelligence tools. This led the Norman Rockwell Museum to talk to its customers as single individuals.

The usage of technologies is favouring a wiser and more aware decision-making process, as the collection and analysis of data are easier and quicker, as stressed by Paneva-Marinova et al. (2010). One of the contributions summarizing all the novel elements for both firms and visitors was authored by Ramos et al. (2018) and it describes the combination of information achieved through business intelligence and the new propositions based on cultural heritage achievable thanks to new technologies. Recently, Liggett and Corcoran (2020) stressed the need to advance new management models to deal with exhibitions designed and provided through technologies as the result of data combination through business intelligence. They stated that it is not only a new way to equip museums and exhibitions but also strategic reasoning behind new service offerings.

Exhibit 2: Museum of Fine Arts—Boston
The Museum of Fine Arts in Boston joined the business intelligence testing programme by Microsoft. The IT company provided greatly relevant funding to support the projects to be run at the museum. An impressive amount of artwork was scanned in different ways and transformed into digital pieces of art.

However, the key transformation stood on supporting the financial management and usage of intelligence for the arts. The new tools were employed to optimize the usage of resources, maximize the results to be achieved through the implementation of new projects, and enhance the overall productivity of the museum. More in detail, the use of business intelligence provided additional chances to manage the artwork available at the Museum of Fine Arts; indeed, the programme was described as an expansion of what was already known as the "encyclopaedic museum", as information was available but shaped and reshaped based on the aim of the offering. The use of business intelligence favoured this continuous recombination based on the data collected and the appreciation achieved for each collection exhibited.

A resource planning system was launched to support the performing of project management, the accounting system, the assessment of investments, and the creation of scenarios based on the projects planned. Moreover, the business intelligence system applied at the Museum of Fine Arts supported the decision-making processes, as the scenarios built into the evaluation stages were then used as a benchmark during the deployment of the projects themselves. The implementation of business intelligence took place with the

(continued)

Exhibit 2: Museum of Fine Arts—Boston (continued)
involvement of other entities, such as donors, providers, and partners, thereby creating a network of a thousand spokes—including datasets and computers—with access from multiple locations hosting the activities of the museum, both behind the scenes and in the realm of service provision.

Most of the results attained in the first stages of the implementation of the business intelligence system were related to how to improve visitors' satisfaction, how to set initiatives for museum members, and how to transform the internal processes in digital ones.

One of the elements representing a novelty in the approach towards shaping cultural services in new ways is the embedding of additional information through the usage of metadata and the combination of various tools (Candela et al. 2017). Scholars highlighted the novelty of these topics and called for further research, especially concerning the approach of firms (Bearman and Geber 2008; Van Der Zee et al. 2018), the consequences for new service features (Ramos et al. 2018), the effects on the combination of smart systems (Angelaccio et al. 2013; Van Der Zee et al. 2018), and users' willingness to use new tools (Aluri 2017). The approach of firms is not based just on what they do on their own, as data are generated from and collected through multiple sources and actors; therefore, proper instruments are needed (Baggio and Fuchs 2018). Indeed, data-driven decisions may offer improvements, expansions, and variations, leading to dynamic strategizing and offerings, as previously proposed by other scholars in a general domain (Costa et al. 2007).

Exhibit 3: La Sagrada Familia
A business intelligence-driven project took place in Spain, in relation to the world famous cathedral La Sagrada Familia, in Barcelona.

The project has been carried out together by public and private entities and began in 2016. The local municipality, Eurecat (a research centre on technology in Spain), the Mobile World Capital Foundation, and the World Association of Mobile Operators (GSMA) participated in this project, aimed at using data to analyze tourists' behaviour while visiting the cathedral and the surrounding area, to get information useful to both local public agencies and private businesses.

The analysis of data showed that most of the tourists in Barcelona (80%) simply pass near the cathedral and spend some time there, without stepping in. Half of the tourists spend 40 min in the area taking photos and visiting, with most of them being there in the morning in the time frame from 10:00 a.m. to noon. Most of the tourists in the area come from France, Italy, and the United Kingdom. The relevance of the information deriving from this data goes beyond tourism management and marketing because the City Councillor for

(continued)

Exhibit 3: La Sagrada Familia (continued)
Enterprise and Tourism stated that the information may prove to be useful for urban planning, public services optimization (such as transport), and offering support to mobility, through signalling and civil agents.

Additionally, this information is even more relevant because it is available in real time. Therefore, services can be adapted to current needs if necessary. Finally, details on the nationalities of tourists can help local actors set proper services; thus, their decision-making process may be steered via the information derived from business intelligence implementation.

5 Social Media Analytics and Cultural Heritage

In line with the above analysis on literature about social media analytics, online and social media presence is part of the museum's objectives to be reached in order to face the current digital transformation in cultural heritage. This relevance of the communication and conservation of cultural heritage had already been recognized by the UNESCO Charter on the Preservation of the Digital Heritage in 2003 with the awareness that "access to this heritage will offer greater opportunities for creating, communicating and sharing knowledge among all peoples" (UNESCO 2003).

Social media represents a source of cultural heritage resources thanks to several kinds of information and knowledge that can be obtained by social media analytics (Cacho et al. 2016; Nguyen et al. 2017). In the case of museums, the needs and expectations of museum visitors become increasingly complex (Marty 2008) and the use of digital tools can help meet these expectations, thereby obtaining an understanding of tourist behaviour (Brandt et al. 2017) and so taking advantage of other organizations (Lê 2019). Vassiliadis and Belenioti (2017), discovering that there is no classification of ways in which social media could affect museums, presented a categorization of four major effects: the opportunities of social media for museum experience and communication; the social media enhancement of museums' learning process; the patterns of social media use in museums; and the problems and barriers attendant to social media integration in museums. However, different scholars (Hausmann 2012) stressed that the introduction of communication systems based on web and social media platforms requires a redesign of the traditional museum in order to adapt products and strategies to the new digital era, promoting new cultural experiences and involving a wider audience of visitors, wherever they are (Padilla-Meléndez and del Águila-Obra 2013).

Exhibit 4: Museum of Modern Art—New York
The Museum of Modern Art in New York (US) is considered one of the most important art museums in the world. It is also considered an early adopter of

(continued)

Exhibit 4: Museum of Modern Art—New York (continued)
social media platforms and also the museum with the best practices in the use of social media analytics, taking into account the high number of followers reached on social networks.

As MoMA began to develop a digital plan to manage its means of communication and its publication of content across various platforms, the museum knew it was of great relevance to first look at its audience data. Social media followers can easily participate in a dialogue with the museum, hardly reachable before the advent of social media, leaving their opinions and feedback on their experiences. These data are analyzed to measure results and improve strategies, generating a series of insights useful for the management. In the case of MoMa, based on the generated insights, the digital team decided to establish several areas of focus to meet visitors' needs, including the development of content for young and international audiences, a re-design of online platforms for the multi-device world, and the propagation online of the whole collection available. The objective is to deliver an immersive experience created by the intertwinement of the physical point with the online one, and leverage this and other data as a source of support for management in their decision-making and in constantly updating their processes.

The spread of social media use and its importance due to the ease of communication and the ability of followers to become involved allows museum organizations to train business intelligence, also called social media intelligence, with the aim of redesigning their strategies of communication and the way in which art is spread. Indeed, social networking can perform a pivotal role in the learning process of informal environments such as museums (Russo et al. 2009) and could be useful in stimulating audience engagement (Fletcher and Lee 2012). Recently, in the literature, it has become clear that the use of tools to train social media intelligence is now necessary and that museums, to keep up with new technologies, must adapt to change their strategies in this digital era.

Exhibit 5: Museum of London
The Museum of London (UK) is a museum composed of two locations, both in London. Although it attracted more than one million visitors per year, it was not a museum easily accessible by visitors.

Therefore, to follow the museum's expansion plan, and consequently attract more consumers, the museum became involved in a challenge as a partner of Cision, an agency that covers all aspects of communication. The main purpose of this challenge was to boost public awareness and increase visitors' engagement using social media intelligence and insights.

(continued)

Exhibit 5: Museum of London (continued)

This research was carried out through a combination of a survey and social media analysis to obtain a complete picture of the museum's target audience in terms of their opinions, feelings, and subjective evaluations contained in messages, posts, exhibitions, and topics. After the first phase of collection, these data were coded to help develop several insights through the use of quantitative and qualitative metrics. Therefore, use of social media intelligence enables the better targeting of the public of the museum, the modification of messages in future announcements based on the results achieved with the previous ones, and the comparison of the statistics year by year to track and connect the number of visits.

In conclusion, social media analysis is an important tool that connects the relationships between museum media and their viewers, developing insights (key performance indicators) useful for monitoring the progress of business processes and building a more tailored experience.

In 2017, thanks to the improvements achieved, the Museum of London and Cision's project won gold at the AMEC awards for "Best Use of a Measurement Framework". The museum has intensified its evaluation service, always through the partnership with Cision, as insights and data are essential to planning and fostering relationships with high-quality media.

As established above, proper tools are needed to study the collected data to compose social media intelligence to obtain detailed information about users' experience inside cultural heritage sites. Indeed, as supported by Clarizia et al. (2018), the importance of data analytics for managers of the sites is strictly connected to the ease in understanding what is (and is not) going well (Clarizia et al. 2018). Thus, thanks to the use of these tools, it is possible to offer new personalized services.

Recently, one of the techniques described above, the sentiment analysis, has become a growing area in museums for the analysis of social media to discover visitors' opinions and feelings, and therefore to correct and improve their strategies.

Exhibit 6: San Francisco Museum of Modern Art—San Francisco (USA)

The San Francisco Museum of Modern Art (SFMOMA), located in the centre of San Francisco, has always been a forefront museum with the use of innovative and successful strategies.

To take steps into the new digital era, the museum is very attentive to the design and implementation of digital strategies. The social media is one of the most important communication channels available to SFMOMA, which allow to reach the success of any exhibition through the right collaboration between

(continued)

Exhibit 6: San Francisco Museum of Modern Art—San Francisco (USA) (continued)

the analysts and the marketing team. Instead, from another point of view, social media represents a way to collect a huge amount of data, which can be analyzed to better understand visitors' behaviour and the success of digital strategies, thus resulting in useful information for museum management.

The SFMOMA confirms the importance of analytics with the use of sentiment analysis algorithms. This technique is commonly used by organizations to identify visitors' sentiments. Indeed, it is used to find and extract subjective information from social media comments or reviews to determine the attitude of visitors.

The museum, in collaboration with Stamen Design Studio, hosted an "Art + Data Day", in which the final instalment was an Art Sentiment Graph generated by SFMOMA's lead software architect through the sentiment analysis of the collected text.

6 Conclusion

The ongoing changes in the technology domain, as well as the rise of competitiveness in cultural heritage organizations, led to novel ways to manage these organizations. Data played a central role in this revolution, as both business intelligence and social media analytics are based on the availability, collection, and analysis of data in supporting decision-making for museum managers and curators. Various initiatives have already been run, but these new tools look very promising and further advances are yet to come.

The literature on business intelligence highlighted various approaches to its definition and implementation. Namely, it can be a set of technologies for data-based operations, a means of supporting decision-making in business processes, and a way to express information due to the whole process of acquiring, interpreting, assessing, and delivering data, process itself favouring competition. The literature on cultural heritage organizations did not offer many advances on the use of BI in museums and exhibitions since Bearman and Geber (2008) stressed the significance of using data-based platforms in the design and offering of services (therefore for both firms and visitors), while recently Ahmed et al. (2019) called for the implementation of artificial intelligence in real business contexts to both test and advance its advantages for the cultural heritage domain. On the other hand, the evidence showed firms from this domain already dealing with BI, even from more than a few years. The use of BI led to the set of predictive models, customized campaigns, real-time data availability, and integration of an offering in a wider context such as an urban space; thus, the implementation of BI has already started and favoured both short- and long-term results for firms and their partners. The role of these latter is relevant due to the advantage in combining several sources of data to expand the data-based processes.

The analysis of the extant contributions on social media analytics favoured a clarification of its main goals and relations with data; indeed, data capturing, data interpretation and understanding, and data visualization are the three steps enabling the use of data as a source, context of analysis, and outcome to gain an advantage in using data. The contributions on this topic highlighted limited details about the usefulness of SMA for cultural heritage organizations, with a general suggestion to make use of data to obtain knowledge about visitors' behaviour in cultural settings (Cacho et al. 2016) and as a way to contrast the increasing complexity shaping this business, as already stated several years ago (Marty 2008). Also with references to SMA, the analysis of real business contexts favoured a better understanding of the already implemented initiatives; indeed, some museums are making use of SMA to collect data and set strategies for audience development, get a more insightful picture of visitors and increase their engagement, and acquire a way to analyze social communication strategies, whose indicators are still under construction for several firms. Therefore, the use of advanced techniques such as opinion mining, sentiment analysis, and visual mapping can improve firms' actions both online and offline in interactions with visitors.

To conclude, the role of data showed its relevance in both BI and SMA, and firms can obtain benefits from the implementation of processes led by these new technologies, to leverage data and improve both decision-making and the derived offerings. Additionally, these advantages can be observed in both small and big firms and in both the short term and the long term. The modularity of these initiatives is a key feature emerging from and depending on the multiplicity of data, the variety of analyses to be run, and the width of usage options available in both internal and external organizational and business processes.

References

Abbasi A, Zhou Y, Deng S, Zhang P (2018) Text analytics to support sense-making in social media: a language-action perspective. MIS Q 42(2):427–464

Ahmed A, Yusof SAM, Oroumchian F (2019) Understanding the business value creation process for business intelligence tools in the UAE. Pac Asia J Assoc Inf Syst 11(3):55–88

Akter S, Bhattacharyya M, Wamba SF, Aditya S (2016) How does social media analytics create value? J Organ End User Comput 28(3):1–9

Ali S, Islam R, Rahman F (2019) Institutionalization of business intelligence for the decision-making iteration. Int J Intell Inf Technol 15(1):101–118

Aluri A (2017) Mobile augmented reality (MAR) game as a travel guide: insights from Pokémon GO. J Hospit Tourism Technol 8(1):55–72

Andryani R, Negara ES, Triadi D (2019) Social media analytics: data utilization of social media for research. J Inf Syst Inf 1(2):193–205

Angelaccio M, Basili A, Buttarazzi B (2013) Using Geo-Business intelligence and social integration for smart tourism cultural heritage platforms. In: 2013 workshops on enabling technologies: infrastructure for collaborative enterprises. IEEE, pp 196–199

Aparicio M, Costa CJ (2015) Data visualization. Commun Design Q Rev 3(1):7–11
Arora A, Bansal S, Kandpal C, Aswani R, Dwivedi Y (2019) Measuring social media influencer index-insights from Facebook, Twitter and Instagram. J Retail Consum Serv 49:86–101
Ayodeji OG, Kumar V (2019) Social media analytics: a tool for the success of online retail industry. Int J Serv Oper Inform 10(1):79–95
Azvine B et al (2006) Real time business intelligence for the adaptive enterprise. In: IEEE joint conference: The 8th IEEE international conference on E-commerce technology and (CEC/EEE'06), IEEE, San Francisco, CA, pp 29–39
Baars H, Kemper HG (2008) Management support with structured and unstructured data—an integrated business intelligence framework. Inf Syst Manag 25(2):132–148
Baggio R, Fuchs M (2018) Network science and e-tourism. Inf Technol Tourism 20:97–102
Balan S, Rege J (2017) Mining for social media: usage patterns of small businesses. Bus Syst Res J Int J Soc Adv Bus Inf Technol 8(1):43–50
Balusamy B, Jha P, Arasi T, Velu M (2017) Predictive analysis for digital marketing using big data: big data for predictive analysis. In Trivedi SK, Dey S, Kumar A, Panda TK (eds) Handbook of research on advanced data mining techniques and applications for business intelligence. IGI Global, pp 259–283
Batrinca B, Treleaven PC (2015) Social media analytics: a survey of techniques, tools and platforms. Ai Soc 30(1):89–116
Bearman D, Geber K (2008) Transforming cultural heritage institutions through new media. Museum Manag Curatorship 23(4):385–399
Brandt T, Bendler J, Neumann D (2017) Social media analytics and value creation in urban smart tourism ecosystems. Inf Manag 54(6):703–713
Brooker P, Barnett J, Cribbin T (2016) Doing social media analytics. Big Data Soc 3(2):1–12
Cacho A, Figueredo M, Cassio A, Araujo MV, Mendes L, Lucas J et al (2016) Social smart destination: a platform to analyze user generated content in smart tourism destinations. In: New advances in information systems and technologies. Springer, Cham, pp 817–826
Candela G, Escobar P, Marco-Such M (2017) Semantic enrichment on cultural heritage collections: a case study using geographic information. In Proceedings of the 2nd international conference on digital access to textual cultural heritage. ACM, pp 169–174
Chen G, Chen K, Jiang D, Ooi BC, Shi L, Vo HT, Wu S (2012) E3: an elastic execution engine for scalable data processing. J Inf Process 20(1):65–76
Clarizia F, Colace F, De Santo M, Lombardi M, Pascale F (2018) A sentiment analysis approach for evaluation of events in field of cultural heritage. In: 2018 fifth international conference on social networks analysis, management and security (SNAMS). IEEE, pp 120–127
Costa L da F, Rodrigues A, Travieso G, Villas Boas PR (2007) Characterization of complex networks: a survey of measurements. Adv Phys 56(1):167–242
Davies PH (2002) Intelligence, information technology, and information warfare. Annu Rev Inf Sci Technol 36:313–352
Dezi L, Santoro G, Gabteni H, Pellicelli AC (2018) The role of big data in shaping ambidextrous business process management: case studies from the service industry. Bus Process Manag J 24 (5):1163–1175
Dinter B, Lorenz A (2012) Social business intelligence: a literature review and research agenda. ICIS
Eriksson M, Ferwerda B (2019) Towards a user experience framework for business intelligence. J Comput Inf Syst 1–10
Fan W, Gordon MD (2014) The power of social media analytics. Commun ACM 57(6):74–81
Fletcher A, Lee MJ (2012) Current social media uses and evaluations in American museums. Museum Manag Curatorship 27(5):505–521
Gandomi A, Haider M (2015) Beyond the hype: big data concepts, methods, and analytics. Int J Inf Manag 35(2):137–144
Gastaldi L, Pietrosi A, Lessanibahri S, Paparella M, Scaccianoce A, Provenzale G et al (2018) Measuring the maturity of business intelligence in healthcare: supporting the development of a

roadmap toward precision medicine within ISMETT hospital. Technol Forecast Soc Change 128:84–103
Gayo-Avello D, Metaxas PT, Mustafaraj E, Strohmaier M, Schoen H, Gloor P et al (2013) Understanding the predictive power of social media. Internet Res 23(5):528–543
George G, Haas MR, Pentland A (2014) Big data and management. Acad Manag J 57:321–326
George A, Schmitz K, Storey V (2018) The BI&A system: building matured business intelligence in organizations. Acad Manag Global Proc 144
Glaser J, Stone J (2008) Effective use of business intelligence: leveraging your organization's business data could improve financial and operational performance—and quality of care. Healthcare Financ Manag 62(2):68–73
Green A (2007) Business information—a natural path to business intelligence: knowing what to capture. J Inf Knowledge Manag Syst 37(1):18–23
Grover V, Chiang RH, Liang TP, Zhang D (2018) Creating strategic business value from big data analytics: a research framework. J Manag Inf Syst 35(2):388–423
Guedea-Noriega HH, García-Sánchez F (2019) Semantic (big) data analysis: an extensive literature review. IEEE Latin Am Trans 17(05):796–806
Hausmann A (2012) The importance of word of mouth for museums: an analytical framework. Int J Arts Manag 14(3):32–43
He W, Wu H, Yan G, Akula V, Shen J (2015) A novel social media competitive analytics framework with sentiment benchmarks. Inf Manag 52(7):801–812
Hu Y, Xu A, Hong Y, Gal D, Sinha V, Akkiraju R (2019) Generating business intelligence through social media analytics: measuring brand personality with consumer-, employee-, and firm-generated content. J Manag Inf Syst 36(3):893–930
Hung SY, Chen K (2020) The role of organizational support and problem space complexity on organizational performance a business intelligence perspective. Pac Asia J Assoc Inf Syst 12 (1):1
Jeble S, Dubey R, Childe SJ, Papadopoulos T, Roubaud D, Prakash A (2018) Impact of big data and predictive analytics capability on supply chain sustainability. Int J Logist Manag 29(2):513–538
Kaplan AM, Haenlein M (2010) Users of the world, unite! The challenges and opportunities of Social Media. Bus Horiz 53(1):59–68
Koontz C, Mon L (2014) Marketing and social media: a guide for libraries, archives, and museums. Rowman & Littlefield, London
Lassen NB, la Cour L, Vatrapu R (2017) Predictive analytics with social media data. In: Sloan L, Quan-Haase A (eds) The SAGE handbook of social media research methods. SAGE, London, pp 328–341
Lê JT (2019) # Fashionlibrarianship: a case study on the use of instagram in a specialized museum library collection. Art Doc J Art Libr Soc N Am 38(2):279–304
Lee I (2018) Social media analytics for enterprises: typology, methods, and processes. Bus Horiz 61 (2):199–210
Leung D, Law R, Van Hoof H, Buhalis D (2013) Social media in tourism and hospitality: a literature review. J Travel Tourism Market 30(1–2):3–22
Li N, Wu DD (2010) Using text mining and sentiment analysis for online forums hotspot detection and forecast. Decis Support Syst 48(2):354–368
Li Y, Xie Y (2020) Is a picture worth a thousand words? An empirical study of image content and social media engagement. J Market Res 57(1):1–19
Liggett S, Corcoran M (2020) Framing the conversation: the role of the exhibition in overcoming interdisciplinary communication challenges. In: Earnshaw R, Liggett S, Excell P, Thalmann D (eds) Technology, design and the arts-opportunities and challenges. Springer, Cham, pp 25–43
Lilien GL (2011) Bridging the academic-practitioner divide in marketing decision models. J Market 75(4):196–210
Lönnqvist A, Pirttimäki V (2006) The measurement of business intelligence. Inf Syst Manag 23 (1):32–40

Mansell IJ, Ruhode E (2019) Inhibitors of business intelligence use by managers in public institutions in a developing country: the case of a South African municipality. S Afr J Inf Manag 21(1):1–8
Mariani M, Baggio R, Fuchs M, Höpken W (2018) Business intelligence and big data in hospitality and tourism: a systematic literature review. Int J Contemp Hospit Manag 30(12):3514–3554
Marty PF (2008) Museum websites and museum visitors: digital museum resources and their use. Museum Manag Curatorship 23(1):81–99
Michalewicz Z, Schmidt M, Michalewicz M, Chiriac C (2006) Adaptive business intelligence. Springer, London
Misirlis N, Vlachopoulou M (2018) Social media metrics and analytics in marketing–S3M: a mapping literature review. Int J Inf Manag 38(1):270–276
Moe WW, Netzer O, Schweidel DA (2017) Social media analytics. In: Handbook of marketing decision models. Springer, Cham, pp 483–504
Montalvo RE (2011) Social media management. Int J Manag Inf Syst 15(3):91–96
Negash S, Gray P (2008) Business intelligence. Handb Decis Support Syst 2:175–193
Nelson GS (2010) Business intelligence2.0: are we there yet. In: SAS Global Forum, paper n. 07
Nguyen TT, Camacho D, Jung JE (2017) Identifying and ranking cultural heritage resources on geotagged social media for smart cultural tourism services. Pers Ubiquitous Comput 21 (2):267–279
Noone BM, McGuire KA, Rohlfs KV (2011) Social media meets hotel revenue management: opportunities, issues and unanswered questions. J Revenue Pricing Manag 10(4):293–305
Padilla-Meléndez A, del Águila-Obra AR (2013) Web and social media usage by museums: online value creation. Int J Inf Manag 33(5):892–898
Paneva-Marinova D, Pavlov R, Rangochev K (2010) Digital library for Bulgarian traditional culture and folklore. In: The proceedings of the 3rd international conference dedicated on digital heritage (EuroMed 2010), pp 8–13
Pang B, Lee L (2004) A sentimental education: sentiment analysis using subjectivity summarization based on minimum cuts. In: Proceedings of the 42nd ACL, pp 271–278
Pang B, Lee L (2008) Opinion mining and sentiment analysis. Found Trends Inf Retrieval 2:1–135
Pirttimäki V, Hannula M (2003) Process models of business intelligence. Front E-Bus Res:250–260
Power DJ, Heavin C (2017) Decision support, analytics, and business intelligence. Business Expert Press, London
Puklavec B, Oliveira T, Popovič A (2018) Understanding the determinants of business intelligence system adoption stages: an empirical study of SMEs. Ind Manag Data Syst 118(1):236–261
Ramos CM., Henriques C, Rodrigues JM (2018) Religious tourism experience model (RTEM): a recommendation model for dissemination of cultural and religious heritage. In: Handbook of research on technological developments for cultural heritage and etourism applications. IGI Global, pp 1–29
Ranjan J (2009) Business intelligence: concepts, components, techniques and benefits. J Theor Appl Inf Technol 9(1):60–70
Revelli C (1998) Intelligence strategique sur Internet. Dunod, Paris
Ribarsky W, Wang DX, Dou W (2014) Social media analytics for competitive advantage. Comput Graph 38:328–331
Roblek V, Bach MP, Meško M, Bertoncelj A (2013) The impact of social media to value added in knowledge-based industries. Kybernetes 42(4):554–568
Rouhani S, Ghazanfari M, Jafari M (2012) Evaluation model of business intelligence for enterprise systems using fuzzy TOPSIS. Expert Syst Appl 39(3):3764–3771
Russo A, Watkins J, Groundwater-Smith S (2009) The impact of social media on informal learning in museums. Educ Media Int 46(2):153–166
Sathiyamoorthi V (2020) An intelligent system for predicting a user access to a web based E-learning system using web mining. Int J Inf Technol Web Eng (IJITWE) 15(1):75–94
Schreck T, Keim D (2012) Visual analysis of social media data. IEEE Comput 46(5):68–75

Schulz M, Alpar P, Winter P (2020) Should data structures look flat for end users? Inf Syst Manag 37(2):150–169
Shmueli G, Koppius OR (2011) Predictive analytics in information systems research. MIS Q:553–572
Shollo A, Kautz K (2010) Towards an understanding of business intelligence. In: ACIS 2010 proceedings - 21st Australasian conference on information systems
Siegel CF (2000) Introducing marketing students to business intelligence using project-based learning on the World Wide Web
Stieglitz S, Mirbabaie M, Ross B, Neuberger C (2018) Social media analytics—challenges in topic discovery, data collection, and data preparation. Int J Inf Manag 39:156–168
Suseno Y, Laurell C, Sick N (2018) Assessing value creation in digital innovation ecosystems: a social media analytics approach. J Strat Inf Syst 27(4):335–349
Sussin J (2015) Market guide: social analytics applications for IT leaders, GARTNER. Available at : https://insidethecomputerindustry.files.wordpress.com/2016/10/market_guide_social_analytic_279553.pdf
Tafesse W, Wien A (2018) Implementing social media marketing strategically: an empirical assessment. J Market Manag 34(9–10):732–749
Tešendić D, Krstićev DB (2019) Business intelligence in the service of libraries. Inf Technol Libr 38(4):98–113
UNESCO (2003) Charter on the preservation of the digital heritage.
Van Der Zee E, Bertocchi D, Vanneste D (2018) Distribution of tourists within urban heritage destinations: a hot spot/cold spot analysis of TripAdvisor data as support for destination management. Curr Issues Tourism, 1–22
Vassiliadis CA, Belenioti ZC (2017) Museums & cultural heritage via social media: an integrated literature review. Tourismos 12(3):97–132
Vercellis C (2011) Business intelligence: data mining and optimization for decision making. Wiley, New York
Vizgaitytė G, Skyrius R (2012) Business intelligence in the process of decision making: changes and trends. Economics 91(3):147–157
Wang Y, Kung L, Wang WYC, Cegielski CG (2018) An integrated big data analytics-enabled transformation model: application to health care. Inf Manag 55(1):64–79
Wedel M, Kannan PK (2016) Marketing analytics for data-rich environments. J Market 80 (6):97–121
Wittwer M, Reinhold O, Alt R, Jessen F, Stüber R (2016) Social media analytics using business intelligence and social media tools—differences and implications. In: International conference on business information systems. Springer, Cham, pp 252–259
Wu L, Barash G, Bartolini C (2007) A service-oriented architecture for business intelligence. In IEEE international conference on service-oriented computing and applications, 2007. SOCA'07, pp 279–285
Yusof NI, Zainuddin NMM, Hassan NH, Sjarie NNA, Yaacob S, Hassan WAW (2019) A guideline for decision-making on business intelligence and customer relationship management among clinics. Int J Adv Comput Sci Appl 10(8):498–505

Part III
Context, Content and Communication

Proximity Marketing and Context-Information Awareness

Anna D'Auria, Tiziana Russo Spena, and Francesco Bifulco

Abstract This chapter investigates the role of new digital devices in marketing initiatives to provide personalized offerings thanks to context-aware information. Despite the scholars' suggestion to create a two-way relationship between provider and user to achieve mutual benefits, the technological tools are used mainly to spread information (i.e. points of interest, opening hours, and other practical information) from an existing database. Some solid evidence related to proximity marketing initiatives in the cultural heritage sector has been further explored. Relying on Nagtode's and Raghunandam's (Integrated digital marketing: the key to understanding your customer. Tata Consultancy Services, 2015) model and the case study exploration, an integrative framework is advanced, based on four elements—information, interaction, tools, and personalization—and the four pillars including people, data, processes, and contexts. The framework can support museum managers in creating a different way to personalize the interaction and engagement with visitors, dynamically.

1 Introduction

The digitalization of marketing processes is playing a central role in the current debate over marketing management (Quinn et al. 2016; Shpak et al. 2020; Zhu and Gao 2019). The new approach leads to a renovated role of the consumer, as he/she is now actively involved in the marketing initiatives through the support of innovative tools. Indeed, thanks to the use of new technologies, organizations can obtain

A. D'Auria (✉) · T. Russo Spena
Department of Economics Management Institutions, University of Naples Federico II, Naples, Italy
e-mail: anna.dauria@unina.it; russospe@unina.it

F. Bifulco
Department of Humanities, University of Naples Federico II, Naples, Italy
e-mail: fbifulco@unina.it

T. Russo Spena, F. Bifulco (eds.), *Digital Transformation in the Cultural Heritage Sector*, Contributions to Management Science,
https://doi.org/10.1007/978-3-030-63376-9_8

information about users' preferences—information that is useful in customizing the service since it started being offered.

In recent years, even more companies operating in the cultural sector are introducing new technologies to their activities, both to shape the offer and to provide the services/products; thanks to the employment of digital tools, organizations can meet a greater number of users at the same time (Lemon 2016). Therefore, the relationship between companies and consumers can be considered multidirectional because it is based on a one-to-many approach or even a many-to-many approach (Liu et al. 2019).

In detail, digital tools are even more frequently used in marketing, sales processes (such as e-ticketing, e-bookshops, or official websites), and administrative activities (such as security and managing archives). New forms of communication and consumption lead to the opportunity to meet users with diversified needs and requests thanks to the direct connection between users and providers during, before, and after the service is experienced.

Communication tools are increasingly based on customer-dominated technologies (Levesque and Boeck 2017), and the diffusion and circulation of data are less controlled by companies. Indeed, thanks to digital devices, customers have the opportunity to share information freely. However, in some cases, organizations can take advantage of the free promotion realized by consumers on their own. Furthermore, information shared by consumers is quite difficult to analyze and categorize because of its variability, with special reference to data obtained implicitly. In this regard, ad hoc digital instruments can be helpful.

In terms of marketing initiatives based on the involvement of consumers, both scholars' contributions and empirical evidence show that the features of the context are highly relevant; in detail, the characteristics of the context can affect consumers' behaviour as well as the decision-making process of the organization (De Mooij 2019; Musumba and Nyongesa 2013).

In general, through new technologies, organizations aim to reduce the physical and cognitive distance between businesses and consumers (Whiting et al. 2017), in order to recognize users' preferences and be able to better define and personalize their offer. Such an approach is defined in the literature as proximity marketing (Allurwar et al. 2016; Fullerton et al. 2019; Levesque and Boeck 2017) and is even more considered in the cultural sector, where the involvement—and, even more, the engagement—of users can strongly affect their perceptions and behaviours.

Dynamism and flexibility are key elements of provider operations and demand trends in cultural business; an example is represented by the "virtual visits" described by Popović and Hromadžić (2008). According to this new trend of consumption, the service is usually provided through the company's website, where employees and customers can interact in line with the co-creation and co-production approach (Lee and Kim 2018; Zhouying 2005).

When talking about proximity marketing initiatives, it must be noted that the provision of such services has to be based on the preferences and attitudes of consumers; therefore, to shape the offering, the firm should be able to outline the profile of the target customer. In this regard, Papandrea et al. (2010) stated that the service is provided "*on the basis of the users' position (e.g., in the nearby to the shops they could enter and buy) and profile (a user receives only advertisements she/he is really interested in)*" (p. 2).

This chapter aims to provide an understanding of proximity marketing in the cultural heritage context (Papandrea et al. 2010; Pavlidis 2019). To frame proximity marketing in the cultural sectors, the analysis of the conceptualization of context is needed because the context in which organizations and users are acting must be considered a set of elements affecting user behaviour.

Thus, the analysis has been conducted by scanning literature contributions on proximity marketing. This topic was firstly analyzed by scholars of engineering, computer and information systems; then the emerging importance of co-creation and digital technologies in service literature (Edvardsson et al. 2014; Lenka et al. 2017) opened up a new interest in service marketing. Furthermore, the chapter focuses on the techniques and tools adopted in the cultural heritage business from both a theoretical and an empirical perspective; indeed, literature analysis has been supported by the observation of some representative case studies (Smirnov et al. 2017) and experiences linked to cultural heritage services. The case studies have been found through the website Google.com, which is usually considered one of the most reliable search engines (Hewson and Stewart 2014) and empirically analysed. Relying on Nagtode's and Raghunandam's (2015) model and the exploration of the case studies, an integrative framework is advanced. It is based on four elements—information, interaction, tools, and personalization—and the four pillars including people, data, processes, and contexts. The framework can support museum managers in creating a different way to personalize the interaction and engagement with visitors, dynamically.

2 The Role of Context-Information Awareness

Increasingly, scholars are paying attention to the topic of context as a key element in shaping proximity marketing initiatives; nowadays, context is no longer considered a physical place but, rather, a "situation in use" (Franklin and Flaschbart 1998; Korper et al. 2018), as it involves a set of elements that could affect users' behaviour. In this regard, Chihani et al. (2011) described context as a combination of various entities such as their identity, activity, location, and mood; their social context may be the nature of their relationship with other persons (e.g. family member, colleague, and friend).

In general, although the context is no longer considered simply as a physical space, it still frames or surrounds an object of analysis; according to Fauconnier (1997), context can be considered a mental space.

As time went by, scholars proposed various frameworks to set up a homogeneous configuration of the concept of context. In 1987, Engeström et al. proposed the "Active Theory" inspired by some psychologists' theories (Leont'ev 1974; Rubinshtein 1973; Vygotsky 1979), suggesting that the action is the key element of the context. In 2004, Kaenampornpan and O'Neill proposed a model based on seven elements—namely, subject, tools, community, division of labour, rules, object, and outcome—as the pillars of the conceptualization of context.

In detail, the authors described each component as follows:

- *Subject*: The information chosen as the main perspective in the analysis.
- *Tools*: Psychological or physical tools that enable the accomplishment of the objective.
- *Community*: Individuals or subgroups that share the same action or objective.
- *Division of labour*: The organization of the tasks realized by members of the community.
- *Rules*: Rules or implicit regulations that regulate the system and can affect the action.
- *Object*: The goal of the activity.
- *Outcome*: The result of the transformation process.

Similarly, Zimmermann et al. (2007) introduced five categories of context, namely, individuality, time, location, activity, and relations.

An interesting contribution is provided by Gilbert (2006), who described context from a cultural point of view, namely, "*a focal event embedded in its cultural setting*" (p. 960).

Therefore, the context has no universally accepted definition, as it refers to many aspects of life and deals with many disciplines; it emerges that the configuration of the context depends on the field of application (Bazire and Brézillon 2005).

In line with the aim of this chapter, the concept of context has been observed through a marketing perspective. Therefore, a reference to the context awareness is needed.

3 Marketing Perspective and Contextual Marketing

In the marketing domain, some scholars identify the elements of the context that can affect consumer behaviour in different ways. For example, Carson and Gilmore (2000) suggested that context is composed of factors that are *inter-dependent*, *inter-related*, and *synergistically influential* and that can be useful in defining marketing processes. Meanwhile, Dinu (2004) in Vlăduțescu (2014) suggested, "*The main dimensions of the context are the spatial, temporal, psychological and social ones*" (p. 197).

With reference to users' behaviour, Shogren et al. (2014) described context as follows: "*referenced to human functioning would result in a delineation of factors that affect both positively and negatively human functioning*" (p. 111). This underlines the relevance of the context in affecting users' choices and shaping services, suggesting that, to improve the quality of their services, companies must detect consumers' preferences and implement initiatives supported by new technologies (Musumba and Nyongesa 2013).

Fig. 1 The main features of context. Source: Authors' elaboration

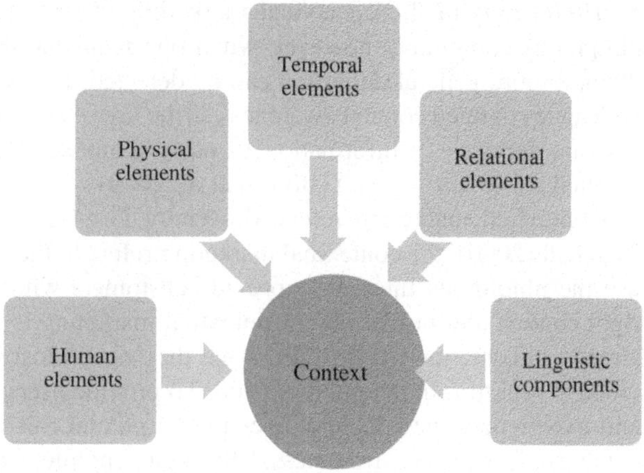

In general, both scholars' contributions and empirical evidence show that the features of the context are highly relevant in shaping services, as users' perception can be strongly affected by circumstances and conditions when they are enjoying the service (De Mooij 2019; Ismagilova et al. 2020; Musumba and Nyongesa 2013). In detail, scholars refer to physical elements, relational elements, temporal elements, human elements, and linguistic components, as represented in Fig. 1. The physical components refer to the concrete environment that has its own set of rules for interactions; the relational elements involve the norms of the group in a particular situation, including the intimacy level and the formality of the interactions; the temporal elements, as the context must "*include, not only the relevant objects and actions taking place at the time, but also the knowledge shared by the speaker and hearer of what has been said earlier, in so far as this is pertinent to the understanding of the utterance*" (Illes 2001; p. 17); the human elements, namely the human acts taking part in the context; and linguistic elements, as the text, in the linguistic communication (Shen 2012).

Thus, context features can affect consumer behaviour in different ways; for example Carson and Gilmore (2000) stated that context is composed of factors that are inter-dependent, inter-related, and synergistically influential and that can be considered as a tool in defining marketing processes. Sampangi and Hawkey (2016) talked about context-dependent attributes, namely, elements that can make a system more dynamic and adaptive. In addition, according to Fuentes et al. (2006) "in several cases, the design and development of effective services should take into account the characteristics of the context from which a service is requested" (p. 1).

3.1 Contextual Marketing

As anticipated, in the present study, context has been analyzed in particular from a marketing perspective.

The origins of the contextual marketing are strictly connected to the field of ubiquitous computing; however, when one scans the literature contribution on the them, a more general definition can be detected; for example in 1999, Abowd and colleagues defined context awareness as the use of contextual information to provide relevant services or information to users (contextual information can usually be labelled using sensor data) (Bowen et al. 2019).

Contextual marketing refers, especially to e-business in line with Kenny and Marshall (2000): the contextual marketing refers to the extent to which e-businesses use the ubiquitous Internet to provide customers with relevant information in the right context and in real time. Contextual marketing is important because users are already information overloaded. What they need most is relevant information provided in real time at the point of need. To provide users with higher quality services and experiences, new technologies play a pivotal role, especially in implementing context-information awareness, through mobile devices, applications, and geolocation tools, useful to obtain contextual information that can be further employed to provide users with personalized services. In this regard, Park et al. (2013) describe context-aware technology as an instrument to analyze the interaction between users and mobile devices to shape users' behaviour. Aided by the emerging technologies, marketers may initiate real-time dialogues with their customers and provide them with interactive services. Such conversations and interactive services may help companies to cut through the market chaos in the marketspace and establish binding relationships with their customers. In the real-time world, traditional marketing connections to customers (e.g. focus groups and consumer surveys) are not enough to build customer loyalty and brand. Instead, companies need to engage, via information technology in a continuous dialogue with customers about product development, experience with the product, service support among suppliers, distributors, and the like. Dialogue with consumers is important in that it is the way firms can achieve context and ultimately obtain greater customer loyalty and superior performance.

However, in practice, contextual marketing—the science of delivering the right content to the right customer at the right moment—is a lot more complicated at location-based level (Grudin 2001; Sampangi and Hawkey 2016). This is particularly because consumers can assume different behaviours based on where they are and what they are doing, especially in the new realm of the connected digital world.

Not surprising, given the extent to which location data is currently changing how people shop, eat, date, and travel, organizations are expected to propose in-the-moment, personalized, relevant experiences to engage the newly connected consumers.

The new contextual insights are gaining importance because businesses can reach their customers on time and at the right place by using contextually relevant, personalized, and multidimensional marketing solutions. Companies can access these data from a wide array of sources that bring depth and diversity to organizational processes, ranging from smartphones to wearables, Internet of Things (IoT) devices to Wi-Fi routers to beacons, and navigation providers (Jamali et al. 2020;

Zafari et al. 2019). As location becomes more central, companies are utilizing this data to reach customers at scale who are in the right context to consider or act.

4 Proximity Marketing

The digitalization of the market has made location-based marketing initiatives increasingly important (Levesque and Boeck 2017; Fullerton et al. 2019; Papandrea et al. 2010). In recent years, both scholars and practitioners started to pay attention to the so-called proximity marketing approach, namely, a set of activities to be implemented to reach the consumer and persuade him/her to make a purchase and create a two-way long-term relationship between provider and user (Smirnov et al. 2017). While location-based marketing communication ensures the quantity of communication with potential customers, the implementation of proximity marketing communication focuses on the quality of communication with potential customers.

The Proximity Marketing (PM) has been defined as a type of marketing that provides the benefit of hyperconnectivity to consumers and helps to provide both a complete sensorial experience and a technological experience. It has been defined as the mobile, wireless, and localized distribution of advertising content related to a specific location. Proximity marketing implies that organizations must dispatch their advertising contents to targeted geographic locations where potential customers have been identified (Bilolo et al. 2015; Levesque and Boeck 2017).

Thus, it would be important to identify the geographical position of the addressee of the communication and create a two-way relationship between provider and user. For example, according to Agostini et al. (2004), the main goal of proximity marketing is to provide targeted, location-aware advertisements about sales on items contained in a user's personal shopping list.

A different perspective in describing proximity marketing has been adopted by Uhrich et al. (2008), who focused on the benefits for consumers, such as time (shopping, cash register, delivery) and money savings (promotion). Finally, one of the most recent and complete definitions of proximity marketing has been provided by Levesque and Boeck (2017; p. 1), who stated, "*Proximity marketing is based on the identification of the customer's geographical position using wireless connectivity. (.......) businesses can send the advertising content to a specific person and a specific location. This contributes to a personalization and customization of the service for an increased experience*".

New technologies emerge as a very relevant element when one is talking about proximity marketing initiatives. According to previous contributions, the most considered devices are Bluetooth, Wi-Fi, QR Code (Quick Response Code) with reference to communication activities, RFID (Radio-Frequency Identification), and GPS (Global Positioning System) with reference to localization processes (González et al. 2015; Levesque and Boeck 2017; Shang et al. 2011). Specifically, new technologies adopt integrated tools to determine the position of a mobile device,

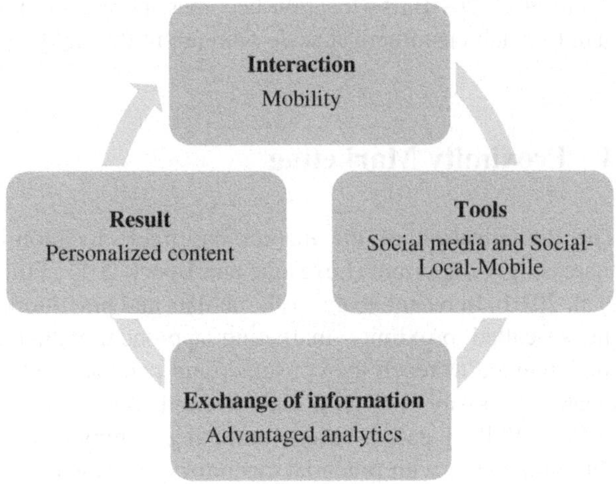

Fig. 2 Elements in proximity marketing initiatives. Source: Authors' elaboration from Nagtode and Raghunandan (2015)

localize the consumer and address him/her needs with the offering based on specific location conditions.

Collaboration and integration of consumer data at the point of their generation are now considered essential aspects in the definition and management of marketing activities, adopting a customer-centric orientation (Viviani et al. 2010). Therefore, the opportunity to detect, collect, and use the right data at the right moment becomes very important.

When implementing proximity marketing initiatives, managers must consider some unavoidable factors, as suggested by Nagtode and Raghunandan (2015). They include:

- Interaction with the context through mobile devices to enjoy proximity marketing activities; "the user base accessing the internet via smartphones has prompted many companies to optimize their online content for mobile devices" (Nagtode and Raghunandan 2015; p. 5).
- Tools as social media and social-local-mobile marketing. The social media can be very helpful in sharing and obtaining information thanks to the direct interaction between providers and customers and among the users themselves (Fan and Gordon 2014; Verhoef et al. 2017).
- Exchange of information, as managers can use digital tools to target marketing strategies through the observation of consumers' behaviour.
- The result consisting of personalized content shaped by the contributions and engagement of consumers (Fig. 2).

By taking advantage of proximity marketing to engage customers, various tools can be implemented with different effects. For example, they include the use of tags, consisting in the use of devices deriving from smart stations, tags that can be a smart card, a badge, and other types of gadgets. The customer must register the station to associate the gadget to the person; from that moment, every interaction will be traced. The purpose is to arouse the interest of the customer. Anyone can spread their own brand considerations on social networks and continue to take advantage of the content related to that brand. Smart tools attract the customer by creating a connection between his/her device and stickers with a QR code and/or an NFC sticker, showing the customers predefined content. Wi-Fi technologies provide the most opportunities for proximity marketing because, thanks to the connection to the Wi-Fi network, it is possible to access all the other engagement strategies, taking advantage of user data. Finally, apps connected to the use of BLE (Bluetooth Low Energy) beacon technology enable interaction with the user's devices in push mode. The app hires the customer through an application, downloadable from its devices, with which to send targeted communications and notify those who circulate in a specific area. The application does not interact on its own when it is located near the store or brand event but, rather, creates a direct channel with the user with whom to interact, even when connected. This can contribute to better promoting the customers' loyalty. Among the advantages offered by proximity marketing, there is also the possibility of implementing selected and creative strategies to ensure customer involvement and provide a more evolved customer experience (Comerio et al. 2015).

4.1 The Recommended Systems Tools

It is clear that to attract consumers and convince them to purchase; it is very important to define the most suitable communication channel and the kinds of information to be shared on the base of the target (Baum and Spann 2014).

In order to accomplish this objective, and according to the new trends of digital and proximity marketing, business and academic literature are paying much more attention to the more frequently introducing recommender systems into organization marketing strategies (Clark 2017). According to Burke et al. (2015), recommender systems represent customer preferences for the purpose of suggesting items to purchase or examine. They have become fundamental applications in electronic commerce and information access, providing suggestions that effectively prune large information spaces so that users are directed towards those items that best meet their needs and preferences. With more than six billion mobile phones in the hands of consumers today, every consumer with a smartphone is potentially susceptible to a proximity marketing campaign (Vlăduțescu 2014).

The main function of these tools is to engage the consumers before, during, and after the experience to obtain information and suggestions that can be useful to improve the offer in the future. In detail, the recommender systems are based on the transformation of various inputs in outputs that can be differentiated on the bases of the preferences of the target. Indeed, Prasad and Kumari (2012) have stated that recommender systems can be defined as people provide recommendations as inputs, which the system then aggregates and directs to appropriate recipients.

Obviously, both the aim of the proximity marketing initiative as well as the characteristics of the information to be introduced lead to the adoption of different techniques and the need to use different languages (de Gemmis et al. 2015; Friedman et al. 2016).

The use of recommender system has a double purpose; on a side, the messages are directed towards potential customers that have no experience related to the offer, or that do not have enough information to decide to buy it or, at least, that cannot achieve information about it (Adomavicius et al. 2013). On the other side, the message transmitted through the recommender system can be addressed to the customers that already have experience about the service to be offered with the aim to improve their fidelity.

It is possible to distinguish different categories of elements that can affect the recommendation process: information about the user, information about the offer, the approach of the consumer, and his/her evaluation of the offer. As it concerns the last point, the evaluation of the consumer can be observed in an implicit way as well as in an explicit way on the bases of the relationship between the organization and the customer as well as the inclination of the customer himself (Adomavicius et al. 2013).

The customer can take advantage of being engaged in the realization process of the offer since, by giving suggestions and sharing opinions, he/she can obtain a personalized service—or product—and then a higher opportunity to be satisfied. Indeed, according to Burke et al. (2015) referring to the relationship between the user and the item, there are five different techniques of recommendation. The most common one is named Collaborative recommendation and is based on a recommender system that aggregate ratings or recommendations of objects, recognize commonalities between users on the basis of their ratings, and generate new recommendations based on inter-user comparisons. More in general, this technique can be described as a collection of valuation proposed by the users, as well as a collection recommendation of objects made by the organization; the analysis of the two categories of the collaborative elements lead to the definition of new proposals and processes (Prasad and Kumari 2012; Burke et al. 2015; Sohail et al. 2017).

Moreover, there are some fewer common techniques that differ from each other. The first one is the demographic recommender system (Al-Shamri 2016; Wang et al. 2015), maybe the most neutral since it is based on pre-existent and unequivocal data such as the demographic information or other clear characteristics of the user. The second one is the content-based recommendation based on the correlation among the information transmitted by the users (implicitly or explicitly) and that can represent his/her preferences. In these cases, it is possible to talk of an *item-to-item correlation* since it is based on the users' preferences (Rosenbaum and Massiah 2007; Ku et al. 2016).

Finally, the utility- and knowledge-based recommendations can be considered the most complicated technique to be used since it is based on elaborated consumers' data that is very hard to manage and share (Burke et al. 2015; Yan et al. 2016).

5 Proximity Marketing in the Cultural Heritage

The marketing approach to cultural heritage is quite different from that of the other sectors, in particular, due to its service-oriented approach (Din and Wu 2014; Kouyoumdjieva and Karlsson 2019; Scuderi and Salvetti 2019).

Proximity marketing initiatives in the cultural sector are based on three essential elements: *People*—namely, users and the providers, as well as the total network of stakeholders involved; *Physical evidence*—the factors enabling one to join the service; and *Process*—leading to the fruition of the service (Cenderello 2015; Christou 2006; Wróblewski 2017). The role of digital tools appears to be significantly relevant because it contributes to highlighting "*the entertainment dimension of the site. It has to be considered that [some] of [the] people visiting cultural heritage sites are not engaged in a deep learning experience*" (Cenderello 2015; p. 10).

Kuflik et al. (2017; p. 1) described cultural heritage as "*an attractive domain for experimenting with novel technologies for various reasons*"—first of all, for the large variety of elements, as well as the high value of the cultural goods. In 2011 Ardisonno et al. stated that "*for more than 20 years, cultural heritage has been a favoured domain for personalization research and as soon as mobile technology appeared, it was adopted for delivering context-aware cultural heritage information both indoors and outdoors*" (Ardisonno et al. 2011 in Lo Bue et al. 2015; p. 2).

In recent years, digital devices—i.e. tablets, smartphones, and applications—have been increasingly used in marketing initiatives related to the cultural heritage sector; as these devices have acquired an essential role in our everyday lives, they are considered the most suitable tools to create a direct interaction between users and attractions (Lewi et al. 2019).

When one scans contributions on the topic, it emerges that the employment of digital tools in cultural heritage is not completely exploited. Indeed, despite scholars' suggestion to create a two-way relationship between provider and user to achieve mutual benefits, and the availability of applications capable of providing personalized cultural propositions thanks to context-aware information, technological tools are used mainly to spread information (i.e. points of interest, opening hours, and other practical information) from an existing database.

6 Research Process

Observation of the above-introduced proximity marketing techniques and tools in the cultural heritage sector has been conducted by analyzing literature contributions and documents providing case studies. However, the novelty of the theme represents a limitation due to the difficulty of finding documents, papers, or practical evidence useful in drawing up the theoretical context.

Attention has been paid mainly to the tools used in situations of proximity marketing activities by selecting the most mentioned in the reports related to practical experiences (Bilolo et al. 2015). The most recognized model with respect to the application of the proximity marketing tools has been analyzed (Levesque and Boeck 2017) to deduce the features that are useful in the depiction of the strategy by merging the different proposals.

An empirical analysis has been conducted by interviewing the manager of three organizations already involved in proximity marketing activities (Doody and Noonan 2013; Healey and Rawlinson 1993). The reason why interviews were performed is related to the need to investigate a new issue—as these new technologies are—with the firms implementing them in a pioneering way. They have provided a useful contribution by offering a brief analysis of the context through observation of the weaknesses and opportunities for enterprises operating in the cultural sector. Secondary data from the web and published reports have also been used to enrich the analysis.

Finally, starting from the analysis of the existing models and the results of the empirical investigation, the proposal of a model has been designed to apply to the cultural heritage sector. In detail, the model proposed by Nagtode and Raghunandan (2015) has been the starting point for developing the proposal. The existing scheme is based on four elements: tools, personalization, interaction, and information; the four pillars, including people, data, process, and context, have been added as pivotal support to sustain the understanding and framing of the proximity marketing activities in the cultural heritage sector.

7 An Integrated Framework

Some solid evidence related to proximity marketing initiatives in the cultural heritage sector has been analyzed. To better address the analysis in the following, we provide a framework to integrate Nagtode's and Raghunandam's (2015) model and update the essential elements of museums' proximity initiatives, i.e. people, process, data, and context (Fig. 3). The figure provides a synthesis, while in the next subsections, some empirical evidence is discussed.

7.1 iBeacon Technology to Enhance Visitors' Experience: Experience of Palazzo Farnese

Since 2014, Palazzo Farnese's museums have proposed proximity marketing activities by employing innovative technologies and tools such as iBeacons and QR Code panels interacting with an app supported by mobile devices. The iBeacons detect the

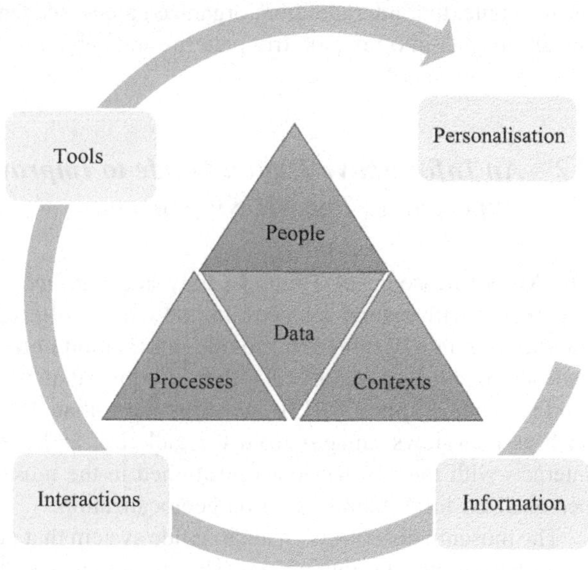

Fig. 3 An integrated framework. Source: Authors' elaboration from Nagtode and Raghunandam (2015)

physical presence of people within approximately 70 m, thereby managing to involve them and provide services and information through the app.

Apart from iBeacons, the museum installed QR Code panels and Bluetooth devices that provide users with additional content such as images or videos based on their physical positions. An app also allows visitors to plan their visits before they arrive thanks to the opportunity to download it when they are at home and get an interactive map, which indicates the locations of all the masterworks. By selecting one of them, the user can find out how to reach it and access additional content, when the visitor is either inside or outside the museum. The visitor can also choose a particular work of art and use the app to trace the shortest route to reach it, as well as receive additional contents. In this way, the museum is transformed into a flexible, open, and multisensory space, providing people with an immersive experience.

It must be noted that both current and future visitors can benefit from the use of this technology, as the opportunity to observe users' behaviour and profile them in line with their preferences enables the shaping of even more suitable and satisfying services and activities. In addition, the suggestions and personalized tour shaped and shared by the visitors provide future users with additional content.

In sum, the attention given to "iBeacons" in the museum industry is due to the possibility of this technology providing an easy-to-implement solution for the indoor location-based solutions. This technology is truly transforming museums because, thanks to the engagement of people, it is possible to provide a wider range of relevant content and personalized services—from art descriptions to educational videos—delivered in real time and based on the exact location in the museum. Furthermore, iBeacons can be used to deliver a contextual interactive guide or self-guided tours, enable contextual interpretation, organize games, scavenger hunts, and quizzes, and obtain insights into visitors' trip patterns and behaviours.

7.2 *An Informative Digital Guide to Improve Users' Experience: The MUSE Museum*

The MUSE Museum of Trento in Italy is a high-tech museum where people can experiment with natural sciences. In line with its offering, the museum launched an interactive guide designed to provide information and content about the exhibition and answer all—or almost all—the questions that may arise during a visit. The guide, named Explora MUSE, contains more than 150 videos and lots of content such as interviews, images from the galleries, and 360° pictures. Furthermore, it interacts with the 116 iBeacons positioned in the museum, providing visitors with personalized information based on geolocalization.

The museum also offers an audio guide system that people can download on their own smartphones through an app. The app interacts with iBeacons so that users can be informed about nearby activities and outline a personalized tour based on their interests and time available. This fosters the availability of information and content, providing visitors with the opportunity to create their own routes through the museum. The app also allows for interactive and personalized content in addition to the short audio blurbs.

For each masterwork, different types of widgets provide additional content such as short explanatory texts, full-bodied in-depth information sheets, photo galleries, videos, and contextual web pages. Through the visualization system, the user can "navigate" the images with a slide of the finger and switch, for example from a picture of a dinosaur's skeleton to that of its musculature, to find out what it looked like. Similarly, the user can view 3D images of a selection of pieces and rotate them to discover and observe the most hidden details.

Finally, a Wi-Fi connection is available, allowing visitors to build his/her own personal logbooks and share the visit experience through social media. The usage of different interactive information and mediums encourages visitors to explore in unexpected ways, which changes how they interact with and interpret what is around them. Furthermore, these tools are used to minimize cultural and age barriers present in traditional exhibitions.

7.3 *Interactive Experience for Visitors: The ARTLENS Gallery*

The Cleveland Museum of Art is a great example of proximity marketing activities, as several and various initiatives have been implemented in the last years. In particular, as explained on the official website, a collection of 20 masterworks of art rotate every 24 months to provide new, fresh experiences. Also, there are 16 innovative games on Composition, Symbols, Gesture + Emotion, and Purpose.

In 2012 Gallery One opened. It is an interactive space providing a new idea of the museum—or art gallery—conceived of as a space able to bring together art and ideas and where art and ideas are connected to better forge connections between art and people, as well as to provide visitors with tools that enhance their permanent collection gallery experiences. This allows and encourages people to use the museum as a place where they can spend time learning, exploring, and having fun.

The experience consists of ten interactives: the Collection Wall, three interactives designed for children and located in Studio Play, and six interactive displays (lenses). The digital wall shows all the masterworks exposed; by touching a piece of art, the visitor can find out what it is and where it is located in the museum. The touch screens allow visitors to discover information about related artwork placed nearby, as well as to engage in unique interactive activities. Visitors also have the opportunity to have interactive viewpoints by viewing the back of a bowl or zooming in on a painting. The six interactive stations, known as "lenses", apart from usual touchscreen technology, also use gesture-sensing projection systems to provide immersive experiences.

In addition, a museum-wide app, ArtLens, is connected to more than 240 iBeacons located throughout every gallery in the museum to ensure the accuracy of description without a paper map. The themes can be changed dynamically by the museum, and the visitors can shape their own individual tours and better understand the artwork through augmented reality and interactive real-time maps. They can also share it through pictures and collages uploaded thanks to commands named Express Yourself, Strike a Pose, and Become an Artwork in ArtLens Exhibition. Moreover, a selection of barrier-free digital and interactive activities makes the offer inclusive and responsible.

In sum, the Gallery provides an engaging environment for visitors with all levels of knowledge of art, promotes major exhibitions, and encourages visitors' interest in themes under development for permanent collection installations, exhibitions, and educational programme development.

8 Conclusion

Today, digital and mobile technology is a significant driver shaping visiting experiences and can affect how visitors interact with the artworks and expositions. This leads to new marketing approaches to creating and providing services, such as proximity marketing, which relies on a renovated role of the consumer, who, thanks to digital tools, is now able to be actively involved in marketing initiatives.

The digital age in which we live has created an array of tools, i.e. tablets, smartphones, and applications—that are changing the visiting experience, favouring, and facilitating visitors in providing target information on arts, galleries, pieces, and so on. Mobile devices are today a constant part of everyday life and most people have a high familiarity with them, so they are properly considered as the most suitable tool to create a direct interaction between the users and the museums' context (Filip et al. 2015).

The way information and content are shared, as well as the way visitors interact with each other and with the artwork thanks to new mobile tools, is transforming museums into more attractive spaces, providing people with relevant and valuable information.

An integrated approach has been proposed based on the Nagtode's and Raghunandam's (2015) model, as well as the analysis of previous contributions.

The integrated framework is based on four elements—information, interaction, tools, and personalization—and the four pillars including people, data, processes, and contexts. It can support museum managers, in creating a different way to personalize the interaction and engagement with visitors, dynamically. To accomplish this scope, museums must acquire ongoing information about consumers' interests and preferences to shape an enhanced experience and provide target solutions to better balance and capitalize on their crossing opportunities. Indeed, through proximity marketing, museums can find a better way to integrate data, processes, people, and contexts, thereby creating a more personalized and dynamic offer for customers.

However, the real challenges still remain, and they involve both technology and human aspect of cultural service interactions. Some aspects can include the following questions: How to search and find publicly available content? How to support customers to share more information? How ongoing adapt offerings to the personal preferences, as well as to the current context (location, social, temporal elements etc.) of the visitor? and, most importantly, How to narrate it and create a coherent, continuous experience over time?

Future studies will be useful for tracing the evolution of such an approach, both concerning the tools adopted and the initiative implemented and for the way in which consumers are involved and their visiting experiences are enhanced.

References

Abowd GD, Dey AK, Brown PJ, Davies N, Smith M, Steggles P (1999) Towards a better understanding of context and context-awareness. In: Gellersen HW (ed) International symposium on handheld and ubiquitous computing. Berlin, Springer, pp 304–307

Adomavicius G, Bockstedt JC, Curley SP, Zhang J (2013) Do recommender systems manipulate consumer preferences? A study of anchoring effects. Inf Syst Res 24(4):956–975

Agostini A, Bettini C, Cesa-Bianchi N, Maggiorini D, Riboni D, Ruberl M et al (2004). Towards highly adaptive services for mobile computing. In: IFIP working conference on mobile information systems. Springer, Boston, MA, pp 121–134

Allurwar N, Nawale B, Patel S (2016) Beacon for proximity target marketing. Int J Eng Comput Sci 15:16359–16364

Al-Shamri MYH (2016) User profiling approaches for demographic recommender systems. Knowledge Based Syst 100:175–187

Baum D, Spann M (2014) The interplay between online consumer reviews and recommender systems: an experimental analysis. Int J Electron Commerce 19(1):129–162

Bazire M, Brézillon P (2005) Understanding context before using it. In Dey A, Kokinov B, Leake D, Turner R (eds) International and interdisciplinary conference on modeling and using context. Springer, Berlin, pp 29–40

Bilolo A, Boeck H, Durif F, Levesque N (2015) The impact of proximity marketing on consumer reactions and firm performance: a conceptual and integrative model. In: Twenty-first Americas conference on information systems, Puerto Rico, pp 1–8

Bowen S, Li Q, Guo Y, Li G (2019) Research of context awareness based accident prevention during mobile phone use. In: 12th EAI international conference on mobile multimedia communications, mobimedia 2019. European Alliance for Innovation (EAI)

Burke R, O'Mahony MP, Hurley NJ (2015) Robust collaborative recommendation. In: Ricci F, Rokach L, Shapira B, Kantor P (eds) Recommender systems handbook. Springer, Boston, MA, pp 961–995

Carson D, Gilmore A (2000) Marketing at the interface: not 'what' but 'how'. J Market Theory Pract 8(2):1–7

Cenderello A (2015) Study Marketing of heritage sites. Heritage Interpretation for Senior Audiences. Available at: http://www.interpreteurope.net/fileadmin/Documents/projects/HISA/HISA_Marketing_Heritage_sites.pdf

Chihani B, Bertin E, Crespi N (2011) A comprehensive framework for context-aware communication services. In: 2011 15th international conference on intelligence in next generation networks. IEEE, pp 52–57

Christou E (2006) A qualitative analysis of consumer attitudes on adoption of online travel services. Turizam: međunarodni znanstveno-stručni časopis 54(4):323–331

Clark EG (2017) Integrating consumer feedback into business marketing strategies. Doctoral dissertation, Walden University

Comerio M, Batini C, Castelli M, Grega S, Rossetti M, Viscusi G (2015) Service portfolio management: a repository-based framework. J Syst Softw 104:112–125

de Gemmis M, Lops P, Musto C, Narducci F, Semeraro G (2015) Semantics-aware content-based recommender systems. In: Ricci F, Rokach L, Shapira B, Kantor P (eds) Recommender systems handbook. Springer, New York, pp 119–159

De Mooij M (2019) Consumer behavior and culture: consequences for global marketing and advertising. SAGE, London

Din H, Wu S (2014) Digital heritage and culture: strategy and implementation. World Scientific, New York

Dinu M (2004) Fundamentele comunicării interpersonale. Editura Bic ALL, Timişoara

Doody O, Noonan M (2013) Preparing and conducting interviews to collect data. Nurse Res 20 (5):28–32

Edvardsson B, Gustafsson A, Pinho N, Beirão G, Patrício L, Fisk RP (2014) Understanding value co-creation in complex services with many actors. J Serv Manag 25(4):470–493

Engeström Y (1987) Learning by expanding: an activity-theoretical approach to developmental research. Orienta-Konsultit OY, Helsinki, Finland

Fan W, Gordon MD (2014) The power of social media analytics. Commun ACM 57(6):74–81

Fauconnier G (1997) Mappings in thought and language. Cambridge University Press, Cambridge

Franklin, D., Flaschbart, J. (1998) All gadgets and no representation make jack a dull environment. In: Proceedings of the AAAI 1998 spring symposium on intelligent environments, pp 155–160

Friedman A, Berkovsky S, Kaafar MA (2016) A differential privacy framework for matrix factorization recommender systems. User Model User Adapt Interact 26(5):425–458

Filip FG, Ciurea C, Dragomirescu H, Ivan I (2015) Cultural heritage and modern information and communication technologies. Technol Econ Dev Econ 21(3):441–459

Fuentes V, Pi NS, Carbo J, Molina JM (2006) Reputation in user profiling for a context-aware multiagent system. In: EUMAS

Fullerton S, Brooksbank R, Neale L (2019) Measuring the effectiveness of technology-based marketing strategies from the consumer perspective. Eur Bus Rev 31(6):813–830
Gilbert J (2006) On the nature of "Context" in chemical education. Int J Sci Educ 28(9):957–976
González JFA, Smith NR, Vargas-Rosales C (2015) A method for identifying multiple RFID tags in high electromagnetic interference environments. Can J Electr Comput Eng 38(4):346–352
Grudin J (2001) Desituating action: digital representation of context. Hum Comput Interact 16 (2–4):269–286
Healey MJ, Rawlinson MB (1993) Interviewing business owners and managers: a review of methods and techniques. Geoforum 24(3):339–355
Hewson C, Stewart DW (2014) Internet research methods. Wiley StatsRef: statistics reference online, pp 1–6
Ismagilova E, Slade E, Rana NP, Dwivedi YK (2020) The effect of characteristics of source credibility on consumer behaviour: a meta-analysis. J Retail Consum Serv 53
Illes E (2001) The definition of context and its implications for language teaching. Doctoral dissertation, Institute of Education, University of London
Jamali J, Bahrami B, Heidari A, Allahverdizadeh P, Norouzi F (2020) Towards the internet of things. Springer, London
Kaenampornpan M, O'neill E (2004) Modelling context: an activity theory approach. In: Markopoulos P, Eggen B, Aarts E, Crowley JL (eds) European symposium on ambient intelligence. Springer, Berlin, pp 367–374
Kenny D, Marshall J (2000) Contextual marketing: the real business in the Internet. Harv Bus Rev 7 (6):119–125
Korper AK, Holmlid S, Lia L (2018) Bridging design-driven and service innovation: consonance and dissonance of meaning and value. In: ServDes2018. Service design proof of concept, Proceedings of the service design 2018 conference, 18–20 June, Milano, Italy. Linköping University Electronic Press, no 150, pp 1130–1143
Kouyoumdjieva ST, Karlsson G (2019) Experimental evaluation of precision of a proximity-based indoor positioning system. In: 2019 15th annual conference on wireless on-demand network systems and services (WONS). IEEE, pp 130–137
Ku YC, Tai YM, Chan CH (2016) Effects of product type and recommendation approach on consumers' intention to purchase recommended products. Pac Asia J Assoc Inf Syst 8(2):1–18
Kuflik T, Lo Bue A, Stock O, Wecker AJ (2017) When will cultural heritage content creation get to the digital age? In: Adjunct publication of the 25th conference on user modeling, adaptation and personalization. ACM, pp 335–336
Lee AR, Kim KK (2018) Customer benefits and value co-creation activities in corporate social networking services. Behav Inf Technol 37(7):675–692
Lemon KN (2016) The art of creating attractive consumer experiences at the right time: skills marketers will need to survive and thrive. GfK Market Intell Rev 8(2):44–49
Lenka S, Parida V, Wincent J (2017) Digitalization capabilities as enablers of value co-creation in servitizing firms. Psychol Market 34(1):92–100
Leont'ev AN (1974) The problem of activity in psychology. Soviet Psychol 13(2):4–33
Levesque N, Boeck H (2017) Proximity marketing as an enabler of mass customization and personalization in a customer service experience. Springer, Cham
Lewi H, Smith W, Vom Lehn D, Cooke S (2019) The Routledge international handbook of new digital practices in galleries, libraries, archives, museums and heritage sites. Routledge, London
Liu G, Xiao Z, Chronopoulos A, Liu C, Tang Z (2019) A many-to-many demand and response hybrid game method for cloud environments. IEEE Trans Cloud Comput
Lo Bue AL, Wecker AJ, Kuflik T, Machì A, Stock O (2015) Providing personalized cultural heritage information for the smart region-a proposed methodology. In: UMAP workshops
Musumba GW, Nyongesa HO (2013) Context awareness in mobile computing: a review. Int J Mach Learn Appl 2(1):5

Nagtode P, Raghunandan H (2015) Integrated digital marketing: the key to understanding your customer. Tata Consultancy Services
Papandrea M, Giordano S, Vanini S, Cremonese P (2010) Proximity marketing solution tailored to user needs. In 2010 IEEE International symposium on "a world of wireless, mobile and multimedia networks" (WoWMoM), pp 1–3
Park HM, Jeon BC, Ryu D (2013) A study for context-awareness based on multi-sensor in the smart-clothing. J Inst Internet Broadcast Commun 13(3):71–78
Pavlidis G (2019) Recommender systems, cultural heritage applications, and the way forward. J Cult Herit 35:183–196
Popović H, Hromadžić H (2008) Media users: from readership to co-creators. Institute for International Relations
Prasad RV, Kumari VV (2012) A categorical review of recommender systems. Int J Distrib Parallel Syst 3(5):73–84
Quinn L, Dibb S, Simkin L, Canhoto A, Analogbei M (2016) Troubled waters: the transformation of marketing in a digital world. Eur J Market 50(12):2103–2133
Rosenbaum MS, Massiah CA (2007) When customers receive support from other customers: exploring the influence of intercustomer social support on customer voluntary performance. J Serv Res 9(3):257–270
Rubinshtein SL (1973) Problems of general psychology. Pedagogika
Sampangi RV, Hawkey K (2016) Who are you? It depends (on what you ask me!): context-dependent dynamic user authentication. In: Twelfth symposium on usable privacy and security (SOUPS)
Scuderi A, Salvetti F (2019) Digitalization and cultural heritage in Italy: innovative and cutting-edge practices. Milano, Franco Angeli
Shang J, Yu S, Gu F, Xu Z, Zhu L (2011) A mobile guide system framework for museums based on local location-aware approach. In: 2011 international conference on computer science and service system (CSSS), pp 1935–1940. IEEE
Shen L (2012) Context and text. Theory Pract Lang Stud 2(12):2663–2669
Shogren KA, Luckasson R, Schalock RL (2014) The definition of "context" and its application in the field of intellectual disability. J Policy Pract Intellect Disabil 11(2):109–116
Shpak N, Kuzmin O, Dvulit Z, Onysenko T, Sroka W (2020) Digitalization of the marketing activities of enterprises: case study. Information 11(2):109. Print of ahead
Smirnov AV, Kashevnik AM, Ponomarev A (2017) Context-based infomobility system for cultural heritage recommendation: tourist assistant—TAIS. Personal Ubiquitous Comput 21 (2):297–311
Sohail SS, Siddiqui J, Ali R (2017) Classifications of recommender systems: a review. J Eng Sci Technol Rev 10(4):132–153
Uhrich F, Sandner U, Resatsch F (2008) RFID in retailing and customer relationship management. Commun Assoc Inf Syst 13(23):219–234
Verhoef PC, Stephen AT, Kannan PK, Luo X, Abhishek V, Andrews M et al (2017) Consumer connectivity in a complex, technology-enabled, and mobile-oriented world with smart products. J Interact Market 40:1–8
Viviani M, Bennani N, Egyed-Zsigmond E (2010) A survey on user modeling in multi-application environments. In 2010 third international conference on advances in human-oriented and personalized mechanisms, technologies and services. IEEE, pp 111–116
Vlăduțescu Ș (2014) Communication environment: context/situation/framework. J Sustain Dev Stud 6(1):193–204
Vygotsky L (1979) Consciousness as a problem in the psychology of behavior. Soviet Psychol 17 (4):3–35
Wang YY, Luse A, Townsend AM, Mennecke BE (2015) Understanding the moderating roles of types of recommender systems and products on customer behavioral intention to use recommender systems. Inf Syst e Bus Manag 13(4):769–799

Whiting RH, Hansen P, Hansen P, Sen A, Sen A (2017) A tool for measuring SMEs' reputation, engagement and goodwill: a New Zealand exploratory study. J Intellect Capital 18(1):170–188

Wróblewski Ł (2017) Application of marketing in cultural organizations: the case of the Polish Cultural and Educational Union in the Czech Republic. Cult Manag Sci Educ 1:79–92

Yan Q, Zhang L, Li Y, Wu S, Sun T, Wang L, Chen H (2016) Effects of product portfolios and recommendation timing in the efficiency of personalized recommendation. J Consum Behav 15 (6):516–526

Zafari F, Gkelias A, Leung KK (2019) A survey of indoor localization systems and technologies. IEEE Commun Surv Tutorial 21(3):2568–2599

Zhouying J (2005) Globalization, technological competitiveness and the 'catch-up' challenge for developing countries: some lessons of experience. Int J Technol Manag Sustain Dev 4(1):35–46

Zhu G, Gao X (2019) Precision retail marketing strategy based on digital marketing model. Sci J Bus Manag 7(1):33–37

Zimmermann A, Lorenz A, Oppermann R (2007) An operational definition of context. In: Kokinov B, Richardson DC, Roth-Berghofer TR, Vieu L (eds) International and interdisciplinary conference on modeling and using context. Springer, Berlin, pp 558–571

Augmented Servicescape: Integrating Physical and Digital Reality

Cristina Caterina Amitrano, Tiziana Russo Spena, and Francesco Bifulco

Abstract This chapter goes in-depth in the analysis of the museum servicescape and discusses it as a new combination of physical and virtual contexts (i.e. mixed reality), including multiple dimensions of visitors' interactions. The chapter proposes a conceptual model of the augmented museum servicescape to analyse how organisations face the increasing complexity in design the customer experience in the cultural heritage sector by integrating multisided aspects of digital and physical contexts. The physical, social, and emotional dimensions are integrated and designed to activate users' roles in an augmented designed environment. Through technologies, servicescape can help users to be guided better by their choices and times, increase their engagement within the virtual exploration, and improve their content understanding through direct and augmented experience.

1 Introduction

Digital technologies are increasingly attracting the attention of business and service scholars, especially in relation to their role in facilitating interactions among actors (e.g., B2C, B2B, C2C) and intensifying customer engagement (Maslowska et al. 2016). In detail, the customer experience appears to be enhanced through the personalisation and interactivity allowed by digital technologies, and the results of

C. C. Amitrano (✉)
PoliS-Lombardia, Milan, Italy
e-mail: cristina.amitrano.bds@edu.polis.lombardia.it

T. Russo Spena
Department of Economics Management Institutions, University of Naples Federico II, Naples, Italy
e-mail: russospe@unina.it

F. Bifulco
Department of Humanities, University of Naples Federico II, Naples, Italy
e-mail: fbifulco@unina.it

T. Russo Spena, F. Bifulco (eds.), *Digital Transformation in the Cultural Heritage Sector*, Contributions to Management Science,
https://doi.org/10.1007/978-3-030-63376-9_9

their use emerge in the form of higher levels of satisfaction and engagement (Parise et al. 2016).

The impacts of these technologies are analysed by scholars from different perspectives. One of these perspectives is the changes and challenges that digital technologies open up to service design (Patrício et al. 2011; Trischler et al. 2018). The physical place where the interactions among actors take place, has been defined as the servicescape (Bitner 1992) and new issues have emerged with the use of the Internet and other digital technologies.

From an experiential perspective, service design has been defined as the process of "orchestrating an integrated series of clues that collectively meet or exceed people's emotional needs and expectations" (Berry et al. 2002; p. 85). The servicescape represents anything in the service experience that can be perceived or sensed by customer in his/her interactions with brands, thus triggering customers' feelings and experiences (Haeckel et al. 2003).

The conditions enabling customer experiences involve the main concept or activity of the experience itself and the context in which experiences occur; furthermore, new technologies and the multiple touchpoints they convey represent recent important aspects for actual service design processes (Harris and Goode 2010).

Physical dimensions were widely investigated in service-design literature in the 1990s, followed by an increasing interest in the social dimensions. In the last years, the servicescape topic has been almost set aside in order to pay attention to digital technologies and their use. The concept of servicescape reappeared only in the twenty-first century (Nilsson and Ballantyne 2014) with a deeper detail in digital services (Ballantyne and Nilsson 2017) and as a call for research for further analysis. E-service design issues are analysed mainly from a theoretical perspective through the use of examples from cases, looking at the differences in this "disruptive" evolution (Ballantyne and Nilsson 2017). Among these studies, the retail industry is the one that has gained more attention (Moorhouse et al. 2018).

During the last decades, several cultural spaces, like museums and art exhibitions, have also offered mobile ICT tools to visitors to extend the boundaries of the customer visit (Kuflik et al. 2015), and computer science and technology are widely considered as disciplines that can support the visiting experience, thereby creating beneficial visitor relationships (Camurri and Volpe 2016). With the rapid diffusion of digital technologies, these trends are likely to continue and grow, but few contributions have paid attention to the link between the real and digital service context in cultural heritage design from a more integrated and strategic perspective. The increasing use of digital technologies in larger business (Parise et al. 2016; Willems et al. 2016) means that customers often form their experiences based on an integrated physical and digital context (Ballantyne and Nilsson 2017) made up of multiple and fragmented channels—i.e. websites, mobile, laptop, and stores. However, most of the recent studies in the cultural heritage sector still focus strictly on the digital environment as a different aspect of cultural service provision. The purpose of this chapter is to analyse, in depth, the museum servicescape in a new mixed-reality era, including multiple interactions between physical and virtual dimensions of visitor interactions. Specifically, the chapter proposes a conceptual model to analyse how organisations face the increasing complexity of managing the customer experience in heritage by integrating multi-sided aspects of digital and physical space of the cultural service provision.

This chapter starts with a literature review on the emerging issues in the servicescape and the roles of virtual and augmented realities in service management design, with a focus on the contributions concerning cultural heritage and cultural service experience. Then, the design of museum servicescape and its link with experience co-creation is further analysed using illustrative case studies. The emerging elements allow for the proposing of a conceptual model of the augmented museums servicescape, with the integration of more traditional and newly emerging technologies features. Finally, implications and conclusions are presented.

2 Servicescape: Interactive and Social Dimensions

The servicescape has traditionally been considered a specific stage of the new service development processes (Edvardsson et al. 2010). The importance of the servicescape in the service marketing literature started with the works of Baker (1987) and Bitner (1992), who stated the relevance of the service environment. Baker (1987) identified three dimensions, namely ambient, design, and social, while Bitner (1992) coined the term "servicescape" and proposed a framework for the analysis of the environmental dimension with the ambient conditions, spatial layout, and signs, symbols, and artefacts. The latter considered the service environment as space where value is simultaneously produced and consumed, especially looking at the influences on customers' responses (i.e. cognitive, emotional, and physiological). The analysis of servicescape has been focused on the effects on both customers' expectation and satisfaction. The first can be unintentionally lower in servicescape where providers have paid less attention to the design of layout and signals or temperature and air quality. At same time, the latter can be higher in servicescape that positively influences customers' service experience (Nilsson and Ballantyne 2014).

The seminal work by Bitner (1992) was further developed by service scholars to expand the framework based only on physical elements. In detail, the specification of five dimensions concerning the environmental variables in retail contexts was introduced by Turley and Bolton (1999). They identified external variables, general internal variables, layout and design, point of purchase and decoration, and human variables. Then, Rosenbaum and Massiah (2011) extended Bitner's model with the addition of another three dimensions besides the environmental one, namely the social, socially symbolic, and natural dimensions of servicescape. The importance of this evolution is related to the understanding of the servicescape as something that providers could not totally manage and delineate following their certainties and ideas of customers' preferences.

However, many other studies focus on the role of technologies and the new perspective on service design (Ballantyne and Nilsson 2017). The focus shifts from a firm-based design approach—an orderly process with a focus on organisation, quality outcomes, and efficient delivery—to an approach recognizing the interactive and experience value-laden dimension of service design (Stuart and Tax 2004). The Service Experience Blueprint (SEB) (Patrício et al. 2011) was presented as a useful technique to deal with some of the new technology challenges. It concerns an interdisciplinary method for the development of technology-enabled service, based on the choice of the best mix of channel interactions leading the customer experience. Further, these scholars identified the design of the service encounter as the third level of an advanced design model—also including the design of the service concept and of the service system—where firms identify the salient moments of the interaction setting, the interaction process, and the role of each participant for each moment. Service design literature recognized that organisations create conditions enabling customers to have the desired experiences. Firms cannot design customer experiences; they can only design the service context for customer experiences (Patrício et al. 2011). The concept of servicescape started to be considered as complex and it is of interest to different disciplines—marketing, psychology, sociology, and humanistic geography (Rosenbaum and Massiah 2011). It addressed the importance of the relationships between people and the surrounding context as "the environment is comprised of contextual, physical and social elements" (Tombs and McColl-Kennedy 2003; p. 448).

Edvardsson et al. (2010) define social servicescape as the relationship between customers and customers, employees and employees, and customers and employees. Johnstone (2012) includes another point: that the social dimension of the servicescape embraces the customers' relationship with the place itself. Johnstone reinforces the idea that social interactions shape the customers' experiences, as it is not the place itself that matters to consumers but the relationship that customers have with the place.

The growing relevance of the context and the idea of it as socially embedded led to a perspective more oriented towards the social service experience, recently highlighted by Nilsson and Ballantyne (2014). They show how service logic is increasingly focused on the role of context in shaping value creation processes (Chandler and Vargo 2011) but without considering it as a physical environment: "the individually and socially constructed meaning of physical place is overlooked" (Nilsson and Ballantyne 2014; p. 376). This social service experience perspective has grown even more in recent studies in which scholars seek to connect and integrate the more physical servicescape (Bitner 1992) with the social servicescape—originally identifiable in Baker's model (1987) and coined by Tombs and McColl-Kennedy (2003)—looking at human density and "the effects of density on consumers' perceptions of the interpersonal aspects of the service" (Hanks et al. 2017; p. 36).

The traditional concept of designing the individual service elements, such as a servicescape or a service encounter at a single point in time, is not more suitable to address the more dynamic and holistic process of interactions between the customers and the service organisation (Zomerdijk and Voss 2010).

3 Digital Servicescape and Emergent Technologies: Virtual and Augmented Reality

Recently, studies on the servicescape have been further developed in relation to the analysis of the impacts of digital technologies on service experience. The contributions started with the study on Internet-based technologies and the related e-servicescape (i.e. electronic servicescape with the online environment factors of Internet websites), focusing on the identification of the main dimensions (i.e. aesthetic appeal, layout and functionality, financial security) and the links to trust and purchase intentions (Harris and Goode 2010), as well as on the analysis of the salient attributes from online shoppers' perspective (Lai et al. 2014). This emerging field of study and the growing importance of the digital technologies reached its peak with the definition of digital servicescape as "interactive digital space in which the customer might be engaged through their smartphone, or a 'mouse click', or through the agency of a supplier generated avatar-presenter, or a participant-generated avatar-persona" (Ballantyne and Nilsson 2017; p. 233).

However, the emergence of the digital era is related to the development of different types of digital technologies. Among them, special interest is devoted to the so-called emergent technologies (Moorhouse et al. 2018) that can be categorised through the *virtuality continuum* from additional information in the physical environment through augmented reality (AR) to virtual reality (VR) that is characterised by all simulated cues. Starting the analysis from virtual technologies, the first VR machine was developed during the 1960s and was followed by head mounted displays (HMD), while the commercialisation of VR devices started in the 1980s (Poppe et al. 2017). In the 1990s, this technology gained the attention of business scholars with the first articles in journals such as *Technological Forecasting and Social Change* or *Internet Research-Electronic Networking Applications and Policy*. Service scholars usually used virtual technologies to study real phenomena such as consumers' attitudes towards online retail (Algharabat et al. 2017) or brand choices (Bigné et al. 2016). Therefore, it appears that virtual reality has not frequently been considered something that must be integrated within the more traditional service experience—in particular the servicescape—except for a few studies looking at the use of digital in-store technologies (Pantano and Servidio 2012; Poncin and Mimoun 2014). VR has been used mainly as a tool to improve and redesign the features of an existing servicescape, with the use of a VR model to test and experiment with design solutions in order to evaluate the most adequate one before the real implementation (Kwon et al. 2015).

However, there are different ways to implement VR—e.g. HMDs, cyber gloves, glasses, cave automatic virtual environment—and among the different VR devices, mobile devices such as tablets and smartphones are widely used, as the mobile VR system "creates the illusion of participation in a simulated environment (...) by replacing real sensory signals that the user perceives with simulated sensory signals through the use of portable technology" (Poppe et al. 2017; p. 313). More in detail, the integration of mobile technologies and emergent technologies through the use of

VR (and AR) on mobile devices allows for the co-creation of the service experience and the sharing of "personalised experience to the online community" (Moorhouse et al. 2018; p. 138).

Beyond VR, the other emerging technology is the augmented reality (AR) that, together with location-based mobile apps, is considered better able to deliver "content-in-context" (Parise et al. 2016) for current customers who are always searching for useful and personalised real-time information concerning the specific context in which they are located. In the retail literature, stores are considered to be smart thanks to the development of mobile AR apps that enhance users' satisfaction and willingness to buy, and provide both hedonic and utilitarian benefits (Dacko 2016; Poushneh and Vasquez-Parraga 2017; Willems et al. 2016). Users' satisfaction through AR mobile apps is also highlighted in contributions on tourism with an additional focus on the learning experience (Moorhouse et al. 2018) and the behavioural intention to recommend the apps as affected by content, personalised service, and system quality (Jung et al. 2015). Moreover, the requirements necessary to implement successful digital marketing strategies through mobile and AR technologies have been identified by Lagiewski and Kesgin (2017) in organisational, human, and technological resources that involve all the actors.

4 Servicescape in the Cultural Heritage Context

Looking at the cultural context, service scholars have traditionally paid less attention to the various implications and evolutions of the servicescape. One of the most-focused-upon contributions was on the museum servicescape, by Forrest (2013), who applied Turley and Bolton's dimensions (1999)—i.e. external variables, general interior variables, layout and design, point of purchase and decoration, and human variables—to a museum context. However, as recently stated by Tubillejas Andrés et al. (2016), "servicescape in the performing arts has not been properly analysed, although there have been exceptions" (p. 592). In fact, in this particular type of service experience, namely the visiting experience, some of the previous studies were those conducted by scholars focused on tourism management, especially looking at the service experience in theme parks. The main contributions emerging in this research are the greater influence on visitors' overall evaluation of functional and mechanical clues of the servicescape (i.e. substantive staging) than human clues with personal and cultural elements (i.e. communicative staging) that, conversely, are more important for the intensification of visitors' behaviour (Dong and Siu 2013). Moreover, recently, Başarangil (2016) has confirmed these results underlining the significant relationships between the servicescape with both experiential quality (strictly related to "surprise") and perceived service quality.

Recently, an emerging trend in service studies has been to look at cultural contexts; this is related to the aforementioned attention on the social dimension of the servicescape in the cultural heritage sector (Tombs and McColl-Kennedy 2003). For example, Tubillejas Andrés et al. (2016) shed light on the importance of interactions in the service experience with the identification of four dimensions of the social servicescape (i.e. employees' characteristics, customers' characteristics, employee and customer interactions, and customers' interactions) and its relationship with positive emotions in the performing arts. The importance of interactions heightens even more with the growing relevance of technologies, as customers—namely visitors—can interact through digital devices and other engaging technologies, as confirmed by Ponsignon et al. (2017). The design of the customer experience in cultural contexts is an under-described phenomenon in which technologies play an important role throughout the four main areas to be considered by service providers (i.e. touchpoints, customer journey, physical environment, and social environment). The integration of participative and immersive areas in cultural contexts can be favoured and enhanced with the use of digital technologies; moreover, mobile tools can support visitors' decisions, regulate flows, and allow service providers to collect useful data to understand preferences and behaviours within a museum (Cuomo et al. 2017).

In addition, the analysis of service literature on AR and VR technologies confirms the statement by Poppe et al. (2017) that "the combination of multiple digital technologies such as VR, AR and mobile devices will re-define the way consumers learn, work, and play" (p. 327). This mixed reality in cultural contexts emerges as the result of an evolution from information technologies (e.g. digitally linked audio guides and interactive kiosks) with an increasing influence of IT dimensions in the "emotional processes (authenticity and cognitive engagement), which in turn influence learning" (Pallud 2016; p. 465), to the ongoing digital transformation with the co-creation of value in more immersive and interactive service experiences. Nonetheless, most of the studies on cultural heritage, especially on museums, have been developed by scholars belonging to the information management (Choi and Kim 2017; Pallud 2016) and engineering (Camurri and Volpe 2016; Chianese et al. 2017; Cuomo et al. 2017) fields of research, while few contributions have been developed to highlight the need to integrate museums' efforts towards mixed-reality technologies—and the servicescape—and visitors' engagement in the digital value proposition.

Looking at the information management studies, Pallud (2016) focuses on how interactive technologies such as digitally linked audio guides and kiosks are perceived by visitors and enhance their experience, while Choi and Kim (2017) underline how digital technologies in cultural tourism experiences and museums are still lacking in storytelling and personalisation. To overcome this issue, the authors propose a framework called "metaverse exhibition experience" based on the combination of the popular Bluetooth-based beacon service and head-mounted displays (HDMs) that mixes augmented reality with virtual spaces and allows for personalisation of the content. On the other hand, engineering scholars underline how technologies can be used in arts to generate mutual benefits (Camurri and Volpe 2016), and focus on the integration of digital mobile technologies and the Internet in cultural heritage through IoT (Internet of Things) sensor networks and mobile applications. That point has been analysed from both an architectural infrastructure point of view and a business intelligence perspective, looking at the huge amount of data collected through the sensors and their elaboration in order to obtain information about visitors' behaviours and obtain suggestions for the allocation of the artwork (Chianese et al. 2017; Cuomo et al. 2017).

Among the few studies on the integration of AR and VR technologies in the cultural context, we can mention Jung et al. (2016). They analyse the relationships among the use of both technologies and the four realms of the experience economy, finding that social presence positively affects visitors' experience, especially the enjoyment that, in turn, influences visitors' intention to revisit.

5 Context of Analysis

The literature review revealed that, among the different kinds of services, the concepts of servicescapes and digital technologies in the visiting experience received less attention than in retail, tourism, and leisure (e.g. theme parks, restaurants, and hotels). Trying to fill this gap, this chapter analyses cultural organisations—in particular, museums in which the growing importance of digital technologies is changing visitors' experience. Three main experiences in the museum design were selected based on the role of physical servicescape and digital technologies, such as VR and AR. They were Casa Batlló (Barcelona), the British Museum (London), and La Citè du Vin (Bordeaux), which correspond to some of the following criteria. First, they are all European museums, and second they are going to renew their role from the traditional functions of collection, exhibition, and research into an emphasis on leisure, education, aesthetic experiences, and entertainment. However, they have something different to offer from other leisure and tourism products, through unique features such as outdoor exhibitions or cultural learning experiences.

Specifically, Casa Batlló is a particular kind of museum—namely a historic house museum—ideated and created by the Catalan architect Antoni Gaudí at the beginning of the twenty-first century. In 2005, the Modernist building joined the list of UNESCO World Heritage Sites along with the other six properties that Gaudí built in Barcelona. It is visited by almost 3000 visitors a day.

The British Museum is the first national public museum in the world, founded in the eighteenth century through the donation of Sir Sloane. Since the nineteenth century, the museum has changed its configuration and expanded the building areas with the famous Great Court, the largest covered public square in Europe, and the World Conservation and Exhibitions Centre. Thanks to these continuous improvements and the wide range of activities and services offered to visitors, the British Museum attracted 6.4 million visitors in 2016 and confirmed its primacy for the 10th year as the United Kingdom's most popular visitor attraction.

La Cité du Vin is a newly created cultural centre dedicated to the culture of wine. It was inaugurated in 2016 in Bordeaux (France). Its iconic architecture hosts a permanent tour that follows a museum-like approach and other initiatives such as temporary exhibitions, events and shows, and workshops and seminars.

The analysis provides evidence of three main aspects that are traditionally related to the servicescape, as the literature shows: i.e. physical, social, and emotional dimensions. All such dimensions are investigated by understanding how technologies impact them and their related opportunities to design an augmented service experience for visitors.

6 The Augmented Museums Servicescape

The conceptual model we propose integrates the three dimensions of the servicescape—physical, social, and emotional dimensions—identified in the literature review and their composing elements, recognised thanks to the illustration of the three case studies.

6.1 Role of the Physical Dimension

A museum's value relies greatly on its physical appearance and the layout of its collections; the service aspect is emphasised, as the offered product is usually intangible. The physical evidence includes, among others, the design of the place, the decor, and the atmosphere created by the service organisation. The importance of the physical environment and spaces in the museum is central to cultural service provision, as they may elevate the value received by the visitors. In this regard, the actual panorama of interactive technologies is increasingly used in the physical space of the museums' exhibitions, and these institutions are designing digital installations and utilising virtual media interactions to enhance visitors' experience, promoting positive relations between them and their publics.

The continuous improvements and transformation of the physical experience by the British Museum represent a typical example in this sense. The complete restyling and refreshment of the buildings and rooms have gone hand in hand with the development of smartphones and tablet PCs, which have had a feature reasonably prominently in the museum strategies. Navigation within the museum and exploration of the collection depend increasingly on mobile technology, and it has been personalised. Visitors can use their device as a complete guide, and the museum has increased its investment to ensure visitors can use their own devices.

The role of technology in transforming the physical evidence in the museum servicescape can also be traced in a recent initiative of Casa Batlló, namely the temporary exhibition "Walking with Gaudí" in Hong Kong, in the Telford Plaza shopping centre, from 12 November 2017 to 1 January 2018. This event represents a particular kind of decentralisation of some physical features of Casa Batlló's servicescape through large-scale reproductions of Gaudí's works, photographs, and explanatory videos.

La Cité du Vin has been designed to be impressive to its customers—even potential ones—with its appealing external structure that reflects the movement of the nearby river, and its visitors with the interior architecture in which curves and wood stimulate the discovery of the worlds of wine. In detail, the created atmosphere allows visitors to perceive a sense of calm, relaxation, and immersion thanks to the use of background music and lights. Moreover, this immersion feeling is balanced with the more interactive and participative spaces inside the centre, where visitors are stimulated to take action. As a cultural institution, it holds vast amounts of information. There has been a tremendous effort over the last years to make more museum data digitally available both online and on the site for everyone to access.

6.2 *Role of the Social Dimension*

Place is not viewed solely as a physical space that people inhabit within a servicescape, as the experiences consumers have in a place are shaped by the multiple kinds of interactions that the consumer can activate. The social nature of the museum environment emerges in terms of how the places or servicescapes are consumed within a social context, how visitors create an experience within it, and in relation to other people within these sites or the influence that visitors' identifications may have on directing museum choice.

The experience in the cultural centre of Cité du Vin has been designed as an autonomous and highly personalised visit during which interactions with employees and among customers are stimulated in a creative way. The visiting experience is carried out using a digital guide with a headset, which facilitate customers' exchange of opinions with other customers. Visitors are interested in sharing their impressions and feelings with other customers inside Cité du Vin, trying to help those who face difficulties and also to resolve emerging tensions in certain situations.

Another interesting perspective on interactions among visitors and between visitors and museum staff is shown in the British Museum through the initiative developed in partnership with Samsung, which created the "Samsung Digital Discovery Centre". This learning and interactive space allow visitors to explore the museum's collection through the active use of digital technologies. It is more like an innovation lab where staff help visitors who interact with each other in the testing of new tools developed for the enhancement of visitors' experiences.

The social dimension of the servicescape has also been further developed through the use of social networks that allow for the passage from live social interactions to online relationships among visitors and between visitors and the museums. In 2018, Casa Batlló tried to take advantage of all the engaging functions offered by Facebook with the uploading and sharing of panoramic photographs, 360° photos and videos, and live telecasts. In particular, the latter allows users to interact, add comments, and ask questions in real time, favouring the co-creation of value, as happened with #GaudíLive for the artist's anniversary. Previously, a focus on the active participation of visitors besides Facebook users was stimulated through the creation of contests, especially photographic ones on Instagram and Twitter, from 2012 to 2017.

The relevance of the social dimension in the meaning of online interactions is confirmed by the "share" option of the audio guide of the British Museum, launched at the end of 2015 and sponsored by Korean Air. The guide allows visitors to publish what they are listening to on social networks such as Facebook, Twitter, Tumblr, Google+, and Pinterest, and via email. Further, visitors can create a digital souvenir of the entire visiting experience through the "My visit feature", which collects the listened-to tracks and the various stops and allows the visitor to send them via email. The online interactions are also confirmed by the sharing initiatives proposed by the museum to its audience with broadcasts on Facebook Live, 360° videos, and Instant Articles, as well as the combination of images and videos on Instagram Stories, with an average of 30,000 views for each story.

The use of social media, especially social networks, is prevalent at La Cité du Vin, which uses social media to promote its initiatives and create stronger interactions with potential customers. This took place with the idea of a "gift" to spread information about the museum's permanent tour and encourage the visiting experience, as well as with the promotion of free events such as conferences and workshops.

6.3 Role of the Emotional Dimension

The increasing use of digital technologies in museums promote the enforcement of the emotional dimension of the servicescape. Technology can be used to create and support new forms of service exchange and participation as well as to shape the processes of service use by impacting visitors' interpretation and understanding.

Casa Batlló seeks to reach the aim of explaining Gaudí's imagination and all the intrinsic meanings of the architectural elements to visitors through the implementation of various digital technologies. First, on the museum's official website, users can take a virtual tour of the building, looking for allusions to nature and special combinations of colours and materials—i.e. stone, glass, and ceramic. The implemented VR technology is easy to use, starts quickly without specific technical requirements, and offers different tools, such as zoom, directions, and rotations. In addition, it contains the floor plan, enabling easy and quick movement throughout the house. This first step in attracting and emotionally engage visitors is strengthened for those users who decide to visit the museum through the development of a mobile app that integrates traditional and indirect AR, integrated into a smartphone that is provided to visitors, along with headphones, at the beginning of the visit. This service is included in the entrance fee and available in 11 languages.

The British Museum has developed initiatives for both interactive digital technologies and VR. Different exhibitions have been set up with the support of technologies, such as displays and 3D visualisations, through auto-playing animations or interactive touchpads. Such has been the case with the recent exhibition

"Ancient Lives, New Discoveries", which is about mummies. Moreover, VR has been widely implemented with two main initiatives. Firstly, since 2015, the partnership with the Google Cultural Institute and its project "Google Arts & Culture" has allowed for the exploration of the British Museum in a virtual tour and the experience of 25 stories and 6802 digitalised elements. The second and most recent initiative started in spring 2017; it is a new and immersive experience within the museum using a VR headset, enabled by collaboration with the company Oculus.

The widespread use of displays is more evident in La Cité du Vin, where technologies enable emotional interactions and visitors' participation during the service experience. In detail, this particular kind of museum has no collections or objects but is made up of themed areas full of digital maps, touch tables, and interactive games that let visitors carry out virtual activities. The museum proposes a platform able to integrate cultural information, including real-time information allowing users to access the stored information from a database while recalling other real-time information from an external source, produced by the gamification activated and running under the platform. These participative areas are balanced with the more immersive ones, in which other types of technologies, such as large mural screens and video projections, permit a more relaxing service experience with fewer physical actions than the interactive areas. There are possibilities for users to select and follow their own storyline or pathway inside the virtual exploration. This allows visitors also to unveil the stories associated with the cultural elements presented in museum, and to contextualise them in the period of their physical visit.

7 Discussion

This chapter conducts an in-depth analysis of the role that the servicescape plays in museums and how new technologies prompt towards a complex integration between physical, social, and emotional dimensions at the basis of its design.

Specifically, the illustration of the case studies has enabled the identification of three main aspects—namely, the physical, social, and emotional dimensions—and the discussion of the main features of each element. Based on these aspects, the proposal of an integrated framework is also advanced to stress how the servicescape in cultural heritage services must move towards a broader configuration of the environmental space (Fig. 1). The augmented servicescape seems to benefit from the application of digital technology. It prevents the digitisation of the museum from bringing with some disadvantages. For example, the physical museum to become more isolated and functionless without visitor's participation; and the audiences to lose the opportunities for sharing and communicating their viewpoint with others. From the user's point of view, the museum augmented servicescape is not to replace the traditional museum; conversely, it allows the digital information to complement the physical museum.

As shown in each case, museums pay attention to how augment their different elements of the physical dimension through technology. The British Museum is

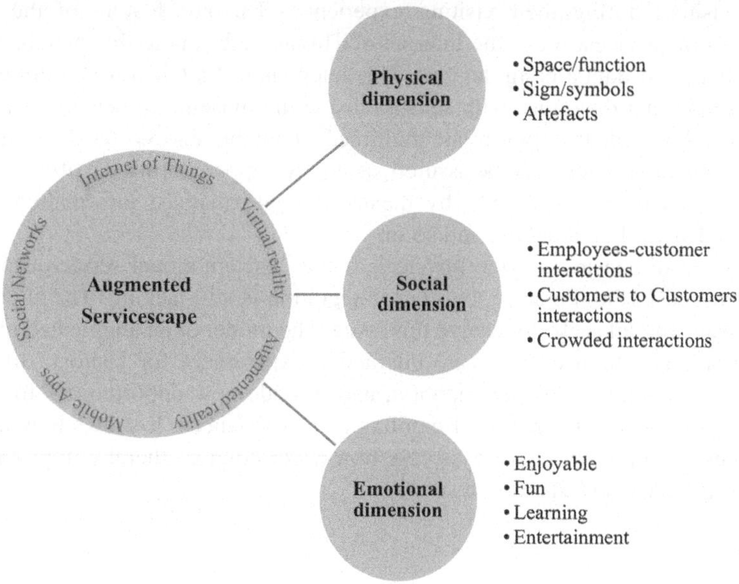

Fig. 1 The augmented museums servicescape. Source: Authors' elaboration

continually developing its space with new galleries or centres and make them easily accessible by smartphone, La Cité du Vin aims to both attract potential visitors thanks to its external structure and satisfy its visitors through opportunities to have access to a great amount of data and Casa Battlò with its particular kind of symbols through the large-scale reconstruction of physical features in decentralised temporary exhibitions. In this regard, all the cases show as the museum experience can be boosted by an interactive and immersive environment.

The investigation of the social dimension of the servicescape has shown the importance of the interactive and new technology-mediated interaction between visitors and employees in two cases, i.e. the British Museum and Casa Battló, as the latter helps visitors throughout their experience and stimulates them to participate and play active roles. A second important social feature in all three cases is visitors' interactions, as the visiting experience appears more and more to be a sharing experience offering the possibility of exchanging opinions and giving suggestions to other visitors; this is a stimulus and driver for the enhancement of visitors' own personal experiences. Such a social element is further evidenced through the importance of social media in the three museums, allowing for interaction between users and museum staff, and for interaction among users.

Finally, the increasing importance of emotional dimension is widely evident in the three case studies thanks to the element of virtual reality. Virtual tours are offered both online through websites (British Museum and Casa Battló) and on-site with headsets (British Museum) or other tools (La Cité du Vin). Another emerging digital element is the augmented reality used in Casa Battló through a mobile app that guides visitors during their visiting experience. The last feature of the digital dimension of servicescape is the Internet of Things, referring to the interconnection and exchange of data among devices. This happens in La Cité du Vin through the mobile guide that dialogues with sensors inside the museum to detect the visitor's position and provide the appropriate multimedia content. Various levels of sensorial experience's integrations can be assured, as it may happen during the observation of an artwork (real or virtualised), by means of contextualised information, audio, tactile feedback, digital actors, and so on.

The three dimensions of the physical, social, and emotional servicescape have been analysed in the literature, but their integration is still lacking. The augmented servicescape model seeks to resolve this issue. The model of an augmented museum servicescape can be used to create interactive experiences for visitors, offer new routes to engagement and participation, and provide new opportunities for visitor interpretation or understanding of exhibits and experiences. It shows how an integrated design approach provides access to a wider context, thereby improving the visitor experience and visitors' responses.

8 Conclusion

The main challenge of today's museums, as well as all other cultural heritage organisations, is to combine the three dimensions of the servicescape in response to the compelling challenges driven by both the digital transformation and the need to face visitors' expectations. An integrated model that takes into account the different dimensions would be an important tool for both academics to analyse other contexts and compare the emerging results and practitioners to delineate an innovative visiting experience. The traditional hierarchy on exposition space, contents, and visitors has been overcome in favour of a more involving immersive and multi-sensorial approach. As museums cannot expose all their collections and pieces at the same time, due to space and resources, VR and AR applications may broaden in time and space the physical museum dimension. They enable users to look at real spaces—through mobile devices—thanks to infinite possible information layers.

The physical, social, and emotional dimensions are integrated and designed to activate users' roles in a mixed-reality environment. Through technologies, users can be "guided" by their choices and times, increase their engagement within the virtual exploration, and favour content understanding through direct and augmented experience. Thus, the visitors' experience is empowered, allowing users to respect their own times and ways to approach the cultural good no forced by guides or predefined visit path. The whole museum environment may become an interactive place, reducing paper-based information in favour of more personal, intimate, and customisable exploration, to be recalled whenever users decide to. This allows a direct way visitor can knowledge through a ludic and immersive experience.

The proposed framework aims at extending the experience of Cultural Heritage through different levels of physical, social, and emotional dimensions and provides an understanding of the augmentation of museum servicescape.

References

Algharabat R, Alalwan AA, Rana NP, Dwivedi YK (2017) Three dimensional product presentation quality antecedents and their consequences for online retailers: the moderating role of virtual product experience. J Retail Consum Serv 36:203–217

Baker J (1987) The role of the environment in marketing services: the consumer perspective. In: Czepiel J, Congram C, Shanahan J (eds) The services challenge: integrating for competitive advantage. American Marketing Association, Boston, MA, pp 79–84

Ballantyne D, Nilsson E (2017) All that is solid melts into air: the servicescape in digital service space. J Serv Market 31(3):226–235

Başarangil İ (2016) The relationships between the factors affecting perceived service quality, satisfaction and behavioral intentions among theme park visitors. Tourism Hospit Res 18 (4):415–428

Berry LL, Carbone LP, Haeckel SH (2002) Managing the total customer experience. MIT Sloan Manag Rev 43(3):85–89

Bigné E, Llinares C, Torrecilla C (2016) Elapsed time on first buying triggers brand choices within a category: a virtual reality-based study. J Bus Res 69(4):1423–1427

Bitner MJ (1992) Servicescapes: the impact of physical surroundings on customers and employees. J Market 56(2):57–71

Camurri A, Volpe G (2016) The Intersection of art and technology. IEEE MultiMedia 23(1):10–17

Chandler JD, Vargo SL (2011) Contextualization and value-in-context: how context frames exchange. Market Theory 11(1):35–49

Chianese A, Marulli F, Piccialli F, Benedusi P, Jung JE (2017) An associative engines-based approach supporting collaborative analytics in the internet of cultural things. Future Generat Comput Syst 66:187–198

Choi HS, Kim SH (2017) A content service deployment plan for metaverse museum exhibitions—Centering on the combination of beacons and HMDs. Int J Inf Manag 37(1):1519–1527

Cuomo S, De Michele P, Piccialli F, Galletti A, Jung JE (2017) IoT-based collaborative reputation system for associating visitors and artworks in a cultural scenario. Expert Syst Appl 79:101–111

Dacko SG (2016) Enabling smart retail settings via mobile augmented reality shopping apps. Technol Forecast Soc Change 124:243–256

Dong P, Siu NYM (2013) Servicescape elements, customer predispositions and service experience: the case of theme park visitors. Tourism Manag 36:541–551

Edvardsson B, Enquist B, Johnston R (2010) Design dimensions of experience rooms for service test drives: case studies in several service contexts. Manag Serv Qual Int J 20(4):312–327

Forrest R (2013) Museum atmospherics: The role of the exhibition environment in the visitor experience. Visit Stud 16(2):201–216

Haeckel SH, Carbone LP, Berry LL (2003) How to lead the customer experience. Market Manag 12 (1):18–23

Harris LC, Goode MM (2010) Online servicescapes, trust, and purchase intentions. J Serv Market 24(3):230–243

Hanks L, Line N, Kim WGW (2017) The impact of the social servicescape, density, and restaurant type on perceptions of interpersonal service quality. Int J Hosp Manag 61:35–44

Johnstone ML (2012) The servicescape: the social dimensions of place. J Market Manag 28 (11–12):1399–1418
Jung T, Chung N, Leue MC (2015) The determinants of recommendations to use augmented reality technologies: the case of a Korean theme park. Tourism Manag 49:75–86
Jung T, tom Dieck MC, Lee H, Chung N (2016) Effects of virtual reality and augmented reality on visitor experiences in museum. In: Inversini A, Schegg R (eds) Information and communication technologies in tourism. Springer, New York, pp 621–635
Kwon RH, Kim KJ, Kim KH, Hong YS, Kim B (2015) Evaluating servicescape designs using a VR-based laboratory experiment: a case of a Duty-free Shop. J Retail Consum Serv 26:32–40
Kuflik T, Wecker AJ, Lanir J, Stock O (2015) An integrative framework for extending the boundaries of the museum visit experience: linking the pre, during and post visit phases. Inf Technol Tourism 15(1):17–47
Lagiewski R, Kesgin M (2017) Designing and implementing digital visitor experiences in New York State: the case of the Finger Lakes Interactive Play (FLIP) project. J Destination Market Manag 6(2):118–126
Lai KP, Chong SC, Ismail HB, Tong DYK (2014) An explorative study of shopper-based salient e-servicescape attributes: a means-end chain approach. Int J Inf Manag 34(4):517–532
Maslowska E, Malthouse EC, Collinger T (2016) The customer engagement ecosystem. J Market Manag 32(5–6):469–501
Moorhouse N, tom Dieck MC, Jung T (2018) Technological innovations transforming the consumer retail experience: a review of literature. In: Jung T, tom Dieck MC (eds) Augmented reality and virtual reality—empowering human, place and business. Springer, London, pp 133–143
Nilsson E, Ballantyne D (2014) Reexamining the place of servicescape in marketing: a service-dominant logic perspective. J Serv Market 28(5):374–379
Pallud J (2016) Impact of interactive technologies on stimulating learning experiences in a museum. Inf Manag 54(4):465–478
Pantano E, Servidio R (2012) Modeling innovative points of sales through virtual and immersive technologies. J Retail Consum Serv 19(3):279–286
Parise S, Guinan PJ, Kafka R (2016) Solving the crisis of immediacy: how digital technology can transform the customer experience. Bus Horiz 59(4):411–420
Patrício L, Fisk RP, Falcão e Cunha J, Constantine L (2011) Multilevel service design: from customer value constellation to service experience blueprinting. J Serv Res 14(2):180–200
Poncin I, Mimoun MSB (2014) The impact of "e-atmospherics" on physical stores. J Retail Consum Serv 21(5):851–859
Ponsignon F, Ponsignon F, Durrieu F, Durrieu F, Bouzdine-Chameeva T, Bouzdine-Chameeva T (2017) Customer experience design: a case study in the cultural sector. J Serv Manag 28 (4):763–787
Poppe E, Gilgen D, Safrudin N (2017) Virtual reality goes mobile in the digital age. In: Oswald G, Kleinemeier M (eds) Shaping the digital enterprise. Springer, Cham, pp 309–330
Poushneh A, Vasquez-Parraga AZ (2017) Discernible impact of augmented reality on retail customer's experience, satisfaction and willingness to buy. J Retail Consum Serv 34:229–234
Rosenbaum MS, Massiah C (2011) An expanded servicescape perspective. J Serv Manag 22 (4):471–490
Stuart FI, Tax S (2004) Toward an integrative approach to designing service experiences: lessons learned from the theatre. J Oper Manag 22(6):609–627
Tombs A, McColl-Kennedy JR (2003) Social-servicescape conceptual model. Market Theory 3 (4):447–475
Trischler J, Zehrer A, Westman J (2018) A designerly way of analyzing the customer experience. J Serv Market 32(7):805–819

Tubillejas Andrés B, Cervera-Taulet A, Calderón García H (2016) Social servicescape effects on post-consumption behavior: the moderating effect of positive emotions in operagoers. J Serv Theory Pract 26(5):590–615

Turley LW, Bolton DL (1999) Measuring the affective evaluations of retail service environments. J Prof Serv Market 19(1):31–44

Willems K, Smolders A, Brengman M, Luyten K, Schöning J (2016) The path-to-purchase is paved with digital opportunities: an inventory of shopper-oriented retail technologies. Technol Forecast Soc Change 124:228–242

Zomerdijk LG, Voss CA (2010) Service design for experience-centric services. J Serv Res 13 (1):67–82

Digital Targeted Communication: An Integrated Approach

Roberta Gargiulo, Francesco Bifulco, and Tiziana Russo Spena

Abstract This chapter deals with digital communication by addressing how, through new digital infrastructure, companies multiply opportunities for information resources accessibility and sharing and customer's co-creative participation. The new cultural heritage audiences grow up through new communication strategies aimed at producing different kinds of digital content (e.g., blog posts, videos, and photos). These create the ability to share and reproduce collections and atmosphere across digital and physical spaces with high and active customer participation. New forms of personalized and targeted communication have moved from businesses "pushing" content toward consumers to consumers "pulling" content.

1 Introduction

Since the 1990s, the Internet and ICT have been big accelerators of innovation. The report "Digital in 2018" revealed that the number of Internet users worldwide (with 195 countries analyzed) has surpassed the threshold of four billion people (Report 2018). This means that today over half (53%) of the world's population is online. The percentage of Internet users has increased by 7%, while the percentage of social media users has increased by 13% and the percentage of mobile users has increased by about 20%. The growth does not stop. As a consequence, audience engagement and communication have profoundly changed: every day, in the world, approximately 300 billion e-mails are sent, five million posts are written, more than 500 million tweets are posted, and 20 billion webpages are viewed.

R. Gargiulo (✉) · T. Russo Spena
Department of Economics Management Institutions, University of Naples Federico II, Naples, Italy
e-mail: roberta.gargiulo2@unina.it; russospe@unina.it

F. Bifulco
Department of Humanities, University of Naples Federico II, Naples, Italy
e-mail: fbifulco@unina.it

T. Russo Spena, F. Bifulco (eds.), *Digital Transformation in the Cultural Heritage Sector*, Contributions to Management Science,
https://doi.org/10.1007/978-3-030-63376-9_10

In this panorama, museums have begun a long process to adjust themselves to these new dynamics. Museums are changing and becoming collective communities that use new languages to dialog with the audience, co-create and share information and activities with them (Bonacini 2012). To satisfy audience expectations, cultural organizations are developing innovative techniques (e.g., gaming, contests on social media, and innovative audio and video guides) to engage users with emotional involvement and not merely provide them with notions about works of art or exhibitions.

In this way, through its infrastructure, digital communication, has multiplied the opportunities for participation, exchange, and accessibility. Today, to reach new audiences, museums have started to produce different kinds of digital content (blog posts, videos, photos, etc.) that they use to share collections and spaces with users to facilitate participative storytelling, through which both museums and users narrate stories about the organization and what it represents. With the advent of social media, personalized communication has moved from businesses "pushing" content toward consumers to consumers "pulling" content themselves. Digital and personalized communication has started to emerge as a new communication approach based on tailoring messages to both achieve business goals and target audiences (Hausmann 2012). In this way, communication can be created and delivered through multiple physical and digital touchpoints.

Consumers have started to become content creators and curators. The rapid growth of social curation communities like Pinterest—where consumers curate their own collections of products—provides businesses with access to deeper insights in near real time—something with which traditional market research simply could not compete.

Looking at the state-of-the-art regarding digital communication, scholars' attention is specifically on three items that allow digital communication to be targeted and customized. The first aspects include eWOM (electronic word of mouth) communication based on platforms, also known as "virtual worlds" (Libai et al. 2010; Hennig-Thurau et al. 2010), which are easily accessible by everyone and, thus, are among the most influential information sources on the web (Abubakar and Ilkan 2016). Then the process of co-creation of content is called into focus. This is different from eWOM because users not only convey content but also create it (Knoll 2015) between companies and customers through UGC (user-generated content) as a new key to customer engagement and participation. Finally, DS (digital signage) is a new marketing tool, i.e., a digital version of the traditional billboard, that, thanks to its versatility, offers a variety of digital devices, is used by numerous industries for different purposes, and can convey different kinds of messages (Wilkinson and Kolodzy 2012). These devices aim to blur the boundaries among the physical and digital worlds and provide a more integrated approach toward targeted communication.

While the topic of digital communication is addressed in the literature, the approach is to consider these aspects individually. The same fragmented situation is found in looking at these concepts in a cultural heritage context: Few studies analyze the three items in-depth in the cultural environment and, even more, there is not a clear boundary among the elements. The museum is presented as just one example of an institution that can make use of digital communication.

This chapter aims to describe how the communication strategy is being changed with the advent of digital technologies through the elements of digital communication. Specifically, it analyses the impact of these changes in a cultural heritage context, using illustrative use cases that provide tools for studying real-life situations and provide better insights into the details of the subjects of interest. In the end, a holistic digital communication model based on the integrations among multiple communication tools and content (eWOM, UGC, DS) dropped in the cultural heritage context is presented and discussed their main practical implications.

2 From Word of Mouth to eWOM

2.1 Word of Mouth

Before the advent of digital communication, there were traditional channels of communication such as TV, radio, and newspapers. To these mass communication channels must be added word of mouth (WOM), a means of social communication that is the oldest and still one of the most effective methods of disseminating information. Rui et al. (2010) stated, "Word-of-mouth (WOM) is the oldest and probably one of the most important channels of information diffusion among people" (p. 2). In this general context, scholars studied how word of mouth, compared to traditional communication channels, influences consumer choices. It has been confirmed that WOM can affect purchase decisions, customer equity, and organizational attractiveness. Throughout the years, many definitions of WOM have arisen: Some of the earliest definitions were introduced during the 1966 by Katz and Lazarsfeld, who described WOM as the exchanging of marketing information between consumers in such a way that it plays a fundamental role in shaping their behaviors and in changing attitudes toward products and services. Arndt (1967) suggested that WOM is a person-to-person communication tool, between a communicator and a receiver, who perceives the information received about a brand, a product, or a service as noncommercial or as face-to-face communication about products or companies between those people who are not commercial entities.

Later, in 1987, Westbrook gave a broader definition of WOM, including all informal communications directed at other consumers about the ownership, usage, or characteristics of particular goods and services or their sellers. Even if he did not specifically define what constitutes "informal communications," his statement clearly indicated that this kind of communication is based on interpersonal relationships, in opposition to those that pass product knowledge from producers/providers to consumers through mass media channels such as advertising. In 1991, Herr et al. described WOM communication as "unmediated communication among consumers, or face-to-face communication." This definition was recovered by Sweeney et al. many years later, in 2008. Over a decade ago, WOM was defined as informal,

Table 1 WOM definitions

Authors	Definition
Katz and Lazarsfeld (1966)	"the exchanging of marketing information between consumers in such a way that it plays a fundamental role in shaping their behaviours and in changing attitudes toward products and services"
Arndt (1967)	"a person-to-person communication tool, between a communicator and a receiver, who perceives the information received about a brand, a product, or a service as non-commercial or as face-to-face communication about products or companies between those people who are not commercial entities"
Westbrook (1987)	"all informal communications directed at other consumers about the ownership, usage, or characteristics of particular goods and services or their sellers"
Herr et al. (1991)	"unmediated communication among consumers, or face-to-face communication"
Harrison-Walker (2001)	"informal, person to person communication between a perceived non-commercial communicator and a receiver regarding a brand, a product, an organization or a service"
Sweeney et al. (2008)	a process of personal influence, in which interpersonal communication between a sender and a receiver can change the receiver's behavior or attitude
Litvin et al. (2008)	the communication between consumers about a product, service, or a company in which the sources are considered independent of commercial influence
Jalilvand et al. (2011)	a process that allows consumers to share information and opinions that direct buyers towards and away from specific products, brands, and services
Huete-Alcocer (2017)	is both the oldest medium for sharing opinions about products or services and the one most likely to influence consumer behavior, due to the high reliability and credibility transmitted by family and friends

Source: Authors' elaboration

person-to-person communication between a perceived noncommercial communicator and a receiver regarding a brand, a product, an organization or a service (Harrison-Walker 2001). Other authors (Hawkins et al. 2004, taken up by Jalilvand et al. 2011) described WOM as a process that allows consumers to share information and opinions that direct buyers toward and away from specific products, brands, and services—a definition that was covered more widely by Sweeney et al. (2008) as an informal communication process that allows consumers to share information about products and services in general. Going more in detail, the same authors, underlined the ability of WOM to influence customers' behavior and attitude too, given by the interpersonal communication between a sender and a receiver. Traditional WOM communication includes unmediated communication among consumers, or face-to-face communication and in general the communication between consumers about a product, service, or a company in which the sources are considered independent of commercial influence (Litvin et al. 2008, Huete-Alcocer 2017) (Table 1).

2.2 Electronic Word of Mouth

The Internet and its evolving technological revolutions have changed the dynamics of WOM communication (Goyette et al. 2010), giving consumers new ways to connect. Today people can interact and share information not only with their friends or parents but also with strangers from a large, geographically dispersed population. Thanks to many technological tools, such as smartphones, and personal computers, people are always connected and can share information very quickly. Due to this digital transformation, WOM has become eWOM (electronic word of mouth or word of mouse) (Yang et al. 2012). The exchange of opinions is no longer done interpersonally (i.e., person-to-person or face-to-face) but, rather, is mediated by ICT. These new alternatives for communication have developed rapidly, thanks to the emergence of online platforms where information is shared. Today, these platforms, such as e-mail, online forums, blogs, wikis, recommendation sites, social networking sites, and virtual reality community sites, which are also known as "virtual worlds" (Libai et al. 2010; Hennig-Thurau et al. 2004, 2010) are easily accessible by everyone. That is why they are the most influential information sources on the Web (Abubakar and Ilkan 2016), for instance, in the tourism industry (Sotiriadis and Van Zyl 2013).

The literature does not propose many definitions of eWOM. The first one was provided by Hennig-Thurau et al. (2004); they emphasized the feature of digital communication as being a one-to-many conversation and indicated that customers' opinions could be positive or negative about a product or company, as in the following: "any positive or negative statement made by potential, actual, or former customers about a product or company, which is made available to a multitude of people and institutions via the internet" (p. 39).

The definition given by Litvin et al. (2008) underlined the feature of digital communication as being informal. Moreover, they focused on the usage of both a good and service. The definition includes communication between producers and consumers as well as communication between consumers themselves—both integral parts of the WOM flow as in the following: "all informal communications directed at consumers through Internet-based technology related to the usage or characteristics of particular goods and services, or their sellers" (p. 461).

Temporally, in the first case, the authors read the eWOM in a perspective way, focusing on potential customers and their opinions about not only a product but about a company too. In the second one, the authors looked at the eWOM retrospectively as a consequence of the usage of a product made by actual consumers. In any case, the second definition, has been considered one of the most comprehensive conceptions proposed in the literature (Huete-Alcocer 2017).

Starting from the very first paper on eWOM (Hennig-Thurau et al. 2004), most of these contributions are focused on products or specific kinds of services business (tourism, hospitality, etc.) Only a few studies have analyzed the marketing role of eWOM in museums, highlighting the possibilities of reaching a high number of people with lower budgets than traditional media. As Hausmann and Poellmann argued (2016), eWOM could be more effective than traditional WOM in museums because of its reach and viral effect. They conducted a study to investigate and determine the personal context, social context, and physical context of George Eastman Museum visitors. Their findings confirmed that recommendations are highly relevant to customers, especially in a social media context, and that the trustworthiness of eWOM on social media depends on the familiarity between the message sender and receiver.

Further, some empirical studies are based on TripAdvisor comments about Canada's penal history museum (Ferguson et al. 2015), the Einstein monument (Owens 2012), and the ten most reviewed museums (Zanibellato et al. 2016), which analyzed customers' positive and negative perceptions of the museum and the monument (Ferguson et al. 2015; Owens 2012) and explored, which attributes of the museum experience led customers to create positive or negative eWOM. This last aspect has been developed by Antón et al. (2018), who focused on the post-visit creation of positive or negative opinions and content, seeking to find a link between visitors' evaluation of the experience and content generation online. Finally, in 2018, Waller and Waller published a qualitative study about negative reviews on the Facebook pages of top art museums. They wanted to identify the key aspects of negative comments made on the Facebook sites and how cultural institutions are monitoring this criticism.

Exhibit 1: Use Cases

In 2017, the Museum of Modern Art of San Francisco won a contest named "museum and web" with a new mobile app. This app, named "SFMOMA," offers, in addition to innovative guided tours, geolocation, and other interesting utilities, synchronization among multiple users. Thus, it allows more people to simultaneously listen to content and share ideas and opinions in real time, favoring WOM and eWOM.

Another museum that has focused on eWOM is the Brooklyn Museum in New York. In 2016 it entered the "museum and web" contest with a new mobile app named "ASK Brooklyn Museum," which allows users to get in touch directly with a team of art historians. Through the app, and due to the proximity of sensors, art historians can locate the user and the work of art he/she is looking for, as well as answer questions and dialogue with the visitor. This innovative method of communication has been very appreciated by many visitors, who appreciate the informal tone of the conversations and the quick, detailed, and personalized answers; that is why this mobile app has received lots of positive reviews online (e.g., iTunes) and has generated a positive flow of eWOM.

2.3 WOM Versus eWOM

Apart from defining eWOM, a debate in the literature was formed about the differences between WOM and eWOM. Some scholars (Filieri and McLeay 2014) consider eWOM as an electronic version of WOM and, thus, very similar to the traditional way of communication. Other scholars (Andreassen and Streukens 2009; Huete-Alcocer 2017) think that, on the contrary, there are many differences between these two ways of communication. However, as Berger and Iyengar (2013) said, very little is known today about the differences across these channels and about how people use them because they are different in terms of capabilities and characteristics (Kaplan and Haenlein 2010; Steffes and Burgee 2009). Digital WOM, in fact, is not a homogenous concept, as it is shared through varied digital channels that fundamentally shape the way consumers interact (Marchand et al. 2017).

Several types of electronic word of mouth exist and differ regarding the number of people they connect, the time, and the mode. eWOM channels such as emails and instant messaging connect one user to another, while web pages or websites, on the contrary, connect one user to many others. Meanwhile, blogs and online communities can create a network of connected people who share interests, content, and information about a product or service to connect one to many or many to many. Another distinction is based on time: While emails or web pages/websites are asynchronous, instant messaging is synchronous; people must be connected at the same time to communicate. This is one of the first differences between WOM and eWOM, as face-to-face communication cannot be asynchronous and use one tool (the mouth) to share information and content.

Furthermore, traditional WOM based on a face-to-face dialogue is more immediate and intimate, more limited in reach (Dellarocas 2003), and less influential than eWOM (Steffes and Burgee 2009). Some features that distinguish eWOM from traditional WOM can be defined as technical features because they are directly linked to Internet properties, i.e., speed and accessibility. In this regard, eWOM is more useful and faster than traditional WOM; when someone needs information about a product or service, there is no need to wait for someone else, as you can go online with your device (smartphone, tablet, PC) and search for what you are seeking. In addition, when going online, a user can find lots of advice or reviews about the same product or service; he/she can use this information to corroborate other information he/she may have received.

Some authors (Andreassen and Streukens 2009) think that WOM and eWOM cannot be similar because of their nature. They say that "electronic dialogues are electronic by nature; there is no face-to-face communication. Rather they entail keyboard-to-keyboard communication, passive reading of a computer screen or active writing of a message" (p. 252). Further, they mentioned what Dellarocas (2003) wrote about the intimacy of face-to-face communication and noticed that while WOM takes place in a private room, eWOM takes place in public rooms. They also observed that WOM is perishable, while eWOM is stored for future reference. Finally, seeking out eWOM is, to a larger extent, more goal oriented than

Table 2 Differences between WOM and eWOM

	WOM	eWOM
Channel of communication	There is only one communication channel, which is the mouth.	Communication is spread through lots of different communication channels and technologies
Synchronism	Face-to-face communication cannot be asynchronous	Communication can be delayed in time and space
Privacy	The conversation is private, interpersonal (via dialogues), and intimate	The shared information is not private and, because it is written down, can sometimes be viewed by others
Power of communication	It is more limited in reach and less influential	It is less limited in reach and more influential
Diffusion speed	Messages spread slowly. Users must be present when the information is being shared	Messages are conveyed more quickly between users and, via Internet, can be conveyed at any time
Accessibility	It is less accessible	It is easily accessible
Nature of communication	It involves active listening and speaking	It involves passive reading and writing
Communication place	It takes place in private rooms	It takes place in public rooms
Persistence over time	Communication is perishable	Communication is stored for future reference
Trust	The receiver of the information knows the communication (positive influence on trust)	There is anonymity between the communication and the receiver of the information (negative influence on trust)

Source: Authors' elaboration on Huete-Alcocer (2017, p. 3)

experientially oriented; the consumer is actively seeking defined discussion forums and, thus, exposing himself/herself to others' experiences with specific products, services, or firms.

Another important topic for understanding the difference between WOM and eWOM is related to trust. The problem is that WOM is a face-to-face dialogue between a consumer and a friend or family member (or, at the very least, someone whom the consumer knows personally), while eWOM is communication among people who do not necessarily know each other. Moreover, users can be anonymous. Luo et al. (2013) have suggested that the anonymity of online messages could have a negative effect on trust and decision-making, and so people trust WOM more than eWOM. Table 2 summarises the main differences between WOM and eWom; it adds some integrations to the list proposed by Heute-Alcocer in 2017.

Finally, another topic concerning the disagreement among authors is the users' motivation and behavior in terms of participating in the communication process. While some authors think that this is one of the few similarities between WOM and eWOM (Hennig-Thurau et al. 2004), others do not agree; they think that consumers may be more open to eWOM because they are actively searching for the information (i.e., motivated to process the information they retrieve) (Andreassen and Streukens 2009). According to some authors, the difference also regards the quality of the information; thanks to all the digital tools that connect people anytime and anywhere, content becomes easier to upload and the quantity of eWOM information available to the digital audience increases significantly (Hennig-Thurau et al. 2010). As a result, the quality of eWOM information may decline because robust information may become a much smaller part of the overall online information resource (Gvili and Levy 2016; Levy and Gvili 2015).

3 User-Generated Content

Today, driven by technological development and rapid user acceptance, user-generated content (UGC) is becoming a new form of brand communication (Dhar and Chang 2009) and an important subject in communication studies. UGC is content made publicly available over the Internet that reflects a certain amount of creative effort and that is created outside professional routines and practices (Organization for Economic Co-Operation and Development (OECD 2007). Resuming this concept, Christodoulides et al. (2012) defined UGC as "any material that is created outside professional practices, reflects effort, and is publicized online" (p. 3), while Daugherty et al. (2008) defined it as "media content that is created or produced by the general public rather than by paid professionals and is primarily distributed on the Internet" (p. 19). The increasing number of communication channels has enabled users to be active in eWOM, generating content, e.g., product or service reviews, real-time feedback, relationship- and community-building, and receiving the same kind of information from the Internet, on virtual platforms or communities. Indeed, one of the most important differences between UGC and eWOM, which are often confused, is that while through eWOM users simply convey a message, through UGC they create the message (Knoll 2015). According to Knoll (2015), user-generated content has three main features:

- UGC must be characterized by a degree of personal contribution. Users can independently create content in different ways: receiving and reading a message (e.g., they are called "readers"; Dellarocas and Wood 2008); forwarding or "liking" a message published by other users; and uploading and creating new messages. In this last group, the author collocates opinion leaders, i.e., users whose reviews and messages are considered more reliable than others from individuals who are followers and fans (Goes et al. 2014; Kaiser and Bodendorf 2012).
- UGC must be published. Users must be able to discuss the content across society or within a group. That is why UGC must be accessible online (OECD 2007).
- UGC must be created "outside the realm of a profession and professional routines" (OECD 2007).

Some contributions to the literature (Lee et al. 2011) are about how the content of a message can affect users' behavior (e.g., purchase attitude and satisfaction). Some authors focus on the relationship between the source of a message and trust, talking about "web-of-trust" (WOT), in which users can choose to "trust" one or more other users, such that content written by the trusted user will be given higher priority when displayed (Goes et al. 2014). Other scholars (Dinçer and Alrawadieh 2017) stress that the quantity and recency of online reviews have an important effect on firms' reputations (in their studies of hotels) and that the emergence of the UGC has radically changed how users evaluate, select, and share experiences (Guo et al. 2017). In this scenario, a few authors (Goldenberg et al. 2001) focus on how UGC platforms, used to convey a positive or negative feeling about a product or experience, can influence marketing decisions and be used by firms as a key success factor to gain a competitive advantage. This is a relevant gap because UGC, social media platforms, provide the opportunity to connect with a much larger number of customers with enhanced speed. Data analysis of UGC could be very useful for firms and assist managers in predicting and projecting a better marketing strategy (Bampo et al. 2008).

Dropping the UGC concept in the cultural heritage context, there are few contributions to the literature. Camarero et al. (2018) recently have focused on museums' communication strategy through two empirical studies of the Facebook pages of 240 museums to understand how different communication strategies could affect users' engagement (first study) and how different content and relational elements could increase positive content co-creation on the web (second study). Their findings show that, to achieve more effective communication, museums must develop a strategy based on co-created content through a constant dialog with their audiences, to the point where they become involved in conversations ensuring a reciprocal engagement (museums-audience). Previously, Bonacini (2012) analyzed the relationship between user-generated content and users' loyalty to the museum: in particular, the author argued that the use of UGC can also be considered a strictly commercial practice that may influence users' satisfaction and institutional websites' traffic. Further, she stressed that UGC can improve the relationship with the audience, favoring involvement, participation, and two-way communication, and can contribute to a definitive transfiguration of the museum institution, perceived by the public as a social, dynamic, multivocal, and participatory place.

Business literature has also started to pay much more attention to the UGC phenomenon. Naiditch et al. (2017) have described, on an online platform (Museum and the Web), the phases of a UGC campaign starting from the moment when a museum asks the audience to share its experiences until this content is added to the other marketing tools in both paid and nonpaid media. This campaign, called #howdoyoumuseum, involved museum visitors and famous influencers on the same social media platforms and produced very positive results. Since February 2016, when the digital campaign was launched, more than 5500 people have shared their own UGC (photos, videos, artwork, and every type of creative content). More than 15 million users have been reached, with an increase in page traffic of over 70%. Videos have had more than 5.6 million views, with more than 100,000 views weekly.

Exhibit 2: Use Cases

In 2015, MoMA (Museum of Modern Art of New York) realized a project named "Playartfully," which consists of a series of games activated on social media that offer users the opportunity to interact with the museum by sharing photos and communicating ideas and suggestions for the improvement of the games themselves. This project has been a huge success and has generated a large amount of content shared and generated by users.

Further, the MAXXI (National Museum of Art of the XXI sec of Rome) launched a contest called "yourXXI" for the creation of the museum's new logo; photographers, graphic designers, or anyone who wanted could send their logo idea by sharing it with the dedicated hashtag #yourXII or by mentioning @museomaxxi. This museum promoted another project for the creation and publication of audio and video guides directly realized by high school students, who became mediators of the museum's cultural heritage. In addition to the project "yourXII," there are other, similar initiatives in collaboration with photographers who were allowed to enter and visit museums at special times and conditions, for the realization of new photos of those museums.

The Metropolitan Museum of Art of New York launched the contest "emptymet," realized in collaboration with Dave Krugman, an image editor and photographer of Brooklyn, that allowed users and Krugman's group of photographers to visit the museum outside of the regular schedule, to realize a series of original shots published directly on social media, thereby creating a great collaboration between the institution and its visitors. This project enabled the museum to reach new followers, increase the amount of traffic on its website, and create awareness and enthusiasm surrounding events and exhibitions.

This project was hugely successful and has been replicated by the Capitoline Museums of Rome with a similar hashtag: "emptycapitolini."

Finally, MACRO (the Museum of Contemporary Art of Rome) has promoted the "MACROego" campaign, through which users have taken and shared selfies that have enriched the museum exhibition. In this way, the users were both artists and works of art in the museum.

4 Digital Signage

Digital transformation has significantly changed communication. Today, dialogues take place in virtual rooms, with people from all over the world who can interact with other unknown users as well as with companies. This change led to the elaboration, introduction, and use of new communication channels. In our contemporary era, digital signage is becoming a more popular, profitable, and influential media channel because it can be considered versatile and its dynamic content captures the attention

Table 3 Digital signage definitions

Authors	Definition
Clarke (2003)	"screen displays located in public spaces showing video material (or private TV channels)"
Schaeffler (2008)	"Pure and simple, digital signage is an answer ... because it presents new opportunities and alternatives for (advertisers) and retailers. [...] remotely managed digital display, typically tied in with sales, marketing and advertising"
Burke (2009)	"the flat panel monitors that show a continuous loop of advertising and editorial material"
Chen et al. (2009)	"a form of electronic display that is being used extensively to advertise targeted and impacting content to large audiences at public venues such as airports, shopping malls, and universities"
Newman et al. (2010)	"screens in public places that may carry a mixture of advertising (that can be similar to national television advertising or, alternatively, more specific to local retail stores and offers) and program content such as news and entertainment"
Bauer et al. (2012)	"a networked,audiovisual information system that allows remote controlling contents—either program-driven or manually—but, in any case, from a centralized system"
Wilkinson and Kolodzy (2012)	"the use of electronic displays or screens (such as LCD, LED, plasma or projection) to deliver entertainment, information and/or advertising in public or private spaces, outside of home"

Source: Authors' elaboration

of observers (Wilkinson and Kolodzy 2012). The first definition of digital signage was proposed by Clarke (2003) and was resumed by Dennis et al. (2012). The authors generically described DS as screen displays in public spaces that transmit videos. Since 2008, almost all authors (Burke 2009; Wilkinson and Kolodzy 2012) underline the marketing opportunities offered by DS that transmit advertising, but only some of these authors (Schaeffler 2008; Bauer et al. 2012) underline the peculiar feature of DS as being remotely manipulated (Table 3).

Digital signage, sometimes known as a digital communications network (DCN) or private plasma screen network, is an effective, easily controlled communication medium. Content typically includes, e.g., advertisements, community information, entertainment, and news (Dennis et al. 2012). DS is an emerging marketing medium that uses digital formats and sometimes replaces billboards, flyers, etc. It is used both in home and out of home (digital out of home, DOOH) media. The most important advantage is that content of these displays can be, if desired, remotely manipulated thanks to SAAS (software as a service) systems (https://www.slideshare.net/ElizabethHay/digital-signage-47752829).

Further recent trends in digital signage include multi-touch, interactive kiosks, gesture recognition, autostereoscopic 3D displays, and wireless interfaces that allow targets to interact with the displayed content and that are capable of linking to smartphones (Mennecke and Peters 2013).

Digital signage is not a passive advertising message. On the contrary, it offers interactions between media, devices, and users (Valli 2008). There are two more crucial components in terms of the "relevance" of DS, i.e., the personalization of the message content and the location of the screens. Users usually prefer screens to be located in places where they have more time to watch content (e.g., waiting areas) (Newman et al. 2010). In 2009, Burke added that the degree of engagement with digital displays depends not only on the content and the context/location but on the quality of exposure. Thanks to its versatility, digital signage uses a variety of digital devices (from giant screens along the highway to modest mobile phone screens and all sizes in between), is used by numerous industries (e.g., hospitals, clinics, doctors' offices, stores and malls, theaters, restaurants, gas stations, casinos, supermarkets, hotels, airports, subway stations, taxis, along highways, and in the streets), for different purposes (e.g., to create information and to engage the audience), and to convey different kinds of messages, such as directions, coupons, schedules, art, and news (Wilkinson and Kolodzy 2012). Traditional signage has evolved into a digital and interactive medium capable of engaging users and getting their attention using an informative and entertaining dimension. Furthermore, many industries are diving into digital signage networks because they are more cost-effective ways to advertise and inform the public (Bauer et al. 2012; Wilkinson and Kolodzy 2012). In the literature, some scholars focused on consumers' affective responses to DS (Dennis et al. 2012, 2014), while few have explored the consequences of DS for retailers themselves (Roggeveen et al. 2016). Nobody focuses on how firms and managers can use digital signage to adapt their marketing and brand strategies.

Today, some museums have started exploiting the advantages offered by DS systems. The literature contains more technical studies (Baglivo et al. 2013) about the step-by-step digital signage implementation to realize a 3D cultural heritage environment that can be explored on desktop, online, and on mobile platforms. A different point of view on this topic is offered by Min et al. (2010), who designed and applied a new model of digital signage tailored to four situations in museums (before visiting, arrival, during the visit, and the end). Their model describes in detail the requirements of customers and museums in the four situations and proposes the appropriate DS strategy to adopt. Finally, other studies (Bearman and Geber 2008; Eid 2016) explored the DS contribution in museums. Bearman and Geber (2008) highlighted how, on the one hand, digital signage can make museum visits fun, interactive, and personalized, and how, on the other hand, it can offer a location-aware service able to improve the entire museum knowledge and experience. Eid (2016) considered DS a tool for the "Museum Innovation Model," which is a framework for innovation in museums that emerged as a result of research about museums in the United States and the United Kingdom, based on three concepts: open innovation, social enterprise, and social innovation.

Exhibit 3: Use Cases

Several museums decided to introduce digital displays in their spaces. It would be useful to divide them into two groups: those whose displays can be managed remotely and those whose screens cannot be remotely run.

Within the first group, we can cite the Science Museum of London, which promoted a project named "What's on Digital Signs" for the creation and distribution of interactive displays that shared information and promotional content tailored to the museum's halls, loaded and managed remotely via the museum's official website.

The Houston Museum of Natural Science in Texas carried out a similar project, called the "Houston Museum of Natural Science lobby and video wall," as did the MoMA, whose project is called the "MoMA digital sign." The latter led to the creation of interactive displays with the aim of favoring, as stated in the project's description, "internal information, menu information, advertising, brand building, influencing customer behavior, enhancing customer experience, [and] enhancing the environment." Further, the Queensland Museum in Australia, as part of its $14.3 million refurbishment program, dedicated some funds to improving the wayfinding and internal promotional capabilities of the museum (e.g., pricing promotions, upcoming and current events, and acknowledgment of the museum's benefactors) through digital signage.

The National September 11 Memorial and Museum in New York installed single screens, video walls, and interactive touchscreens, located throughout all seven floors of the subterranean museum, to feed informational and interactive content. Regarding the second group, the New York Historical Society Museum introduced displays which share content, such as information about exhibits and artists, prices, and wayfinding, while the Chrysler Museum of Art has screens that share primarily information about upcoming events and exhibitions, for which it is not specified whether the content can be remotely managed.

Finally, the Estonian National Museum carried out a project called "Estonia National Museum display network" to enhance visitors' experience in the museum. These displays are interactive to the extent that they allow users to change the language, but they are not managed remotely; in essence, they replace the traditional information panels, making them more enjoyable.

5 The Role of Credibility in the Digital Communication

Credibility is another relevant item which influences communication, as it can sometimes be an issue that is significantly increased by the advent of digital (Levy and Gvili 2015). Credibility is based on personal acquaintance, believability, and the trust relationship that exists between the message sender and receiver (Bampo et al.

2008; Keller 2007). In the digital environment, credibility is defined as "the extent to which one perceives other consumers' recommendations or reviews as believable, true, or factual or believable" (Cheung et al. 2009, p. 12 who resume Nabi and Hendriks 2003). The problem is that digital communication, in most cases, eliminates the receiver's ability to judge the credibility of both sender and message. In particular, the information is perceived as more credible if the message sender is highly identified and recognized, and the senders' credibility can be extended to all channels if this relationship becomes friendlier and of longer duration (Chu and Kim 2011). The consumer can be worried about manipulation of the message, misinformation, and intentionally misleading and out-of-context messages (Steffes and Burgee 2009). Further digital communication includes many different communication channels that are based on a variety of technologies with different features that can influence consumers' behavior and the evaluation of the channels' informativeness, entertainment, and level of irritation, which influence users' perceptions of credibility (Levy and Gvili 2015). Several features can positively influence credibility perception:

- Some channels can indicate the closeness of the connection between participants (e.g., LinkedIn displays the number of mediators between the sender and the receiver), encouraging a sense of long-lasting community and a trust-based relationship.
- The capability of some channels (e.g., social networking sites and forums) to give receivers access to senders' history of posted opinions enables receivers to judge senders' consistency and message potential reliability. Facebook, for example, keeps track of message flow as the message travels throughout a series of individuals and allows participants to track a message back to its source.
- Most forums employ moderators who oversee the communication activity and enforce rules of conduct. These capabilities of eWOM channels may increase their potential perceived credibility (Bampo et al. 2008; Keller 2007; Yang et al. 2012).
- The richness of information included in eWOM messages positively affects message credibility, as it may reduce consumer uncertainty and, in turn, increase message credibility (Hung et al. 2011; Yang et al. 2012).

Other features influencing credibility perceptions have been analyzed by Levy and Gvili (2015). These authors resumed a model realized by Brackett and Carr (2001), which introduces trust and credibility as an influencing element of consumers' behavior and message value. Additional elements impacting users' trust in the message have been considered in the model, i.e., entertainment, fun (Kaplan and Haenlein 2011; Woerdl et al. 2008), emotive content (Golan and Zaidner 2008; Lance and Golan 2006), informativeness (Dao et al. 2014; Logan et al. 2012), and annoyance (Hennig-Thurau et al. 2004). According to the authors, credibility serves as both a mediator and an antecedent of the general attitude toward eWOM and the impact on consumer behavior in the case of eWOM, because this form of communication is often created by a large number of unknown participants and, in many cases, concerns products that cannot be observed first-hand (Fan and Miao 2012).

The authors also demonstrated that a channel's informativeness and entertainment impact on eWOM have value only if they are perceived as being credible. As a result, credibility influences the user's perception of the message more than other communication features, i.e., the richness of information, the pleasure of using a website, or social networking.

While studies on credibility have confirmed the important role, it plays in users' perceptions and decisions, there are few studies on this topic in the cultural heritage context. Amin et al. (2009) investigated how displaying the credibility ratings of cultural heritage sources affects the user's confidence and time to search for information. Starting from the consideration of how the complexity of having to deal with multiple information sources can influence the user's ability to select the appropriate information, these scholars realized this empirical study analyzing multiple cultural heritage sources (e.g., museum websites and art blogs); their findings showed that when the source credibility ratings are available and explicit, people's confidence significantly increases, including for novice users (Amin et al. 2009). A qualitative study on Latvian museums published in 2014 analyzed the topic from the point of view of professionals and specialists working in different museums and confirmed that credibility is an element, which influences the entire digital communication process in the social network museum world (Lotina 2014). They started studying the different forms of online participation based on the viewpoints of professionals and specialists working in different museums. During the interviews, the topic of credibility frequently emerged, as museum specialists, based on their experiences, consider it an element that influences the entirety of digital communication in the social network museum world.

6 Discussion: The Proposal of an Integrated Approach

The analysis of the literature and the use cases presented emphasizes that companies and museums are trying to find new communication strategies to engage and involve customers, taking advantage of the possibilities offered by new digital technologies. The wider point of view on the actual digital environment includes many different communication channels that are based on a variety of technologies with different features that can influence consumers' behavior. Some of these digital channels, such as chatting and text messaging, are more immediate and intimate, while others, like social networks and online communities, create the possibility of sharing and distributing information among groups of users. Some channels allow users to recognize the source of the message and, thereby, more easily judge its credibility (Steffes and Burgee 2009), while in other channels, message senders often remain anonymous (e.g., online comment boards), which greatly affects the credibility issue. As a consequence, companies must focus not simply on how there will be differentiation in message delivery across digital channels but also on how customers perceive the messages systemically, and which are their willingness to interact and their credibility perceptions.

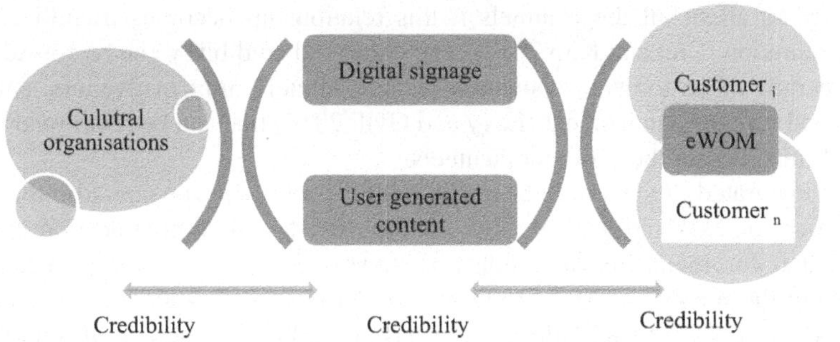

Fig. 1 Integrated digital communication approach. Source: Authors' elaboration

This observation led to the elaboration of a holistic digital communication model in which the three items are related to one another.

Digital communication can follow three directions: from the museum to the customers through digital signage, between the museum and customers through user-generated content, and among consumers through electronic word of mouth (Fig. 1). When the company is involved in the dialogue, the communication can be unidirectional or bidirectional: DS is a digital tool used unidirectionally by companies to engage customers, thereby making their visit experiences (if we consider digital signage used to provide information about the artwork and the museum's collection) or their information research (if we consider DS that provides tickets or servicescape information) easier and more enjoyable. On the other hand, UGC is communication that starts from the company, which asks consumers something about a product or service, but is bidirectional, as customers are invited to provide company answers and suggestions in a process of the co-creation of content.

In particular, about eWOM, the communication can be one to one (customer i to customer j) or one to many (customer i to customer n). eWOM influences the customer experience before, during, and after the visit to the cultural place. People who want to visit a cultural place search for information before the visit and take into account mostly other users' opinions. People who visit the cultural place usually share their experiences on digital platforms, which can generate and feed new eWOM.

Starting from these considerations, the credibility can be seen as a moderator able to enhance or decrease digital communication in all three directions: the one from the museum to the user, the one among users, and the one from users to the museum and vice versa.

Taking into account the relations and directions of communication and the crucial role of credibility, companies can find new routes to engage and involve customers in a long-term relationship, while consumers can take advantage of the dialogue with organizations and other users. Credibility is based on many-to-many communication (among people who interact on social platforms, websites, chats, etc.) from a wider point of view. In particular, the information is perceived as being more credible if the message sender is highly identified and recognized; senders' credibility can be extended to affect all the channels if this relationship becomes friendlier and of longer duration (Chu and Kim 2011). The perceived credibility can be considered as the outcome of customers' evaluation of the channels' informativeness, entertainment, and level of engagement (Levy and Gvili 2015) that can be reinforced when it is confirmed across the different channels.

The integrated model could be useful both for scholars who can drop this model into other contexts and analyze how this holistic digital communication approach works and for managers, to employ a strategy using all of these technologies following the models of MoMA, the State Hermitage Museum in St. Petersburg, or the Museo del Prado in Madrid, which have introduced to their organization charts a dedicated department that works on digital communication from a holistic approach.

References

Abubakar AM, Ilkan M (2016) Impact of online WOM on destination trust and intention to travel: a medical tourism perspective. J Destination Market Manag 5(3):192–201

Amin A, Zhang J, Cramer H, Hardman L, Evers V (2009) The effects of source credibility ratings in a cultural heritage information aggregator. In: Proceedings of the 3rd workshop on Information credibility on the web. ACM, pp 35–42

Andreassen TW, Streukens S (2009) Service innovation and electronic word-of-mouth: is it worth listening to? Manag Serv Qual Int J 19(3):249–265

Antón C, Camarero C, Garrido MJ (2018) What to do after visiting a museum? from post-consumption evaluation to intensification and online content generation. J Travel Res 75 (7):920–935

Arndt J (1967) Word of mouth advertising: A review of the literature. The advertising research foundation Inc., New York

Baglivo A, Ponti FD, De Luca D, Guidazzoli A, Liguori MC, Fanini B (2013) X3D/X3DOM, Blender Game Engine and OSG4WEB: open source visualisation for cultural heritage environments. In: Digital heritage international congress (DigitalHeritage), vol 2, October. IEEE, pp 711–718

Bampo M, Ewing M, Mather D, Stewart D, Wallace M (2008) The effects of the social structure of digital networks on viral marketing performance. Inf Syst Res 19(3):273–290

Bauer C, Dohmen P, Strauss C (2012) A conceptual framework for backend services of contextual digital signage. J Serv Sci Res 4(2):271–297

Bearman D, Geber K (2008) Transforming cultural heritage institutions through new media. Museum Manag Curatorship 23(4):385–399

Berger J, Iyengar R (2013) Communication channels and word of mouth: how the medium shapes the message. J Consum Res 40(3):567–579

Bonacini E (2012) The participatory museum on the Web: forms of user participation in cultural production and the creation of cultural value. Stud Value Cult Herit 5:93–125

Brackett LK, Carr BN (2001) Cyberspace advertising vs. other media: consumer vs. mature student attitudes. J Advert Res 41(5):23–32

Burke RR (2009) Behavioral effects of digital signage. J Advert Res 49:180–185

Camarero C, Garrido MJ, San Jose R (2018) What works in Facebook content versus relational communication: a study of their effectiveness in the context of museums? Int J Hum Comput Interact 1–16

Chen Q et al (2009) Interacting with digital signage using hand gestures. In: Proceedings of international conference on image analysis and recognition (ICIAR 2009), 6–8 July, Montreal, pp 347–358
Cheung MY, Luo C, Sia CL, Chen H (2009) Credibility of electronic word-of-mouth: informational and normative determinants of on-line consumer recommendations. Int J Electron Commerce 13 (4):9–38
Christodoulides G, Jevons C, Bonhomme J (2012) Memo to marketers. Quantitative evidence for change: how user generated content really affects brands? J Advert Res 52:53–64
Chu SC, Kim Y (2011) Determinants of consumer engagement in electronic word-of-mouth (eWOM) in social networking sites. Int J Advert 30(1):47–75
Clarke R (2003) Question: when is a retailer not a retailer? Answer: when it's a media owner. Eur Retail Digest 38:20–23
Dao WV, Le AN, Cheng JM, Chen DC (2014) Social media advertising value: the case of transitional economies in Southeast Asia. Int J Advert 33(2):271–294
Daugherty T, Eastin MS, Bright L (2008) Exploring consumer motivations for creating user generated content. J Interact Advert 8(2):16–25
Dellarocas C (2003) The digitization of word of mouth: promise and challenges of online feedback mechanisms. Manag Sci 49(10):1407–1424
Dellarocas C, Wood CA (2008) The sound of silence in online feedback: estimating trading risks in the presence of reporting bias. Manag Sci 54(3):460–476
Dennis C, Michon R, Brakus JJ, Newman A, Alamanos E (2012) New insights into the impact of digital signage as a retail atmospheric tool. J Consum Behav 11(6):454–466
Dennis C, Brakus JJ, Gupta S, Alamanos E (2014) The effect of digital signage on shoppers' behavior: the role of the evoked experience. J Bus Res 67(11):2250–2257
Dhar V, Chang EA (2009) Does chatter matter? The impact of user-generated content on music sales. J Interact Market 23(4):300–307
Dinçer MZ, Alrawadieh Z (2017) Negative word of mouse in the hotel industry: a content analysis of online reviews on luxury hotels in Jordan. J Hospit Market Manag 26(8):785–804
Eid H (2016) The museum innovation model: a museum perspective on innovation. In: Museums and the web. MW2016: museums and the web
Fan YW, Miao YF (2012) Effect of electronic word-of-mouth on consumer purchase intention: the perspective of gender differences. Int J Electron Bus Manag 10(3):175.
Ferguson M, Piché J, Walby K (2015) Bridging or fostering social distance? An analysis of penal spectator comments on Canadian penal history museums. Crime Media Cult 11(3):357–374
Filieri R, McLeay F (2014) E-WOM and accommodation: an analysis of the factors that influence travelers' adoption of information from online reviews. J Travel Res 53(1):44–57
Goes P, Lin M, Yeung C (2014) "Popularity effect" in user-generated content: evidence from online product reviews. Inf Syst Res 25(2):222–238
Golan GJ, Zaidner L (2008) Creative strategies in viral advertising: an application of Taylor's six-segment message strategy wheel. J Comput Mediated Commun 13(4):959–972
Goldenberg J, Libai B, Muller E (2001) Talk of the network: a complex systems look at the underlying process of word-of mouth. Market Lett 12(3):211–223
Goyette I, Ricard L, Bergeron J, Marticotte F (2010) E-WOM Scale: word-of-mouth measurement scale for e-services context. Can J Adm Sci/Revue Canadienne des Sciences de lAdministration 27(1):5–23
Guo Y, Barnes SJ, Jia Q (2017) Mining meaning from online ratings and reviews: tourist satisfaction analysis using latent dirichlet allocation. Tourism Manag 59:467–483
Gvili Y, Levy S (2016) Antecedents of attitudes toward eWOM communication: differences across channels. Internet Res 26(5):1030–1051
Harrison-Walker LJ (2001) The measurement of word-of-mouth communication and an investigation of service quality and customer commitment as potential antecedents. J Serv Res 4:60–75
Hausmann A (2012) The importance of word of mouth for museums: an analytical framework. Int J Arts Manag 14(3):32–43

Hausmann A, Poellmann L (2016) eWOM in the performing arts: exploratory insights for the marketing of theatres. Arts Market 6(1):111–123

Hawkins DI, Best R, Coney KA (2004) Consumer behavior: building marketing strategy, 9th edn. Boston, McGraw-Hill

Hennig-Thurau T, Gwinner KP, Walsh G, Gremler DD (2004) Electronic word-of-mouth via consumer-opinion platforms: what motivates consumers to articulate themselves on the Internet? J Interact Market 18(1):38–52

Hennig-Thurau T, Malthouse EC, Friege C, Gensler S, Lobschat L, Rangaswamy A, Skiera B (2010) The impact of new media on customer relationships. J Serv Res 13(3):311–330

Herr PM, Kardes FR, Kim J (1991) Effects of word-of-mouth and product attribute information on persuasion: an accessibility-diagnosticity perspective. J Consum Res 17:454–462

Huete-Alcocer N (2017) A literature review of word of mouth and electronic word of mouth: implications for consumer behavior. Front Psychol 8:1256

Hung K, Li SY, Tse DK (2011) Interpersonal trust and platform credibility in a Chinese multibrand online community. J Advert 40(3):99–112

Jalilvand MR, Esfahani SS, Samiei N (2011) Electronic word-of-mouth: challenges and opportunities. Procedia Comput Sci 3:42–46

Kaiser C, Bodendorf F (2012) Mining consumer dialog in online forums. Internet Res 22 (3):275–297

Kaplan AM, Haenlein M (2010) Users of the world, unite! The challenges and opportunities of Social Media. Bus Horiz 53(1):59–68

Kaplan AM, Haenlein M (2011) Two hearts in three-quarter time: how to waltz the social media/ viral marketing dance. Bus Horiz 54(3):253–263

Katz E, Lazarsfeld PF (1966) Personal influence: the part played by people in the flow of mass communications. Transaction, Piscataway, NJ

Keller E (2007) Unleashing the power of word of mouth: creating brand advocacy to drive growth. J Advert Res 47(4):448–452

Knoll J (2015) Advertising in social media: a review of empirical evidence. Int J Advert 35 (2):266–300

Lance P, Golan GJ (2006) From subservient chickens to brawny men: a comparison of viral advertising to television advertising. J Interact Advert 6(2):4–33

Lee J, Park D-H, Han I (2011) The different effects of online consumer reviews on consumers' purchase intentions depending on trust in online shopping malls. Internet Res 21(2):187–206

Levy S, Gvili Y (2015) How credible is E-word of mouth across digital-marketing channels? The roles of social capital, information richness, and interactivity. J Advert Res 55(1):95–109

Libai B, Bolton R, Bügel MS, De Ruyter K, Götz O, Risselada H, Stephen AT (2010) Customer to customer interactions: broadening the scope of word of mouth research. J Serv Res 13 (3):267–282

Litvin SW, Goldsmith RE, Pan B (2008) Electronic word-of-mouth in hospitality and tourism management. Tourism Manag 29:458–468

Logan K, Bright LF, Gangadharbatla H (2012) Facebook versus television: advertising value perceptions among females. J Res Interact Market 6(3):164–179

Lotina L (2014) Reviewing museum participation in online channels in Latvia. Museum Manag Curatorship 29(3):280–292

Luo C, Luo XR, Schatzberg L, Sia CL (2013) Impact of informational factors on online recommendation credibility: the moderating role of source credibility. Decis Support Syst 56:92–102

Marchand A, Hennig-Thurau T, Wiertz C (2017) Not all digital word of mouth is created equal: understanding the respective impact of consumer reviews and microblogs on new product success. Int J Res Market 34(2):336–354

Mennecke BE, Peters A (2013) From avatars to mavatars: the role of marketing avatars and embodied representations in consumer profiling. Bus Horiz 56(3):387–397

Min W, Ketai H, Hua H (2010) Research on using of digital signage in museum visiting navigation. In: 2010 IEEE international conference on optoelectronics and image processing, pp 327–330

Nabi RL, Hendriks A (2003) The persuasive effect of host and audience reaction shots in television talk shows. J Commun 53(3):527–543

Naiditch M, Gertz R, Chamorro E (2017) How do your museum? Marketing user-generated content to engage audiences. Museum and the Web. Available at https://mw17.mwconf.org/paper/how-do-you-museum-marketing-user-generated-content-to-engage-audiences

Newman A, Dennis C, Wright LT, King T (2010) Shoppers' experiences of digital signage-a cross-national qualitative study. J Digit Content Technol Appl 4(7):50–57

Organisation for Economic Co-operation and Development (OECD) (2007) Participative web and user-created content: Web 2.0, wikis and social networking. OECD, Paris

Owens T (2012) Tripadvisor rates Einstein: using the social web to unpack the public meanings of a cultural heritage site. Int J Web Based Communities 8(1):40–56

Report (2018) Digital in 2018 global overview. Hootsuite, Available at https://wearesocial.com/it/blog/2018/01/global-digital-report-2018

Roggeveen AL, Nordfält J, Grewal D (2016) Do digital displays enhance sales? Role of retail format and message content. J Retail 92(1):122–131

Rui H, Liu Y, Whinston AB (2010) Chatter matters: how twitter can open the black box of online word-of-mouth. In ICIS-international conference on information systems proceedings, paper 204

Schaeffler J (2008) Digital signage: software, networks, advertising, and displays: a primer for understanding the business. Frostburg State University's catalogue, ACM, pp 1693–1698

Sotiriadis MD, Van Zyl C (2013) Electronic word-of-mouth and online reviews in tourism services: the use of twitter by tourists. Electron Commerce Res 13(1):103–124

Steffes EM, Burgee LE (2009) Social ties and online word of mouth. Internet Res 19(1):42–59

Sweeney JC, Soutar GN, Mazzarol T (2008) Factors influencing word of mouth effectiveness: receiver perspectives. Eur J Market 42(3):344–364

Valli A (2008) The design of natural interaction. Multimedia Tools Appl 38:295–305

Waller DS, Waller HJ (2018) An analysis of negative reviews in top art museums' Facebook sites. Museum Manag Curatorship 1–16

Westbrook RA (1987) Product/consumption-based affective responses and postpurchase process. J Market Res 24:258–270

Wilkinson JS, Kolodzy J (2012) Digital signage. In: Grant AE, Meadows JH (eds) Communication technology update and fundamentals, 13th edn. Waltham, MA, Focal, pp 133–144

Woerdl M, Papagiannidis S, Bourlakis M, Li F (2008) Internet-induced marketing techniques: critical factors in viral marketing campaigns. J Bus Sci Appl Manag 3(1):35–45

Yang J, Kim W, Amblee N, Jeong J (2012) The heterogeneous effect of WOM on product sales: why the effect of WOM valence is mixed? Eur J Market 46(11/12):1523–1538

Zanibellato F, Rosin U, Casarin F (2016) Art experiences and eWOM: exploring the content of museum reviews, paper no. 15

The manufacturer's authorised representative in the EU is Springer Nature Customer Service Centre GmbH, Europaplatz 3, 69115 Heidelberg, Germany. If you have any concerns regarding our products, please contact ProductSafety@springernature.com

Printed and bound by CPI Group (UK) Ltd, Croydon, CR0 4YY
28/09/2026
02224091-0006